the Secret Stream

the Secret Stream

Christian Rosenkreutz and Rosicrucianism

Selected Lectures and Writings

Rudolf Steiner

Edited with an Introduction and an Afterword by Christopher Bamford

℮ Anthroposophic Press

Published by Anthroposophic Press

Library of Congress Cataloging-in-Publication Data

Steiner, Rudolf, 1861–1925.
   [Selections. English. 2000]
   The secret stream : Christian Rosenkreutz and Rosicrucianism : selected lectures and writings / Rudolf Steiner ; edited with an introduction and an afterword by Christopher Bamford.
      p.   cm.
   Includes bibliographical references.
   ISBN 0-88010-475-9
   1. Rosicrucians.   I. Bamford, Christopher.   II. Title.

BF1623R7 S715 2000
133'.43 – dc21

                                                                  00-060900

Printed in the United States of America

Contents

Part 4
ROSICRUCIANISM AND MODERN INITIATION

Part 5
ROSICRUCIAN MEDITATION

"Who Added the Roses to the Cross?"

1. The Cross and the Rose

Access to Rosicrucianism has always been difficult. Layers of mystification, like heavy dew, dampen the understanding of all but the most stalwart researchers. Chaos and confusion likewise abound at every turn, drawn to a subject that, like the proverbial jewel in the dung heap, has protected itself from the merely curious by taking refuge in the nether regions of occultism. Consequently, most serious people have always preferred to avoid the subject rather than risk contamination.

Therefore, it is difficult to write straightforwardly about the Rose Cross. This is unfortunate, because Rosicrucianism is vital not only for an understanding of the history of Western spirituality, science, and culture but also — as this collection of Rudolf Steiner's lectures makes very clear — for the promise of its future.

Stated most simply, since true knowledge is suffering (we can truly know only what we have suffered), Rosicrucianism — which is the union of the Cross and the Rose — stands for the union of *science* (knowledge) and *love*. The Rosicrucian question, first formulated by Goethe in his poem "The Mysteries," and repeatedly posed by Rudolf Steiner, therefore becomes *who added love to knowledge?* Or, *who added compassion to suffering?* And how do you do it?

The tensions and struggles demanded by this union have determined much of our intellectual history. Indeed, this may be read as a series of successive attempts (and failures) to achieve the union of these two poles.

To use a different metaphor, we might say that from the beginning the problem and the task have been to unite the *inner,* mystical path of self-knowledge with the *outer,* alchemical path of knowledge of the world. In other words, Western civilization has sought to realize

1

that the path to the divine at the center of the soul and the path that encounters the divine through a progressive unveiling of nature are *one* path.

Putting it yet differently again, we may say that the task has been to realize a perfect fusion of nature and grace. This is the union of what human beings accomplish by their own power (*reason*) and what conversely they must gratefully depend upon — what comes from "other power" by *faith* and listening. Chemistry, for instance, is an example of a purely rational science, while alchemy (at its best, as the Rosicrucians and Rudolf Steiner understood it) represents the attempt to fuse nature and grace in a higher empiricism.

Alchemy is, for this reason, the paradigmatic Rosicrucian science. As a general rule, wherever one finds alchemy in the West upon a Christian basis, the true Rose Cross is not distant. From this point of view, Rudolf Steiner's anthroposophy, to the extent that it is Rosicrucian, is alchemical.[1] Alchemy in this sense is the science of the transmutation of substances, the "resurrection" of matter. As Steiner put it: the task of the earth — of human beings on the earth — is to transform wisdom into love. *The substance of the earth must become love.* Human beings must become priests of a new liturgy, a new eucharistic sacrifice that extends beyond bread and wine to include the whole of nature. This is the very meaning of the Incarnation. Therefore the medieval alchemist, actualizing the Word of Christ to the letter, proclaimed the Gospel to all creation: "The Stone is Christ."[2]

Another word for the fusion of nature and grace, "own power" and "other power," upon which alchemy depends, might be *sacramentalism*. Technically, a sacrament is the union of the visible sign with the invisible grace. Sacramentalism believes that God can work through created things to help, heal, and sanctify them. From this point of view, not only familiar, archetypal things like star, rock, plant, bread, salt, or wine, but also anything and everything from "atoms to galaxies" can be channels of grace. In other words, the impact of Christianity, centered on the sacrament of the Eucharist, the perpetual death and resurrection — *the transforming life* — of God in the world, was to suggest the possibility of a universal sacramental science, one that would transmute the world (matter) as such and as a whole.

Something else is at stake here, too. It is well known that the farther back in history one goes, the more closely what we call science, religion, and art are one. Rudolf Steiner often claimed that in the ancient mysteries these three fundamental human gestures (knowing, praising, and making) were a single reality. In ancient times, you could not separate out some one human activity and claim it was art, not religion, or religion, not science, or science, not art. Culture, like the human being, was a complex, seamless whole. Beauty, truth, and goodness were indivisible though distinguishable. Writing of musical theory and ancient cosmology, Ernest McClain, says: "In ancient Mesopotamia, music, mathematics, art, science, and poetic fantasy were fused."[3]

What does it mean when art, science, and religion are not three but one?

Or when the path in search of the self and the path in search of the world are seen as mutual and complementary, rather than as opposed and antithetical?

2. *Some Precursors*

Ancient Greece recognized the possibility of adding roses to the cross.

They knew the cross as the world soul crucified for the sake of creation. Plato in his *Timaeus* tells how the creator sought to make the world "a living creature truly endowed with soul and intelligence by the providence of God." He writes how, when it came to fitting soul together with the body, the creator mixed it from the appropriate elements and proportioned it musically, dividing it "lengthwise into two parts, which he joined to one another at the center like the letter *X*."

Thus, for the ancient Greeks, the world bore within it a kind of crucifixion that made it sing.

As for the rose, the Greeks derived it from *rhodein,* to flow. They saw in the precious flower something active, sacred to Aphrodite, the Goddess and the Mother of Love. Aphrodite was the foam-born one, daughter of heaven by her father's testicles, falling to Earth, crashing into the surging sea. Eros was her son, so that the rose was associated with him, too. Together, mother and son were responsible for "the madness of Love" which, as Plato said, was the highest form of madness, leading human beings by beauty from the world of becoming toward the world of being.

The Greeks then knew both the cross of the world, and the rose leading out of it. However, they only intuited the possibility of saving, that is, transforming, the world by uniting the Cross and the Rose. They did not yet possess the possibility of doing so. They already knew the union could exist, however, and even sought to bring the two — knowledge and love — together.

The first to try to do so was Pythagoras of Samos (born about 569 and died about 475),[4] whose life spans the so-called "axial" period. This is the epoch that saw the revolutionary human activity of (among others) Lao-Tzu, Confucius, Gautama Buddha, Mahavira the Jain, Zoroaster, and the Hebrew prophets of the Exile. Pythagoras, too, belongs among these revolutionaries of consciousness.

His "school," founded toward the end of his life at Crotona in southern Italy, presents for the first time in the West the idea and practice of a living synthesis of science, religion, and art. Pythagoras is revered as the founder of Western science, but the School that he founded was not a scientific institution in our sense. Rather, it was a spiritual and esoteric organization, the fundamental tone of which was *religious*. The science flowed from the religion. For example, there was a probationary period of seven years of silence, in which one could listen but not speak. The aspirant sacrificed speaking in order to hear. Once accepted, he or she (Pythagoras held that women were more naturally suited to piety than men) became one of the *mathematikoi* or *practitioners;* the practice was simultaneously cognitive — or scientific — and ethical. At the same time, there were specific ethical practices and beliefs: nonviolence, vegetarianism, and reincarnation. And there was *study*. To study, to practice, to learn number theory, geometry, music, and astronomy in the Pythagorean sense was to investigate the world and oneself at the same time. And it was *healing*. Furthermore, such knowledge (which was both world-knowledge and self-knowledge) sought, and depended upon union with the divine. Pythagorean science was also a practice of praise.

The Pythagorean life was open to all. In it, many now apparently separate human activities (which we associate with science, religion, and art) were conceived of and *practiced* as one. Pythagoreanism was a radical venture, one that depended upon each human beings' capacity for direct, unmediated contact with God and nature through the activity of the spirit of *meaning* (the *Logos*) — which Pythagoras expressed in the language of number, proportion, and harmony.

The Pythagorean School failed. It established no permanent institution or culture. This was most immediately so, perhaps, because Pythagoras became involved with politics. Henceforth, it became a rule that esotericism and politics should never mix — a rule that many have unfortunately disregarded to their detriment. Or perhaps

Pythagoras failed because he could not succeed — because no one had yet added "the roses to the cross."

Pythagoras is regarded not only as the father of modern science but also as the father of Western esotericism, one of the *prisca theologia or* "ancient theologians" (along with Orpheus, Hermes, Moses, and Zoroaster). His influence may be seen in all communal movements from the Essenes, through monasticism, to the Rosicrucians. In other words, Pythagoras, who created the idea of the esoteric school, succeeded for a time in uniting knowledge and love, science and religion, in an artistic form.

Subsequently, this communal ideal was rarely attempted and never successfully. Schools of love (monasteries, philosophical schools) and schools of knowledge (if such existed) went their own way. The Pythagorean sciences (arithmetic, geometry, astronomy, music), as well as alchemy, astrology, and "magic," continued to be studied and practiced of course, but by individuals, not groups, so that the history of the transmission is underground and elusive. Although attempts were made to heal the split, this split between love and knowledge was to continue right up to the Rosicrucian attempt to bring them together.

The twelfth-century renaissance, for instance, saw a great renewal of cosmological, that is, scientific, thinking at the Cathedral School of Chartres. There, foreshadowing the Renaissance proper, major philosophical figures (like Bernardus Sylvestris, Alain de Lille, and Bernard of Chartres) forged the powerful beginnings of a synthesis between ancient Platonic-Hermetic cosmology and Christian theological metaphysics. Drawing on very few texts — basically extracts from Plato's *Timaeus* and fragments of the *Poimandres* dialogue of the *Corpus Hermeticum* — these thinkers began to create a new way of thinking about nature that utilized the full resources of both faith and reason.

Joseph M. Zycinski, Archbishop of Lublin, states the issue very clearly (1988):

A consistent and well-considered theological justification for natural science may be found in treatises worked out by the influential School of Chartres in the Twelfth Century. It was William of Conches who categorically denied attempts to oppose theology and the study of nature. In his arguments, God the creator of human intellect and the order of nature is to be glorified through our understanding of the natural order. Theological recognition of the importance of physical regularities was based on the Vulgate translation of the Epistle to the Romans (13.1) *quae a Deo sunt, ordinata sunt,* whatever is from God is ordered. For many reasons, the Platonic picture of the cosmic order described in the *Timaeus* appealed to the theologians who belonged to the School of Chartres and inspired their works on the harmony of natural and supernatural values. Alain de Lille impressively depicted the beauty of this harmony. In his description of nature, which is subordinate to the divine Mind that brings order out of chaos, we find anticipation of both Blake's poetry and St. Francis's cosmic mysticism.

In the religious hymns of the School, fascinating descriptions of nature unite both theological and physical perspectives. This integration does not yield uncritical physical theology, but instead provides a beautiful description of cosmic harmony that embraces aesthetic, moral, and existential values. Germs and light, human love and physical laws are united in Alain's philosophy of nature. His philosophical and physical descriptions disclose the theological dimension of nature presenting the physical world as the domain of the presence of the immanent God.

[And yet] the image of nature proposed by the Chartres School met violent opposition from some medieval scholars. William of Saint-Thierry, for instance, attacked the very idea of uniting biblical doctrine with the pagan philosophy of the *Timaeus.* Despite the categorical protests of William's followers, however, the School provided intellectual patterns in which harmonious synthesis replaced the isolation of different cultural traditions. With these patterns of new harmony, the world of natural phenomena was no longer an agent of alienation. It appeared . . . as "the beautiful book and heaven and earth offered to every person."[5]

Much lies hidden in these innocent remarks. William of Saint-Thierry, cited by Zycinski as a leader of the opponents of the School of Chartres, was an early Cistercian, a colleague of St. Bernard. Now, by any estimation, the renewal of monasticism undertaken by the Cistercians was every bit as remarkable, spiritually and intellectually, as the School of Chartres. St. Bernard towers over the age (the School of Chartres included) not only as a mystic, but also as a theologian, a philosopher, and even as a practical Platonist. Bernard was, after all, a magnificent composer and superb architect whose motto was "No iconography, only geometry!" Unexcelled in his knowledge of acoustics, Bernard exercised in both fields an amazing understanding of number, ratio, and proportion in relation to matter. St. Bernard in other words *knew* what the Chartrians only *talked about.* Yet he could not abide them; they were the enemy. There were philosophical and ethical reasons for this, but essentially it was a question of love. For St. Bernard and William, the Chartrians lacked love in the sense that the monastics in their schools of love sought to realize it. There are two ways of looking at this. On the one hand, the Cistercians felt the Chartrians placed faith in jeopardy because they lacked love. On the other hand, the "practical," that is, empirical, nature of monastic spiritual discipline seemed to have no place in (or at least seemed to confuse) the intellectual, speculative serenity of the scholars of the School of Chartres.

The medieval university — which grew out of the Cathedral schools — inherited much of this confusion, which would be temporarily and disastrously resolved for the modern age by the reductionism of the "scientific revolution." This, of course, created the pseudo-objectivity of a material world resting upon the assumption of the absolute and radical separation of quantity from quality, of "physical" science from "humanistic" ethics and theology.

This dichotomy of what would become, in C. P. Snow's phrase, "two cultures" was long in the making and may be seen germinating in many places. We may note, for example, the fate of alchemy in the medieval university. Chiara Crisciani has raised the question as to why alchemy (so fundamental to Rosicrucianism, as Steiner's essay on *The Chemical Wedding* makes clear) was not part of the university syllabus in the Middle Ages. The alchemists, for their part, certainly kept abreast of what was happening in the universities. Crisciani claims that the exclusion of alchemy from the academic curriculum was based on the very nature of alchemical knowledge, which was essentially and radically "operative." Alchemy was *practical,* "rooted in contact with matter and its activity." And learning was then considered to have nothing to do with "practice" in this sense ("practical medicine," too, lay outside university studies). Worse still, *epistemologically,* the alchemist's "technological dream" included the transformation of the alchemist — that is, it was practical in quite another dimension, namely, as affecting *consciousness.*

How and where (in what groups) was alchemy then transmitted, if not through university culture? Crisciani's most telling hypothesis is that it was among the religious orders, most likely the Franciscans. Certainly Roger Bacon, Arnold of Villanova, Constantine of Pisa (author of one of the earliest alchemical texts, one with clear reference, too, to the School of Chartres) — and other early alchemical writers — had Franciscan associations, or were Franciscans.[6] And certainly Franciscan incarnationalism bears unmistakable affinities with the hermetic philosophy of alchemy. On the other hand, Basil Valentine (so important to Rudolf Steiner) was reputedly Benedictine. For our purposes, the specific affiliation is unimportant. What matters is the realization that knowledge of the kind that alchemy presupposes cannot be acquired outside a context of "love" and the practice of love.

The meaning and practice of love had, in fact, been broadening and deepening throughout the epoch leading up to the Rosicrucian phenomenon. What else is the meaning of Christianity? Christianity is the religion of the incarnation of love. For Christians, Christ's coming marked a new era of creation in which the creator entered creation, transforming it utterly. No longer outside, beyond, above, God was now within creation, dissolving and overturning the cosmic norms of above, below, inside, outside, beginning, and end.

Initially, none of this was evident. It would not become so, in fact, until the "Second Coming," when history would close and a Golden Age begin — signs of whose approach would be read on every side. As the first Rosicrucians stated: "God hath most certainly and most assuredly concluded to send and grant to the World before her end, which presently shall ensue, such a Truth, Light, Life, and Glory, as the first Man Adam had."

For Christians, then, love's incarnation is a cosmic event. Love enters creation, becomes flesh, penetrating the entrails of matter to become all in all. Love enters, not for the comfort of skin-bound human beings, but for the sake of the cosmos. Love prays that human beings might assume once more their cosmological function as cosmic beings, becoming again participants in and coworkers with God, capable of raising up the cosmos and hence also God himself who is now one with it.

None of this, of course, could be accomplished all at once. According to Joachim of Fiore, the prophet of Calabria:

> The first age was that of knowledge, the second that of understanding, and the third will be the period of complete intelligence. The first was servile obedience, the second filial servitude,

and the third will be freedom. The first was affliction, the second action, and the third will be contemplation. The first was fear, the second faith, and the third will be love. The first was the age of slaves, the second the age of sons, and the third will be the age of friends.

In other words, history would culminate in the pouring out of the spiritual intelligence of the Holy Spirit: the Spirit of Love. When this "pouring out" would begin was the great question. For the first Rosicrucians, who were assiduous students of Joachim, their own time bore the unmistakable sign that "the Lord Jehovah... [was] turning about the course of nature." For Joachim himself, this moment of turning-about coincided with the coming of the Third State, that of spiritual humanity, when the "spirit of the Lord will be poured over the orb of the earth." And the fact that Joachim, who was no prophet, had been able clearly to understand the meaning of the Scriptures — and hence also of history — merely by the gift of spiritual intelligence, meant that the great moment could not be far off. It meant, too, that the Antichrist likewise stood in the wings and beside him Elijah, or Elias, the type of the Holy Spirit, who "will come and restore all things" and usher in the great *renovatio,* or reformation.

"Behold — it is Elias who was to come!" For the Rosicrucians, there are two great contenders for the role of Elijah or *Elias Artista* who returns to inaugurate the great period of "reform" — Luther and Paracelsus. (In the end, both were seen as only "precursors.")

Luther was the first to take as his emblem the Rose and the Cross: a large five-petaled white rose, enclosed within the blue circle of the world which is bounded by gold, at whose center lies a heart, wherein sits a black cross. The rose is white, he writes, because white is the color of all angels and blessed spirits. The fact that it is so, and not red, the color of incarnation or embodiment, and single, not seven-fold, shows that Luther was more a mystic than a proto-Rosicrucian. Nevertheless, Luther appreciated alchemy (the hallmark of Rosicrucian science as we have said) not only for its many uses "but also for the sake of the allegory and secret signification...touching the resurrection of the dead at the Last Day." He understood that alchemy, too, in the final analysis, depended upon the Cross, Christ crucified. In the words of the Lutheran Khunrath, "the whole cosmos is a work of Supernal Alchemy," performed in the crucible of God.

Since Christ's Incarnation — for Luther, as for the Rosicrucians — the Cross is everywhere. It is in human beings and in nature.[7] It is the very substance of things, the root fact of existence, closer to us than we are to ourselves. If this is so, one can easily understand why this reality — the Cross — makes a mockery of any institutions or speculative philosophies that seek to "mediate" between this central fact of existence and human existence as such. God and nature, nature and grace, grace and gnosis or revelation are two sides of a single coin. As we have seen: the task is to realize this. Therefore Luther reaffirmed the possibility of each soul's having direct, unmediated access to God and God's nature and processes. What had been separated before was now united in the Cross. To pass through the Cross, to enact the Cross, was to participate in the transmutation that the Cross alone made possible.

Paracelsus, for his part, felt that Luther had dogmatized his revelation so that it had become a justification of privilege and election. Paracelsus took his stand on experience, against all authority. On this basis, he espoused the interdependence of radical religious and intellectual freedom, freedom of the will, pacifism, the unity of humanity. Fighting for these, he was on the side of the poor and the oppressed: everything he did was motivated out love for the fallenness of creatures, and the goal of all his work was to hasten the great redemption or healing he felt was possible. Thus, while disapproving of Luther, he shared the Reformer's insight into the Cross as the Rosetta Stone of the Great Work.

Paracelsus's accomplishment — for which he was forever invoked as the great precursor — was to unite the mystical and the alchemical, the religious and the cosmological, in a life completely given over to service of humanity and the world. Medieval mystics sought a mystical exchange or union of three hearts — their own, that of Mary-Jesus, and that of Christ. Paracelsus understood this could be unfolded with practical consequences as the union of human nature with cosmic nature and the divine. It is from Paracelsus that we derive the image of the alchemist as a kind of universal lay priest, celebrating a healing Mass in which not just bread and wine were transformed, but nature and human nature in their entirety. Paracelsus, indeed, was the type of the new priest who realizes the identity of macrocosm and microcosm. And on the basis of this knowledge, he understands the world from within as a complex field of signatures, and acts in it, healing and transforming it.

As for his "religion," it is really an attempt to reinstate the Golden Age, a radically individualist "Church of the Spirit," in which there is direct connection between the human being, Nature, and God.

Nature, God, and the "Star" in the human being (imagination): no more was needed. "One man seeks the Gospel among the Papists in Rome, another among the Zwinglians, a third one among the Lutherans, a fourth one among the Anabaptists.... *Do not believe any of these, because it can never be found there.*"[8]

It is questionable, in fact, whether such a "religion" as Paracelsus proposed — a religion of two lights (the Light of Grace and the Light of Nature), "the Book of Nature and the Book of Grace joined together," as Oswald Crollius put it — is socially possible or viable. Certainly, it cannot provide the unifying function of religion, anymore than an esotericism without exotericism can. Indeed, it is unlikely that, without a common rite, accessible at many levels and to all people, a religious revolution could occur. And indeed, it did not. The Rosicrucian experiment disappeared from public view in the maelstrom of the Thirty Years War — which was, needless to say, a war of religion.

3. The Primary Documents[9]

The first of the three documents that attest to the existence of Christian Rosenkreutz and the mystery of the Rosy Cross began circulating, in manuscript, in Lutheran circles, in Tübingen, Germany, at the turn of the seventeenth century. The first of these (published anonymously in 1614 in Kassel), the so-called *Fama Fraternitatis,* or "Rumor of the Brotherhood," struck Europe like a lightning bolt, creating a cultural riot, the so-called Rosicrucian *furore.* Written in German and "Addressed to the Learned in General and to the Governors of Europe," the *Fama* called for scholars, scientists, philosophers, artists, and mystics to unite in the cause of a "general reformation, both of divine and human things." The time was ripe, the author or authors believed, for a global transformation. With the help and blessing of "the only wise and merciful God," it claimed, humanity was poised on the cusp of an evolutionary leap and wanted only to come together in the great work of bringing all the arts and sciences to perfection.

Within the short compass of a few pages employing the full paraphernalia of mystery, metaphor, and mythology, the *Fama* sought to raise into general awareness the new possibilities for spiritual knowledge and cultural, scientific, and religious evolution opened up by the Renaissance and the Reformation. The *Fama*, however, was not unique in believing, as it put it, that

> ...The only Wise and Merciful God in these latter days hath poured out so richly his mercy and goodness to Humankind, whereby we do attain more and more to the perfect knowledge of his Son Jesus Christ and of Nature, that justly we may boast of the happy time wherein there is not only discovered unto us the half part of the world, which was hitherto unknown and hidden, but He hath also made manifest unto us many wonderful and never-before seen works and creatures of Nature, and, moreover, hath raised human beings, endued with great wisdom, which might partly renew and reduce all arts (in this our spotted and imperfect age) to perfection, so that we might thereby understand our own nobleness and worth, and why we are called microcosmos, and how far our knowledge extendeth in Nature.

Others, too, had sensed the reality of "these latter days" when "the only Wise and Merciful God... has poured out so richly his mercy and goodness." We find evidence of this in many mystics and scientists of the period. Of these, the Polish alchemist Michael Sendivogius's *Statues for a Society of Unknown Philosophers* is perhaps most closely related to the Rosicrucian documents. Sendivogius proposes an international and democratic society of alchemists, all of whom are devout, practicing Christians, love virtue, and "have the proper frame of mind for philosophy." Those who have taken holy Orders, however, are excluded, for "philosophy demands people with free minds who are free to do as they wish." Behavior of members is specified: one must have strong faith, strong hope, be generous, have good business sense, be honest, persevering, nonviolent, and free of "unhealthy connects with wine or women." One must have a natural curiosity, and be able to keep a secret, for "secrecy is an essential condition." The founding document, not published until 1691, goes into much detail on the procedure for admitting members, and describes the rules and activities pertaining to "the making of the [philosophical] stone," which is the end and purpose of the society. It is unclear whether the society ever actually functioned, but its existence, if only in Sendivogius's mind, gives evidence of the tenor of the times that brought Rosicrucianism to the stage of history.[10]

The Rosicrucian intention for its part, as described in the *Fama*, was ascribed to "the founder of the Fraternity," one "C.R.C., who was born in 1378, a mysterious German," also called "Father" and "our Brother." According to some unverifiable sources, he was born on the border of Hesse and Thuringia into a Cathar household called Germelshausen.[11] His tomb was opened in 1604. This was one hundred and twenty years after his death — which would therefore have occurred (one year after the birth of Luther) in 1484, when he was 106 years of age.

This C.R.C., having been placed by his parents at the age of five (1383) in a cloister, where he "learned indifferently the Greek and Latin tongues," determined at an early age to undertake the journey to the Holy Sepulchre in Jerusalem. This was a legendary pilgrimage to the East in search of initiation. It took him to Damascus, Damcar in Arabia, Egypt, and Fez in North Africa. Wherever he went, he met with the Wise of those lands who initiated him into the secrets of God, Nature, and Humanity.

C.R.C. went first to Cyprus, where P.A.L., his companion, died. From there, C.R.C. continued on his own to Damascus, then a haven for the learned of Persia and Iraq fleeing the Mongol invasion. Seeing all the sages, philosophers, and physicians gathered there, C.R.C. soon gave up the idea of proceeding to Jerusalem. Instead, he decided to stay a while in Damascus and, having learned Arabic, study with the assembled Masters. Thence, after three years, he proceeded to Arabia, to Damcar (a word supposedly meaning "monastery in the sand"), where he translated into Latin the *Book M,* and met with many scientists, alchemists, astrologers, theologians, and mathematicians. Accepting this account — that he studied "mathematica, physic, and magic" with Sufi hermetists and spiritual masters of Islam — we may say that C.R.C. was initiated into the group known as the *Ikhwan al Safa* or *Brethren of Purity* and studied their fifty-two *Epistles,* which constitute a "Summa" of the sacred sciences.

Thereafter, he went to Egypt and to Fez in North Africa, through which the great Ibn Arabi had just passed. As a fifteenth-century historian wrote: "In Fez one finds masters of all branches of intellectuality, such as grammar, law, mathematics, chronometry, geometry, metaphysics, logic, rhetoric, music, and these masters know all the relevant texts by heart. Whoever does not know by heart the basic text relating to the science about which he speaks is not taken seriously."

Returning to Europe, C.R.C. then sought to gather together scholars and scientists who would unite their work on the sure footing he had discovered. He began in Spain, "but it was to them a laughing matter." Sadly, this was generally true as he traveled north: "The same song was sung to him by other nations." Disappointed, he withdrew to his homeland, Germany. There he built a house in which he ruminated on his journey and his philosophy, reducing them together into a true memorial. After five years of intense study, science, and inner work, the task of "general reformation" returned to him with pressing urgency. And so he called from his childhood cloister three of his former friends: Brothers G.V., J.A., and J.O.

Thus, the Fraternity of the Rose Cross began with four members. These four created a "magical language," a series of *Axiomata*, a mysterious *Rota* (Wheel) and a secret dictionary. They worked intensively with the *Book M* (*Mundus,* or *World*) and completed the house, now called *Sancti Spiritus* (Holy Spirit). Then four new members were inducted, bringing the total to eight — "all bachelors and of vowed virginity." These then dispersed into several countries. Before they did so, however, they drew up certain laws or agreements.

The first rule was to profess no other thing than to cure the sick, and that *gratis*. This rule, as stated, is a rule of love. "Compassion," wrote Paracelsus, "is the true physician's teacher." In addition, however, we should also note that the orientation is outward, toward healing the world — that is, toward other beings, for we can love and heal only other, living beings. These Rosicrucians worked for the sake of healing the world, not for the redemption of the individual soul. That is, the Rosicrucians rule affirmed the primacy of service and action. A true Rosicrucian walks "the true thorn-strewn way of the cross — the renunciation of selfhood — for the sake of the redemption of the world, that is, the building of the New Jerusalem."

This healing must be understood in the largest sense to include nature. As the *Fama* makes clear, nature, like humanity, fell with Adam and is sick and needs healing. Like humanity, nature is not the unity it ought to be. It was to heal this disease, to renew the unity of nature in and through humanity, that Christ came. Indeed, as the Rosicrucian Prince Lapoukhin writes, Christ not only "mystically sprinkled every soul with the virtue of his blood, which is the tincture proper to the renewal of the soul in God . . . but he also regenerated the mass of immaterial elements of which he shall make a new heaven and a new earth."

The second rule is stated as follows: That no one should be obliged to wear any kind of distinctive dress but should adapt to the customs of the country At its simplest, this is the injunction to live anonymously, unpretentiously, plying some ordinary trade, drawing no attention to oneself. At another level, since chief among the customs of a country is its language, this rule invokes the "gift of tongues," so often mentioned as a Rosicrucian characteristic. This gift, which is a gift of the Holy Spirit, is said to mean that the possessor of it addresses everyone in their own language, in the way and at the level appropriate to their understanding. The person who has attained the Rose Cross is attached to no form, no language, no name, not even his or her own — some sources adding that the second rule includes the injunction to change one's name with each country one visits.

Here, then, is the meaning of the designation "cosmopolitan" found throughout Rosicrucian literature. True Rosicrucians are at home everywhere and nowhere. It should be remarked, too, that this rule of nonattachment to phenomenal forms extends in principle also to beliefs. As Ibn Arabi notes: "The true sage is bound to no particular belief."

The third rule enjoins "that every year on Christmas Day they meet together at the House Sancti Spiritus or write the cause of their absence." Sancti Spiritus or Holy Spirit is the name Rosenkreutz gave to his "building," naming it after what it housed. In other words, the "mother house" — the Church or Temple of the Rose Cross — is invisible. It is the Temple of the Spirit, the Inner Church, the Church of the Fire of Love. Prince Lapoukhin, writing of *The Characteristics of the Interior Church,* after having discounted faith, prayer, fasting, the seeing of visions, the gift of prophecy, miracles, and even humility as distinctive — for these can be deceptive — concludes that the only true sign is love. "Love is the manifestation of Christ's spirit, which can only exist in love, and can only work by love." Only what proceeds from the spirit, the fire, of love is good and true. The heart is the Temple of the Rose Cross.

The last three rules seem simpler: first, each Brother must choose a successor. In other words, there is to be no Rosicrucian school or institution. The Rosicrucian, working alone, anonymously, for the sake of humanity and the world seeks one intimate friend to continue the work. Second, the word C.R. should be their seal, mark, and character. As their seal, the Rose Cross is stamped on their heart: it has become their heart, their work. As their mark, it radiates from them like the light of six thousand candles. As their character, it affirms that they will be known by their fruits of love. Finally, the last rule: they shall remain secret one hundred years.

Hence, as the *Fama* goes on to affirm, in 1604, the tomb was opened. Complexly constructed, an altar lay at its heart. On the altar was inscribed:

"This compendium of the universe I made in my lifetime to be my tomb."

Around its rim: *Jesus mihi omnia,* Jesus my all.

In its center: *Nequaquam vacuum,* no vacuum anywhere. *Legis Jugum,* the yoke of the law; *Libertas Evangelii,* the freedom of the Gospel. *Gloria intacta,* the perfect glory of God.

Much more, of course, lay within the vault. Many things were to be found there — volumes of Paracelsus, mirrors, burning lamps, artistic songs, a parchment book called *T* (Testament), whose last page contained a eulogy of Christian Rosenkreutz ("a seed buried in the bosom of Jesus.") This repeated his story, then described how he died — how, having passed the century of years, though oppressed by no disease, but summoned by the Spirit of God, "amid the last embraces of his brethren he rendered up his illuminated soul to God his Creator. *A beloved Father, a loyal friend, he was hidden here by his disciples for 120 years.*" Below this, the names of the first eight members of the Rosicrucian Brotherhood were appended, the whole being completed with the following three short sentences (brilliant jewels to which Rudolf Steiner returns repeatedly throughout his esoteric work) that magisterially resume in the briefest possible compass the entire radical message of the Christian revelation.

Ex Deo nascimur, In Jesu morimur, Per Spiritum Sanctum revivi- scimus.

From God we are born, in Christ we die, through the Holy Spirit we are reborn.

The *Fama* then closes with a repeated call for all those wishing to work with the R.C. for a general reformation to make themselves known.

The companion document, the *Confessio,* appeared a year later in 1615, also anonymously in Kassel. This time the text was in Latin, although a German version soon followed. Basically, the *Confessio* repeated the message of the *Fama,* now giving "thirty-seven reasons" for the existence of the Rosicrucian Brotherhood and for the imminence and necessity of the general reformation, as well as adding further claims of the possession of secret knowledge.

In response to these calls, between 1614 and 1622, about two hundred responses were published across Europe, mostly anonymously. At the same time, leading authors like Robert Fludd, Michael Maier, Theophilus Schwieghart, published works in support of the Brotherhood. Others, such as the philosopher René Descartes, sought in whatever way they could to enter into relationship with the Brotherhood, while still others, like Van Helmont and later, Thomas Vaughan, skillfully kept the ball rolling.

The final text of the Rosicrucian oeuvre, *The Chemical Wedding of Christian Rosenkreutz* (published 1616), was of a different order — a sophisticated alchemical text, masquerading successfully and with great artistry as a romantic allegory, a fiction, a masque. It tells the story of the narrator, Christian Rosenkreutz, so-named for the first time, who describes his experiences as the guest at the wedding of a king and queen. The story covers seven days and takes place in and around a marvelous castle. The central theme is that of alchemical transmutation.

4. Dramatis Personae

The Chemical Wedding was also published anonymously. However, it is now known to be the youthful work of a Lutheran theologian of Tübingen, Johann Valentin Andreae, who though later acknowledging authorship of the work, disowned its content, calling it a *ludibrium* or jest.[12] Andreae, however, allows us to begin to unfold the milieu through which Rosicrucianism entered the stage of history.

The place (womb or crucible), therefore: most likely, Tübingen, Germany.

The time: the turn of the seventeenth century. Metaphorically, we may say it was the end of the Renaissance — Giordano Bruno was burned at the stake in the Piazza di Fiore in Rome in 1600. One hundred and fifty years before, in Florence, under the aegis of Cosimo de Medici, Marsilio Ficino began to translate and transmit the works of ancient theologians like Orpheus, Zoroaster, Hermes, Pythagoras, Plato, Plotinus, Iamblichus, and Proclus. Thus the *Hermetic* tradition was first enabled to encounter the new, heart-centered, Christic mysticism not only of mystics like Hildegard of Bingen, Margaret of Porete, Francis and Clare of Assisi, and Meister Eckhart, but also the more hidden traditions represented by the Cathars, the Troubadours, and the Brethren of the Free Spirit.

The actors: most likely, Christoph Besold (1577–1638), Tobias Hess (1558–1614), and Johann Valentin Andreae (1586–1654). Andreae came to Tübingen after the death of his father in 1601. He entered the university as a student, receiving his baccalaureate in 1603 and his master's degree in 1605. He was a talented writer, and wrote

plays. *The Chemical Wedding,* first drafted when he was sixteen in
1602/3, came down as part of this youthful inspiration. Then, in
1607, involved in a scandal, he broke off his studies. He was twenty-
one. We hear nothing more of him for seven years, when at the age
of twenty-eight, in 1614, he marries Agnes Gruningen, the daughter
of a well-known Lutheran, Joshua Gruningen.

In his eulogy of his friend Tobias Hess, printed in 1616, Andreae
describes how the best anatomists in Europe came to find out why
he had died and made the following diagnosis:

> The heart was healthy and saturated with the clear red blood of
> Christ; a small trace of the contagious fluid of original sin was to
> be found only in the foremost chamber. His lungs had been filled
> to the full with the breath of God the Holy Spirit — the presence
> of only a few tiny ulcerations of academic science was detected.
> His Christian liver had so well distributed the finest virtues over
> his entire body that only a small number of weaknesses of cor-
> rupt human nature could be found. His spleen had cooked only
> the best blood of charity . . . his kidneys . . . had remained totally
> chaste. . . .

Christoph Besold was a law professor, a lifelong friend of Kepler
(who attended university in Tübingen), and the possessor of a four-
thousand-volume library that included many hermetic and heterodox
writings, which he put at Andreae's disposal. Tobias Hess, for his
part, was a close friend of Simon Studion (1543–1605), author of the
celebrated *Noametria,* (completed 1596) and founder of an alliance
called the Crucesignati, or "those marked by the Cross." *Noametria,* meaning "Temple Measure," is a vast, rambling work combining
mathematics, prophecy, and natural laws in the building of an allegorical temple. H. Spencer Lewis writes; "a great part of the book is
devoted to the history of the cross and its real spiritual and mystical
significance, to the rose and its symbolical meaning, and to the special significance of the rose and the cross when united." *Noametria* is
dated 1604 (the date of the opening of Christian Rosenkreutz's tomb,
and therefore also one hundred and twenty years after Luther's birth
in 1483). It was also significant astrologically. According to Tobias
Hess, 1604 marked the beginning of a new epoch. Hess, according to
Ritman, was "the heart, the pivot, the architect of the manifestos."
They were created and written in his house, and kept there until publication, handwritten copies circulating for a number of years among
a chosen circle of friends.

Publication itself was probably precipitated by the death of Tobias Hess in 1614, which, as we have seen, was also the year of Andreae's marriage. It was also when he assumed his "new" role as Lutheran theologian — a guise in which he had no choice but to deny the reality of what he had been involved in. Nevertheless, he always remained true, in a sense, to the spirit of it.

What are we to make of this whole story? Is the whole thing a concoction, a literary and philosophical hoax, a revolutionary squib? Certainly, the situation is extremely ambiguous. However, it is not unique. The case of Dionysius the Areopagite, called the *Pseudo - Dionysius*, is similar. Here, too, there are texts that have had an enormous historical impact on Christian mysticism, theology, and esotericism.[13] Steiner refers to them constantly as the foundational teachings of esoteric Christianity. The writings purport to be by Dionysius, who was converted by St. Paul in Athens and became his disciple, and was also the friend of the Evangelist St. John (Dionysius writes him a letter on Patmos!). However, the documents (and therefore their author) do not appear on the stage of exoteric history until the sixth century. Scholars therefore claim that they were written not by the disciple of St. Paul but by a Neoplatonist of the period, probably a student of Damascius, who, following Justinian's closing of the Platonic Academy, hoped to ensure the survival of Neoplatonic teaching within Christianity. Certainly, the Dionysian writings are suffused with Neoplatonism; nevertheless, they also authentically transmit a profound and esoteric Christian teaching. It is as if both were true: they were written in the fifth century, and they do convey authentic esoteric Christian teaching.

We may say the same of the Rosicrucian texts: they were "created" by Tobias Hess, Christoph Besold, and Johann Valentin Andreae; but they are also "true." As stated in the documents, there really is/was a Christian Rosenkreutz, an initiate, who lived a life, founded an esoteric order, and has a world mission, which continues to unfold. This certainly is Steiner's position in the lectures printed in this book.

This is not surprising, for Steiner places his work, especially that part of his work that has to do with science/knowledge and with religion/Christianity under the sign of C. R. More than that, however, for Steiner the whole work of the West is inspired and guided by two *individualities,* Christian Rosenkreutz and the "Master Jesus." These two figures are, as it were, Christ's two hands in the West for the sake of the transformation of the world.

For the "mission" concerns the world. It is for the sake of the

world, a work of service, of love. That is why Rosicrucianism strives
to bring together science, religion, and art — grace and nature, faith
and reason, invisible and visible — into a new unity, the unity of *love*.
Gerhard Dorn beautifully expresses this:

> First, transmute the earth of your body into water. This means
> that your heart, which is as hard as stone, material, and lazy
> must become supple and vigilant. . . . Then spiritual images and
> visions impress themselves on your heart as a seal is impressed
> on wax. . . . This liquefaction must transform itself into air. That
> is to say, the heart must become contrite and humble, rising
> toward its Creator as air rises toward heaven. . . . Then, for this
> air to become fire, desire, now sublimated, must be converted
> into love — love of God and neighbor — *and this flame must
> never be extinguished.* . . .

This is what the old alchemists — Steiner always calls them "the
old philosophers" — meant when they spoke of transforming oneself
"from dead stones into living philosophical stones."

5. *Transmission*

The transmission of this path of Rosicrucian wisdom occurred along
two lines, in two dimensions. Historically, a continuous lineage of
personalities and texts — from the founders through the eighteenth
century to H. P. Blavatsky and Rudolf Steiner at the turn of our own
"new age" — transmitted a historical Rosicrucianism shot through
with human frailty. At the same time, intersecting with this and
guiding it (more or less), an invisible transmission has been continuously occurring through the spiritual reality of F.R.C., including the
periodic incarnations of the individuality "Christian Rosenkreutz."[14]
Historically, the Thirty Years' War silenced Rosicrucianism in Germany. It continued, however, to make itself known in England, where
Thomas Vaughan produced printed translations of the *Fama* and the
Confessio in 1652. Ezechiel Foxcroft's translation of *The Chemical Wedding* followed in 1690. Elias Ashmole, too, speaks of the
Brotherhood in mid-century, even suggesting a link with the emerging movement of Freemasonry. (Freemasonry also arrives on the scene
in the seventeenth century, though obviously it began earlier. Its origin seems to be Scotland, rather than Germany. Ashmole, who was
possibly also a Rosicrucian, witnesses to the existence of Masonry in

1646.)[15] Masonry, then (which officially dates from St. John's Tide, 1717), will, in turn, in the eighteenth century assimilate Rosicrucianism as one of its "grades." In colonial America, too, Rosicrucians were active, as the Harvard historian of science William Newman describes in his book on "Eirenaeus Philalethes," *Gehennical Fire: The Lives of George Starkey, an American Alchemist in the Scientific Revolution.*[16]

Rosicrucianism reentered public consciousness in Germany in 1710 with a book by one "Sincerus Renatus" (Samuel Richter), a Protestant, Pietist pastor from Silesia. The book was called *The True and Complete Preparation of the Philosophical Stone of the Brotherhood of the Order of the Gold and Rosy Cross.*[17] The Brotherhood referred to was, however, by no means identical with the original "Brotherhood" of the previous century. For instance, it lacked the original's anti-papal spirit, allowing Roman Catholic members to join. This is probably just a matter of the changing context; a case can be made that the quasi-fanatical Protestantism of the manifestos was more a "sign of the times" than an essential part of the teaching. More significant, therefore, is the *alchemical* emphasis. Alchemy was always an extremely important part of the Rosicrucian program. Indeed, it could be called its hallmark. Now, however, it began to assume the central, doctrinal position previously held (at least overtly) by the more polemical apocalyptic and "reformist" elements. Again, like ecumenicism, this is far from being out of character. Taken historically, in fact, both — ecumenicism and alchemy — were always central to the Rosicrucian mission, as they were always central to Rudolf Steiner.

Throughout the eighteenth century, Rosicrucianism, now virtually synonymous with alchemy, was carried both within the burgeoning Masonic movement and within religious movements of the "Inner Light" like Pietism (which safeguarded and transmitted the works of Paracelsus and Jacob Boehme).[18] At the same time, self-appointed Rosicrucian and alchemical groups proliferated. Important alchemical and Rosicrucian works were continuously published — for instance, the famous *Secret Symbols of the Rosicrucians* (1785), a work that Rudolf Steiner studied closely, recognizing in it a major Rosicrucian moment — equivalent to H. P. Blavatsky's *Isis Unveiled* one hundred years later. [19]

Equally important is the way in which Rosicrucianism entered "exoteric" consciousness through "Romanticism." Romanticism is all too often considered merely as a literary or artistic movement. It was certainly that; but it was also much more. Romanticism, that is, the production of literary works by masters such as Herder, Lessing, Goethe, Novalis, Hegel, and Schelling in fact brought the Rosicrucian impulse to a new social, scientific, and cultural level. It was like a second Renaissance, raised to another degree, at once more idealistic and more realistic. Science, art, poetry, medicine, law, religion, philosophy — all seemed poised to embody a new lived synthesis based upon what the philosopher Fichte called "the transcendental I" and the poet William Blake, "Jesus the Imagination." Something of immense promise then seemed poised to enter evolution: a new science of the human heart, and a new language, the holy vernacular of the true I, the experience of what Franz von Baader calls the "it thinks."

The premises and methodology underlying all of Goethe's major works, for instance, stem largely from hermetic and Rosicrucian sources, to which his Pietist friend Fraulein Von Kettenberg introduced him.[20] This is true of the other Romantics also. Rudolf Steiner drew upon and referred continuously to this tradition in its German form, inspiring Owen Barfield to call anthroposophy "Romanticism come of age." Steiner in fact estimated Goethe so highly that, besides spending more than ten years of his life in Goethean studies, he many years later named the headquarters of his anthroposophy (which we may call postmodern Rosicrucianism) the *Goetheanum*. This was more than just a literary allusion. For Rudolf Steiner, Romanticism was the earthly resonance of a much higher reality. He frequently referred to an event in heaven that marked the coming together of the spiritual School of the Archangel Michael.[21] Romanticism was the reflection of this spiritual event. This was Steiner's way of speaking of the heavenly paradigm of the spiritual path of humanity appropriate for our time. Souls now descending to earth passed through the Michael School and in it participated many of the souls who had been part of the tradition we are studying.

Romanticism, however, was not just a German phenomenon. In England, there were Blake, Keats, and Coleridge, all profound students and transformers of the hermetic tradition; in America, Thoreau, Emerson, and Melville; in France, Nerval, Hugo (even parts of Balzac and Baudelaire); in Russia, Pushkin; in Poland, Mickiewicz; and so forth.

It was Pushkin, in fact, who asserted that Romanticism is called so after the first "romantics," the troubadours, who wrote in the romance tongue, their vernacular, mother tongue, rather than dead

Latin. To be romantic, in other words, is to take one's stand in experience, rather than theory or speculation. And experience knows no bounds. As Keats puts it:

> Where's the poet? Show him! Show him!
> Muses nine, that I may know him!
> 'Tis the man who with a man
> Is an equal, be he King,
> Or poorest of the beggar clan,
> Or any other wondrous thing
> A man may be 'twixt ape and Plato;
> 'Tis the man who with a bird,
> Wren or eagle, finds his way to
> All its instincts: he hath heard
> The Lion's roaring, and can tell
> What his horny throat expresseth,
> And to him the tiger's yell
> Comes articulate and presseth
> On his ear like mother-tongue.

In this sense, the poet is a true Rosicrucian:

> He passes forth into the charmed air
> With talisman to call up spirits rare
> From plant, cave, rock and fountain. To his sight
> The husk of natural objects opens quite
> To the core, and every secret essence there
> Reveals the elements good and fair
> Making him see where learning hath no light...

Keats writes of the poetical character that "it has no self — it is everything and nothing — It has no character; It enjoys light and shade; it lives in gusto, be it foul or fair, high or low, rich or poor, mean or elevated.... A poet is the most unpoetical of anything in existence, because he has no identity — he is continually informing and filling some other body." Keats himself, it is well known, could even fill a billiard ball. He lived in "gusto" (a word that connotes the quintessential energy of things). Keats, exemplary in this, seeks everywhere to enter into "Havens of intenseness," in which time and space collapse into a single image-meaning. The language that he uses for this makes it clear what this energy is. It is love. It has to be: for it is love that joins us to what is living and creative. The

famous "pleasure-thermometer" lines from "Endymion" express it
most clearly:

> Wherein lies happiness? In that which becks
> Our ready minds to fellowship divine,
> A fellowship with essence; till we shine,
> Full alchemized, and free of space. Behold
> The clear religion of heaven! Fold
> A rose leaf round thy finger's taperness,
> And soothe thy lips; hist, when the airy stress
> Of music's kiss impregnates the free winds,
> And with a sympathetic touch unbinds
> Aeolian magic from their lucid wombs;
> Then old songs waken from enclouded tombs;
> Old ditties sigh above their father's grave;
> Ghosts of melodious prophesyings rave
> Round every spot where trod Apollo's foot...
> Feel we these things? — that moment have we stepped
> Into a kind of oneness, and our state
> Is like a floating spirit's. But there are
> Richer entanglements, enthrallments far
> More self-destroying, leading, by degrees,
> To the chief intensity: the crown of these
> Is made of love and friendship, and sits high
> Upon the forehead of humanity.
> All its more ponderous and bulky worth
> Is friendship; whence there ever issues forth
> A steady splendour: but at the tip-top
> There hangs by unseen film, an orbed drop
> Of light, and that is love: its influence,
> Thrown in our eyes, genders a novel sense,
> At which we start and fret; till in the end,
> Melting into its radiance, we blend,
> Mingle, and so become part of it
> Nor with aught else can our souls interknit
> So wingedly. We combine therewith,
> Life's self is nourished by its proper pith,
> And we are nurtured like a pelican brood...

During this same period, Rosicrucianism also moved more covertly.
Sigismund Bacstrom, for instance, was an alchemist and doctor at the
end of the eighteenth century. Probably of Scandinavian origin (he

was born around 1740 and lived in Amsterdam from 1763–1770), Bacstrom worked as a ship's physician, traveling the world and finally, in 1790, settling in London. Living in Marylebone, he practiced alchemy and gathered around him a small group of spiritual seekers. Among these, he circulated his own translations of important alchemical texts and, in this way, became one of the seminal influences behind the so-called occult or theosophical revival in Britain at the end of the nineteenth century. (Madame Blavatsky, for example, knew Bacstrom's work, and printed his translation of the "Golden Chain of Homer" in the theosophical journal *Lucifer* in 1891.)

Bacstrom, though practically unknown except to a few specialists in the field of esoteric studies, is a remarkably interesting figure on two counts at least. His knowledge of the history, theory, and practice of alchemy was rare and deep; and he almost certainly came by it through the Society of the Rose Cross (into which Comte Louis de Chazal initiated him on the Island of Mauritius in 1794.

The Count was then ninety-four years old and appears to have obtained his alchemical knowledge (and perhaps Rosicrucian initiation) in Paris in the 1740s, possibly from the great Comte de St. Germain himself. We know this because a copy of a document attesting to Bacstrom's admission in the society survived in the library of the nineteenth-century occultist Frederick Hockley, where it was found by A. E. Waite, the mystic and scholar of the Western esoteric traditions. Later, in 1980, Adam McLean, the contemporary guardian of alchemical literature, discovered another version of the same document (this time attesting to the admission of a certain Alexander Tilloch into Bacstrom's Rosicrucian Society) in the Ferguson Collection at Glasgow University Library. [22]

This initiation text therefore lies, as it were, midway between the first historical appearance of Rosicrucianism and its manifestation in the anthroposophy of Rudolf Steiner. As Adam McLean points out, "Perhaps we have in Bacstrom a direct connection through Chazal and the Comte de St. Germain with a continuing stream of Rosicrucian mystery wisdom." He adds, "We should come to see behind [Bacstrom] this esoteric order of the Rose Cross which provided him with the material and impulse to continue and develop the alchemical science. . . . " As the present collection shows, the same is true in some degree of Rudolf Steiner also.

From the Bacstrom document, we learn (as we do from Rudolf Steiner) that the Rosicrucian path is *Christian, alchemical,* and profoundly *modern.* The Christianity is implicit throughout and explicit

in its opening, for the document begins by invoking "Jehovah Elo-
him, the true and only God manifested in Trinity." It goes on to
affirm that "the Brethren believe in the grand atonement made by
Jesus Christ on the Rosy Cross, stained and marked with his blood
for the Redemption of Spiritual Nature." And then adds, in a foot-
note, that this same *grand atonement* "laid naked at the same time
our universal microcosmical subject, the best magnet for continually
attracting and preserving the Universal Fire of Nature, in the form of
incorporeal Nitre, for the regeneration of matter.... "

Various articles that the candidate swears to uphold follow. As is
to be expected, candidates begin by vowing to conduct themselves
as worthy members, and never to gossip about their membership
in the Society or publicly reveal any knowledge they may have
acquired. Then comes the promise that each member, before depart-
ing this life, will find and initiate a worthy successor. This, too, is
to be expected. Having stated it, however, the document takes an
unexpected turn:

> And as there is no distinction of sexes in the spiritual world, nei-
> ther amongst the blessed Angels nor among the rational spirits
> of the human race; and as we have had a Semiramis, Queen of
> Egypt, a Myriam the prophetess, a Peronella, the wife of Flamel,
> and lately a Leona Constantia, Abbess of Clermont, who was
> actually received as a practical member and master into our So-
> ciety in the year 1736, which women are believed to have been
> all possessors of the Great Work, consequently Sorores Roseae
> Crucis and members of our Society by possession, as the posses-
> sion of this our art is the key to the most hidden knowledge. And
> moreover as redemption was manifested to mankind by means
> of a woman (the Blessed Virgin), and as salvation, which is of in-
> finitely more value than our whole Art, is granted to the female
> sex as well as to the male, *our Society does not exclude a worthy
> woman from being initiated,* God himself not having excluded
> women from partaking in felicity in the next life. We will not
> hesitate to receive a worthy woman into our Society as a mem-
> ber apprentice (and even as a practical member or master if she
> does possess our work practically and has herself accomplished
> it), provided she is found, like Peronella, Flamel's wife, to be
> sober, pious, discreet, prudent, not loquacious, but reserved, of
> an upright mind and blameless conduct, and withal desirous of
> knowledge. (Italics added)

Needless to say, this is extraordinarily liberal and very unusual in its freedom from the dominant "patriarchalism" of the time and sets Bacstrom's stream of Rosicrucianism apart from Freemasonry and similar occult movements of the time.

Thereafter, throughout nineteenth-century Europe, Rosicrucianism remained something to conjure with. In a way, it stood for the ideal of an independent Christian esotericism — an authentic, true Christianity, apart from institutional religion, in direct contact with the spiritual powers. With nothing (or very little) to guide one but one's own "inner lights," great discretion was needed, for, as Wittgenstein wrote, "Does not the origin of the idea of the devil lie in the fact that our intuitions are not always correct." The field thus often belonged to the foolhardy (and the crazy), as well as to the truly courageous, loving, and wise. Manifestations, groups, initiates, and lineages sprung up everywhere, both above and below ground in Germany, France, England, America and so forth. It is unclear, however, how many (or whether indeed any) of these were Rosicrucian or alchemical (hermetic) in the true sense and not simply either para-Masonic (like the Asiatic Brethren, the *Fratres Lucis,* an offshoot of the Gold and Rosy Cross) or what we might call "Masonic-magical" or "kabbalistic-occult "(like Eliphas Levi, Bulwer-Lytton, the Hermetic Brotherhood of Luxor, or the Golden Dawn, for instance).[23]

Certainly, then, the nineteenth century left an extremely rich, well-prepared, and fertile ground upon which the Teachers of the New Age of Light — H. P. Blavatsky and Rudolf Steiner — could build.

6. *The Secret Stream*

Edith Maryon was an English sculptor who came to Rudolf Steiner and accepted him as her teacher just before the outbreak of the First World War. She had previously been a member of the Order of the Golden Dawn. This was the prestigious English hermetic "Rosicrucian" ritual order (it was affiliated with the *Societa Rosicruciana in Anglia,* the Rosicrucian Society in England.)[24] Luminaries as different as the poet W. B. Yeats, the mystic, Evelyn Underhill, and the novelist (and Inkling) Charles Williams — not to mention not necessarily lesser luminaries like MacGregor Mathers, Aleister Crowley, A. E. Waite, and Arthur Machen — all belonged to this order. Steiner was familiar with it and, on occasion, representatives of the Golden

Dawn had approached him for teaching. Apparently, then, the two
sides had something in common. And yet, in a letter to Edith Maryon
on her coming to Dornach, Steiner, while by no means disparaging
the Golden Dawn (in fact, he speaks of it as if it were a kind of distant
cousin), quite clearly states that it belongs to "a different stream."

What, then, was and is the stream to which Rudolf Steiner and
anthroposophy belong?

Certainly, it was the stream that came to light with the primary
Rosicrucian documents of the early seventeenth century. For Steiner,
these documents are true. They derive from the spiritual being of the
Rose Cross and the narratives they tell actually occurred. As the *Fama*
and the *Confessio* recount it, there was a Christian Rosenkreutz, who
traveled widely and created the Fraternity. But that, still, is only the
beginning (or is the end?) of the true story. In the words of George
Adams, "As a hidden fraternity the Rosicrucians lived and worked in
Europe ever since the fourteenth century....But the spiritual preparation for their work goes back to an even more hidden event that
took place a thousand years before. Rudolf Steiner in the last chapter of *The East in the Light of the West* describes it as one of the
greatest conferences that have ever taken place in the spiritual world
belonging to the earth."[25] This was in the fourth century. Three of
the greatest initiates were called together by a fourth, who was "even
greater" than they. The three were Zarathustra, Gautama Buddha,
and Scythianos; the fourth was Manes, the founder of Manicheanism.
In Steiner's words:

> Manes called these three together to consult with them as to how
> the wisdom that had lived through the turning-point of post-
> Atlantean time [the Incarnation] might gradually come to life
> again and unfold ever more gloriously into the future.... In that
> council, the plan was agreed upon that all the wisdom of the
> Boddhisattvas of post-Atlantean times should flow more fully
> and strongly into the future of the earth. And the plan for the
> future evolution of earthly civilization that was then decided
> was preserved and carried over into those European mysteries,
> which are the Mysteries of the Rose Cross....

To understand this we must grasp that, for Steiner, Zarathustra
represents simultaneously the alchemical path through the macrocosm or outer nature and the protection and development of the life
or etheric body. Now, from this perspective, the Buddha has to do

with the catharsis of the astral body and Scythianos with the "mysteries of the physical body." Thus the presence of these three indicates the primacy of the Rosicrucian engagement with the whole human being: body, soul, and spirit. But what, then, of Manes? Manes, the greatest of all according to Steiner, is the teacher who understood the primacy of ethics, of the active engagement of the heart as the central, redemptive, cognitive and discriminative organ. This has to do with the fundamental fact of creation being light and darkness, good and evil — of the task being the transformation of darkness into light (evil into good, lead into gold, matter into light). Consciousness surely has no other role or function. George Adams therefore concludes his essay, "The Rose Cross is not so much an *ascetic* path; it may even be described as an *aesthetic* path in the literal sense of the word. It leads us, to use Schiller's phrase, 'through the gateway of beauty into the morning land.'" This beauty, as Adams says, is not merely Luciferian, but is achieved consciously, by the training of inner spiritual senses. And, just as it is aesthetic, involving beauty and the senses, so it is also *ethical,* involving right action. For, as the French philosopher Levinas has so movingly shown, it is the "face" of the other (whether another human being or the face of nature) that calls forth from us, if we *see* it, the ethical response that allows us to become who we truly are.[26]

Mention of Schiller (whom Adams here links with Dürer, Goethe, and Rembrandt), together with the notion of aesthetics, allows us to connect not just Romanticism, but the central stream of European art and culture since the Renaissance with the Rosicrucian impulse. There is a danger here that Rosicrucianism could become everything "good," that is, anything one wants. One must beware of that. For that reason, Steiner himself in these lectures is at once very circumspect and precise. And it is to these that we should now turn.

Part 1

ROSICRUCIANISM

— one —

Tao and Rose Cross

This opening piece may be read as a kind of prologue to the book as a whole. It is taken from Steiner's first talk as spiritual teacher to the Esoteric Class, following the separation of the German Theosophical Society (of which he was the general secretary) from the Esoteric School of Theosophy (Adyar, India). Hence, the sharpness of his delineation of the Rose Cross as the Western way.

Steiner here links the Rosicrucian outward path in nature with the ancient wisdom of Atlantis, which he sees as intimately connected with the Northern mysteries. At the same time, he reveals Christian Rosenkreutz's great task to be precisely the uniting of "Eastern and Western cultures" — "Eastern" here being above all Hebraic and Christian, as in the Old and New Testaments — with the ancient Atlantean teaching of the Tao.

— ◆ —

. . . Esoteric students must be quite clear about the fact that they are always surrounded by invisible beings — invisible to ordinary people.

This is the text of Rudolf Steiner's first Esoteric Class after the German group's separation from the esoteric school of Theosophy; *From the History and Contents of the First Section of the Esoteric School, 1904–1914*, Munich, June 1, 1907 (*Zur Geschichte und aus den Inhalten der ersten Abteilung der Esoterischen Schule 1904–1907*, GA 264), translated by John Wood (revised).

Just as we walk through air, we also constantly walk through count-less invisible beings. They are there wherever we turn. Every single thing that surrounds us is the expression of such beings. When we breathe we inhale not only air, but, at the same time, a high spiritual being, whose physical body is composed of air, which streams into us and entirely fills our organism. When we exhale, this being flows out of us again.

We should be aware that with every breath we take a divine spir-itual being takes up residence within us, and we should realize that we shall one day become such a being ourselves. This being that in-carnates into the air is at a much higher stage of development than we are today, but at one time it was at our present stage, and there will come a time when we shall have progressed as far as it has.

When we belong to an esoteric school, the exercises, however they are given, are arranged so that we gain a living consciousness of the instreaming spirit. So what is it that says "I" in us? It is the stream of the inhaled air. It creates the red blood within us, and only after the red blood started to flow in our bodies could we learn to say "I" to ourselves. But it is not only within the instreaming air that a spiritual being works in upon us. Spiritual beings are at work in every part of our body — in muscles, nerves, and bones. Knowledge of this, however, does not yet make us into esotericists.

If I say to myself, "The air penetrates my body," I am a materialist. If I know and recognize the fact that a spiritual being penetrates me when I inhale, that makes me a "knower," but it does not yet make me an esotericist. When, full of awe and filled with the deepest reverence toward the divine being that penetrates my organism, I allow the instreaming breath to flow into me, and a living consciousness of this higher being entirely fills me, then I am an esotericist.

What is this air-embodied spirit doing in me? It enters my blood, penetrating my whole organism, so that a body composed of air is formed within me, surrounded by bones, muscles, sinews, and so on. Through the exercises I do — I do them with this in mind — I become quite conscious of this airy body. It is the same as what says "I" within me. If one carries out the exercises in this way, one becomes more and more free. It is as though a different human being were born within. I then no longer say "I" to my bones, muscles, and sinews. I feel entirely united with this body built of air. I discover myself in the spirit of this God incorporated into the air.

What are we actually doing when we perform exercises? We must be quite clear about this. When we do exercises we are living the way everyone will live at some time in the future. During the exercises, esoteric pupils find themselves in a future state of humankind. In the future, some, but not all, people will do this. Only in a very far distant future will it be the natural thing for all human beings to breathe in this way. But when that time comes, human bodies will have become quite different. They will have developed so that it will be quite natural to breathe as esotericists sometimes do today. An esoteric pupil is actually doing something in anticipation of what will happen later. It is, in a certain sense, not yet quite timely. The physical body is not yet adapted for it. Esotericists thus live ahead of their time and work into the future.

But only in this way can progress occur. Our Earth would never develop further if it were not inhabited by people who live as all of humanity will live in a far distant future. If no one on Earth was willing to do esoteric exercises, Earth would become more and more rigid. It is true that everyone shares in the transformation of Earth during the *devachan* stage of life after death, but if those incarnated on Earth merely tried to preserve everything as it is now, and, at the same time, those in devachan tried to transform the earth, then there would be no harmony in their respective efforts. The human beings on Earth would cause Earth to become quite bonelike and rigid, whereas the efforts of those in devachan who wish to transform the rigid earth would finally split it up and disintegrate it. Therefore esotericists must be quite clear about the sacred duty they have to fulfill for the progress of humankind when they do esoteric exercises.

In itself, it is paradoxical, at least in the present circumstances, for the esotericist to live in a way that will be natural only in the future. Yet only in this way can progress be achieved. Human beings always find it necessary to use the bodies that are natural and possible for their stage of evolution. A being that ought to belong to Jupiter or Venus [epochs of Earth evolution] according to its stage of development must, nevertheless, make use of the physical bodies available to all humankind if it would live among us. But spiritually such a being leads a life belonging to a distant future, thereby gradually bringing this future down into us and enabling us to attain it.

Some people might ask if it would not also be possible to go through such development on their own, without any esoteric school? Certainly it would. Everyone will, for example, undergo a transformation of the breathing process during the course of development. But that is like saying you would like to study mathematics completely on your own without a teacher. You would then, of course, also have to forego the use of any textbooks. Certainly you could learn mathematics in this way, but it would take about three thousand years to learn what could be picked up in about five months with the aid of a teacher.

In itself it would be quite possible — yes, certainly it would — to find out for oneself all that can now be learned through esoteric exercises. For all the exercises are basically a part of human nature. Only it would not be three thousand years, but many hundreds of thousands of years that would be needed. The way can be shortened through esoteric training. Esoteric training has no other purpose than that. By undertaking such esoteric exercises a person grows spiritually toward the future and experiences within what will come to pass in the future; what one thus experiences is what is known to us as "the higher worlds." The higher worlds represent future human conditions. At every moment, therefore, we must be conscious of our sacred duty. With every breath we must experience the Divine that pours into us. The Godhead flows into us with every inhalation, but with every exhalation we kill its body by making the air unusable. But ultimately our exercises will gradually teach us how to exhale the air in the same purity as we inhaled it. Those not inclined to learn this through exercises will, of course, eventually attain it by natural means, but they will have to wait until the human body has been so transformed in the future that this kind of breathing will come as naturally as the way we now breathe comes through our present constitution.

The air flows in and out of us today and transforms the used-up blood into blood that can be reused. Was that always so? No! There was a time when everything that today constitutes the warmth of our blood was not within us, but streamed in and out of our organism as air does today. Just as the air spirits flow into us today, so the fire spirits flowed into us at that time. Then human beings inhaled and exhaled warmth. And just as warm blood could be formed through the influence of the air spirits, so another kind of substance flowed through us when the fire spirits were at work on our organism: milk. What flows in all beings who suckle their young is a remnant of that time; but the functions within the human body connected with milk are directed by other spirits.

During the time when a young humankind was developing on Earth — for example, at the time of Atlantis and the first eras following — its leaders were not yet human, but were fire spirits. It is to them, therefore, that we must first turn when we try to advance.

Today not all people advance at the same rate. Some remain behind, and so it was then as well. A number of the fire spirits remained behind the others and created a resistance to new development. The spirits of the air and wind had already succeeded the fire spirits and begun their activity among humankind when the retarded fire spirits obstructed their way. The Northern sagas give us a notion of what these retarded spirits were like in the myth of the God Loki. He represents such a retarded fire spirit; he opposes the Aesir and was the cause of Baldur's death. Wotan, the one who lives in the flowing air, is a god of the winds. He was experienced by the ancient Northern peoples when they heard the storm brewing, and when they drew breath into their bodies.

These Northern peoples were not without their Mysteries. We know how the peoples of our post-Atlantean era poured out of the West toward the East from ancient Atlantis. The Mysteries that had flourished in Atlantis also remained in the new era being formed. Four cultural eras have formed our fifth root race: (1) the Indian; (2) the Persian; (3) the Chaldean-Babylonian-Egypto-Semitic; (4) the Greco-Roman.

But not all of the multitudes coming from Atlantis reached the regions in the East. Some of them stayed in western areas belonging to modern Europe. This group also had its Mysteries, which developed later into what we know as the Druidic and Drottic Mysteries.

Western culture did not remain isolated from what grew up in the East. What eventually blossomed in the East culminated in the foundation of Old and New Testament wisdom. It reached the West and united with what had developed quietly there with great impact. This impact brought untold blessings.

We must clearly see that Atlantis is the source of all Eastern and Western wisdom.

Atlantis was a land thickly shrouded in mists. These mists had a very special connection to humanity. Human beings of that time experienced something through the mists; their souls were made receptive toward the speech of the Gods. In the bubbling springs, in the rustle of leaves, the people of Atlantis heard the voice of God speaking to them. And when they were alone and sunk into their own inner beings, they could perceive a sound that was the voice of God speaking to them. They did not need laws and commandments. God told them what they had to do. And the sound reverberating throughout Atlantis and echoing out of the hearts of those people during silent hours of communion was later fixed in Egypt into the *Tau* symbol: T.

This is also the original form of the Cross.

We must be clear about the way these mists provided a link with the Divine — so that people could take up into themselves and understand divine wisdom in a direct way. Bearing this in mind, let us then turn our attention to the water that flows today in our country.

If we look at a drop of dew glistening on the grass in the morning sunlight, our hearts are filled with piety. This tiny glistening dewdrop is a reminder for us — a reminder of those times in Atlantis when fogs covered the land and when people had an inkling of the divine wisdom that enveloped them.

The wisdom of Atlantis was embodied in the water, in a drop of dew. And the word *dew* [*Tau* in German] is nothing other than the ancient Atlantean sound.[1] Thus we should view with awe and reverence every drop of dew that glistens on a blade of grass, and regard it as a sacred legacy of the time when the link between human beings and the gods was not yet broken. The Tau symbol, the ancient sign of the Cross, is *Crux* in Latin. And what is the name for dew in Latin? *Ros: Ros-Crux* is our "Rose Cross." Now we recognize its true significance. It is the *Tao* of Atlantis, the wisdom of Atlantis, that twinkles at us today from every dewdrop.[2] The Rose Cross conveys exactly this to us. It is the symbol for the new life that will blossom forth in spirit in the future.

Thus our Northern race remained in intimate connection with ancient Atlantis. It was different in the case of those races that wandered toward the East and formed the four epochs of India, Persia, Egypt, and Greece/Rome. They developed independently. Yet it is a rule of the spiritual world that every culture that evolves independently through its own efforts must also perish if it cannot receive a new impulse from the regions it sprang from, from its mother country. So it was necessary for the exalted culture of the East to receive an impulse from our territories, to merge itself with the spiritual culture that had grown up quietly in our lands.

The exalted spiritual individuality who recognized this fact was Christian Rosenkreutz. In the thirteenth and fourteenth centuries, he took up the great task of uniting the Eastern and Western cultures. He has always lived among us and he is still with us today as the leader of the spiritual life. He brought the spiritual culture of the East, revealed in its greatest blossoming in the Old and New Testaments into intimate harmony with the ancient wisdom of Atlantis.

Thus he gave us the form of Christianity that was also prepared and introduced through that mysterious "Stranger from the Highlands" who visited Johannes Tauler.[3] "Highlands" is the name for the spiritual world, the Kingdom of Heaven. That spiritual individual who was concealed in the "Stranger from the Highlands" was none other than the Master Jesus himself, in whose body the Christ had lived on Earth. He is also still with us today.

The Master Jesus and the Master Christian Rosenkreutz have prepared two paths of initiation for us: (1) the Christian-esoteric path, and (2) the Christian-Rosicrucian path.

These two paths have existed since the Middle Ages. But spiritual life disappeared more and more from human consciousness when materialism arose. At the end of the last century, materialism had reached such a degree that a new spiritual impulse was required if humankind were not to perish.

A single personality, through her psychic capacities, could perceive the voice of the Masters. This was H. P. Blavatsky. Not all esoteric traditions had been lost by the time she began her work. The Eastern brotherhoods had received esoteric knowledge, but in a rigid, ossified form, without any life in it. When Blavatsky wrote *Isis Unveiled,* these brotherhoods assumed that this was their knowledge, for they were familiar with many symbols and teachings, and they tried in every way to put obstacles in her way.

So H. P. Blavatsky was hindered in the worst possible way in accomplishing her work in the sense of Christian esotericism as she originally intended. She really had to suffer terrible things at that time. And those esoteric brotherhoods actually succeeded in forcing her to present what she had to offer in her second work, *The Secret Doctrine,* in an Eastern guise.[4] We are still accustomed to receiving most of our esoteric terminology in Eastern language. But this Eastern form of truth is not for us Western peoples. It can only restrict us and divert us from our goal. Here in the West are the people who will form the nucleus for the coming epochs.

That should be the true answer to what was proclaimed recently as the voice of the Masters from the East. Our Western Masters have also spoken, even though it was accompanied by less fanfare. And we would inscribe what they have said deep into our hearts. They summoned us to share in the future development of humankind, to remain steadfast and endure in all the battles that remain ahead of us, and to hold on to what we possess of the sacred living tradition. This summons will continue to sound in our souls. But no one should believe that there is disharmony between the Masters of the East and those of the West — although an incisive change has occurred lately regarding the esoteric schools of the East and those of the West.

Until now, both schools have been united in a large circle under the combined leadership of the Masters. Now, however, the Western school has become independent, and there are two comparable schools: one in the East, the other in the West — two smaller circles instead of the one large one. The Eastern school is being led by Mrs. Annie Besant, and those who feel more attracted to her in their hearts can no longer remain in our school. People should sound exactly their hearts' longings to discover which way they are being led. At the head of our Western school there are two Masters: the Master Jesus and the Master Christian Rosenkreutz. And they lead us along two paths: the Christian and the Christian-Rosicrucian way. The Great White Lodge leads all spiritual movements, and the Master Jesus and the Master Christian Rosenkreutz belong to this Lodge. Let that be the answer — the true, factual answer — to the question that many of you must have been asking because of the most recent events.

We stand at the dawning of the Sixth Day of Creation. We have to develop the sixth and seventh cultural eras out of ourselves. The future in its rising light is already present within us. . . .

Notes from memory relating to the final part of the same lesson on June 1, 1907:

. . . In 1459 Christian Rosenkreutz saw it was necessary for the wisdom of the *Tau* to unite with Christianity so that it could be led into the new evolution. He brought to the people of Middle Europe the wisdom of the *Tau* or *Ros-Crux* that united with the wisdom of the Old and New Testaments.

At the time of Johannes Tauler, a personality lived who was called "the Stranger from the Highlands." This person instructed Johannes Tauler, who then preached so powerfully that some of his audience were left as if dead. The individuality that appeared in this personality was the individuality of the Master Jesus, who has always been the leader of the development of the West — although this has been concealed. Together with this individuality there was another Master-Individual at work in the West: Christian Rosenkreutz. They are still the Masters of the West, who guide the development of Middle Europe. A brotherhood is formed by the Lodge of the Masters, but the work they perform for human progress is nevertheless varied. Just as the other two Masters are working for the East [Kut Hoomi and Morya], so these two Masters work for the West.

Of all the learned ones living in the West during the last third of the nineteenth century, none were suited to the task of introducing the new spiritual impulse, which the Great White Lodge found necessary in order to protect the Western world from destruction by materialism. But in H.P.B. the Masters found the desired tool to introduce the new teachings to the world — the wisdom that would bring in the future. H.P.B. incorporated the Western wisdom, given her at that time, in *Isis Unveiled*. This is an important work, containing great treasures of the highest truth, but in part they are portrayed in a distorted way. That is why H.P.B. was not understood in the West then.

There are also great occult brotherhoods in the West. Many of them were not in agreement with what H.P.B. was doing. Among these brotherhoods, a strong persecution arose against her, causing H.P.B. to suffer immensely, in a way of which no one has any inkling. These occult brotherhoods were anxious to propagate occult knowledge only in an orthodox sense. They therefore joined together to oppose H.P.B., who merely wanted to bring future knowledge to the West; but because she was not understood she turned to the East and allowed herself to be inspired by Eastern wisdom, which she wrote down in *The Secret Doctrine*. That is Eastern wisdom. At first, she just wanted to bring Western future knowledge....

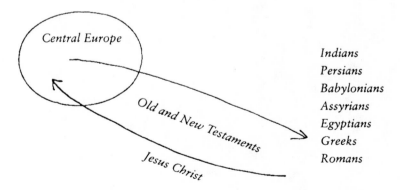

Central Europe

Old and New Testaments

Jesus Christ

Indians
Persians
Babylonians
Assyrians
Egyptians
Greeks
Romans

From the end of other notes from memory of the same lesson:

... The Masters also must incarnate physically to aid development. The Master of the "Sixth Dawn" is Christian Rosenkreutz. Jesus of Nazareth — Christian Rosenkreutz. If we try to take that into our feelings and allow it to become perception, we will understand why there must be an esoteric school of the West and an esoteric school of the East. They stand side by side, of equal value. Each possesses its two Masters: Mahatma K [Kut Hoomi] and Mahatma M [Morya]; Master Jesus of Nazareth and Master Christian Rosenkreutz. One of these schools is led by Mrs. Besant, the other by Dr. Steiner. But we have to decide which one to follow.

— two —

Who Are the Rosicrucians?

Berlin, March 14, 1907

In these first lectures, Steiner introduces the subject of Rosicrucianism. As the lectures unfold, readers will notice a certain repetition. However, this repetition does not seem boring. Rather, as now-familiar ideas keep recurring in different contexts, with different nuances and overtones, one's understanding seems to penetrate ever more deeply into the unspoken meaning of Steiner's message.

He begins with Rosicrucianism as a spiritual discipline — a path of knowledge or initiation. "To be initiated means to awaken faculties that sleep in every soul." This takes effort, of course, but it is available to all; and having made the effort, one can begin to penetrate nature's secrets.

Steiner is clear that there are many paths to initiation, all of which lead to the truth; but, he says, there is one path above all that is appropriate for modern Western human beings and that is the Rosicrucian path of initiation.

After speaking briefly about rules, Steiner then turns to a description of Rosicrucian training in seven stages. In so doing, he speaks most movingly of the Rosicrucian understanding of the Grail.

— ◆ —

Few people have even remotely adequate ideas about today's subject, the Rosicrucians. Indeed, it is not easy even to say what the name means. It remains extremely vague for most people. Books tell us that the Rosicrucians are believed to be some sort of sect that flourished in the early centuries of German culture. Some say it is impossible to verify that anything serious or rational ever existed behind the fraud

Supersensible Knowledge, lecture 11 (*Die Erkenntnis des Übersinnlichen in unserer Zeit*, GA 55), translated by Rita Stebbing and revised.

41

associated with the name. On the other hand, some learned books do offer a variety of information.

If what is written about Rosicrucianism is true, one could only come to the conclusion that it consisted of nothing but idle boasting, pure fraud, or worse. Even those who have attempted to justify it, do so with a patronizing air, even though they may have found that Rosicrucianism is able to throw light on certain subjects. But what they have to say about it — for example, that it is involved with alchemy, with producing the philosophers' stone, the Stone of the Wise, and other alchemical feats — does not inspire much confidence.

For the genuine Rosicrucians, however, these feats of transformation were only symbols for the inner moral purification of the human soul: the transformations represented ways that inner human virtues should be developed. When the Rosicrucians spoke of transforming base metals into gold, they meant that it was possible to transform base vices into the gold of human virtue.

Those who maintain that the great work of the Rosicrucians should be understood symbolically are met with the argument that Rosicrucianism is therefore trivial. Such people argue that it is difficult to see the necessity of all these alchemical inventions — such as the transformation of metals — if their purpose is merely to demonstrate the obvious fact that we should be moral and change our vices into virtues. Rosicrucianism, however, involves something far more important that.

Rather than offer more historical material, I will present a factual account of Rosicrucianism. Its history need not concern us aside from the fact that Rosicrucianism has existed in the West since the fourteenth century, and that it goes back to the legendary figure of Christian Rosenkreutz, about whom much is rumored but history says little.[1]

The various accounts share one basic feature. This may be summarized by saying that Christian Rosenkreutz (this is only the name by which he is known) traveled the world around the end of the fifteenth and the beginning of the sixteenth centuries. On his journeys through the East, he became acquainted with a book, called *M———*. Mysteriously, by means of this book, Paracelsus, the great medieval physician, mystic, and alchemist, gained his knowledge — or so we are told. This account is true, but only initiates know the true nature of this book *M———* and what it means to study it.

Conventional knowledge about Rosicrucianism stems from two writings published at the beginning of the seventeenth century, the so-called *Fama Fraternitatis,* published in 1614, and the *Confessio,* published a year later. These texts are much disputed by scholars. However, these disputes have been by no means confined to the usual kind of controversy surrounding texts — whether the author really was Valentin Andreae, for instance, who in his later years was an ordinary normal clergyman. Scholars have also disputed whether the author intended his books to be taken seriously or as a lampoon — a "ludibrium" — meant to parody a certain secret brotherhood known as the Rosicrucians. These first two publications were followed by many others offering all sorts of information about Rosicrucianism.

When people with no knowledge of the true background of Rosicrucianism pick up the writings of Valentin Andreae (or indeed any other Rosicrucian document), they do not find anything exceptional in them. In fact, until now, it has been impossible to gain even elementary information about this spiritual stream, which still exists and has existed ever since the fourteenth century. All that has been published, written, and printed are merely fragments, surrendered into public hands by a kind of betrayal. Not only are these fragments inaccurate, they have suffered all manner of distortions by charlatans and frauds. They have been the butt of incomprehension, and sheer stupidity. Throughout its entire history, in fact, true Rosicrucianism has been passed on orally to members who have been sworn to secrecy. That is why nothing of great importance found its way into public literature.

Today, I will address certain basic aspects of Rosicrucianism that can now be spoken of publicly for reasons that, for now, would take me too far afield to explain. Only when they are known can one make any sense of what is found in writings that are for the most part exaggerated, sometimes to the point of being merely comical, and that are often fraudulent as well.

Rosicrucianism is a way or method of attaining what is known as initiation. We have often discussed the nature of initiation in our circles. To be initiated means to awaken faculties that sleep in every human soul. Such faculties enable us to see into the spiritual world that exists behind our physical world. The physical world is an expression of the spiritual world of which it is a product. Initiates are those who have applied the method of initiation — a method as exacting and scientific as any applied in chemistry, physics, or other sciences. The difference is that the method of initiation is not applied to begin with to anything external but only to the human being himself or herself; we ourselves become the instrument, or tool, through which knowledge of the spiritual world is attained. Those who genuinely strive to attain knowledge of the spirit recognize the deep truth contained in Goethe's words:

> Mysterious in day's broad light,
> Nature retains her veil, despite our imprecations,
> and what she won't reveal to human mind or sight
> levers, screws or hammers
> cannot wrench from her.[2]

Deep indeed are the secrets of nature, but not as impenetrable as people maintain because they are too comfortable to exert the effort. The human spirit is certainly able to penetrate nature's secrets — not through the soul's ordinary faculties, however, but through higher ones, which are attained when the soul's hidden forces have been developed through certain strictly defined methods. Those who prepare themselves incrementally will eventually reach the point where knowledge attainable only through initiation is revealed. Then, to use the language of Goethe, the great secret is revealed, the secret of what ultimately holds the world together — a revelation that is truly a fruit of initiation.

It has often been explained that anyone may go through the early stages of initiation with no danger whatever. But the higher stages require the very highest conscientiousness and devotion to truth in spiritual research. When we approach the portals through which we look into very different worlds, we realize the truth of what is often emphasized — that it is dangerous to reveal the holy secrets of existence to large groups of people. However, such secrets can be revealed, but only to the extent that modern human beings are able, through inner preparation, to find their way gradually to the highest secrets of nature and the spiritual world.

The movement of spiritual science is a path that guides human beings to the higher secrets.[3] Numerous such paths exist. This does not mean, however, that the ultimate truth attainable assumes different forms. The highest truth is one, no matter where or when human beings ever lived or live. Once they reach the highest truth, it is the same for all.

This truth may be compared to the view from a mountaintop, which is the same for all who reach it, regardless of whether they chose different paths to get there. When you are standing at a certain spot on the side of a mountain and see a path, you do not walk round the mountain to look for another path. The same applies to the path of higher knowledge, which must accord with a person's nature. This consideration is too often overlooked — that is, the immense differences in human nature. The inner organization of people in ancient India was different from that of people nowadays. This difference in the higher members of the human being can be seen by spiritual research, but not by conventional physiology or anatomy. Because of this, a wonderful spiritual knowledge as well as a method for achieving initiation — the path of yoga — has been preserved right up to today. Those who are constituted like the people of ancient India may be led along this path to the summit of knowledge. For contemporary Europeans, however, it makes no more sense to seek that path than it would, when hiking a peak, to leave the path we stand on and walk to the other side of the mountain and use a path there. The nature of modern Europeans is completely different from human beings in ancient Asia. Likewise, a few centuries before the Christian era, human nature was different from what it would become a few centuries later. And today it has changed again.

Initiation, as I have said, is based on awakening certain forces in human beings. With this in mind, we must acknowledge that we must consider our individual nature when developing methods through which we become instruments for perceiving and investigating the spirit world.

The great way of yoga developed by the Rishis, the great spiritual teachers in ancient India, is still valid for Indians. At the beginning of the Christian era, the appropriate method was the so-called Christian gnostic path. But those who stand fully within today's civilization need a different method. That is why over the course of centuries and millennia the great masters of wisdom who guide human evolution change the methods that lead to the summit of wisdom.

The Rosicrucian method of initiation is especially appropriate for today's humanity. It meets the needs of modern conditions. Not only is it a Christian path, but it enables those who strive to recognize that spiritual research and its achievements harmonize completely with modern culture and with the whole outlook of human beings today. For many centuries to come, Rosicrucianism will be the right method of initiation into spiritual life.

When Rosicrucianism was first inaugurated, certain rules were established for its adherents — rules that are essentially still valid.

And because these rules are strictly observed, Rosicrucians are not recognized by outsiders.

The first rule (which only recently has been slightly modified) is never to reveal that one is a Rosicrucian.[4] The wisdom is fostered in narrow circles, but its fruits should be available to all humanity. That is why, until recently, Rosicrucians never divulged what enabled them to investigate nature's secrets. Nothing of the knowledge was revealed; no hint was given, theoretically or otherwise. Instead, work was done that furthered civilization and implanted wisdom in barely noticeable ways to others. That is the first basic rule; to elaborate it further would go beyond our subject. It is enough to say that this rule has been relaxed somewhat, but that higher Rosicrucian knowledge is not revealed.

The second rule concerns conduct and may be expressed in this way: Become a real part of the culture and people to which you belong; be a member of the class in which you find yourself. Dress normally, not in something different or conspicuous. Thus, you will find that neither ambition nor selfishness motivates the Rosicrucians. Rather, they strive wherever possible to improve aspects of the prevailing culture, all the while keeping in view the much higher aims that link them to the central Rosicrucian wisdom.

The other basic rules need not concern us here. For the moment, I want to look at actual Rosicrucian training or schooling as it is practiced today and has existed for centuries. Anything I can say about it, however, of course concerns only the elementary stages of the whole system of Rosicrucian training. I should add something, too, about this training that also applies to spiritual scientific training — it should not be undertaken without knowledgeable guidance. You will find what is to be said about this subject in my book *How to Know Higher Worlds: A Modern Path of Initiation.*[5]

Preliminary Rosicrucian training involves seven stages, which need not be accomplished in the sequence enumerated here. The teacher will lay more emphasis on one point or another according to the individual and special needs of the student. Thus, it is a path of learning and inner development, adapted to the particular student. These are the seven steps:

1. Study (in the Rosicrucian sense of the word);

2. Acquisition of Imagination knowledge;

3. Acquisition of the esoteric script;

4. Bringing rhythm into life (also described as "preparing the philosophers' stone," which has nothing to do with the nonsense
   written about it);

5. Knowledge of the microcosm, our essential human nature;

6. Becoming one with the macrocosm, or great universe;

7. Attaining beatitude.

The sequence in which the student passes through these preliminary stages of Rosicrucian training depends on the student's
personality, but they must all be accomplished. What I have said
about it thus far (and also what I am about to say) must be seen
as a description of the ideal. Do not imagine that such things can be
attained from one day to the next. One can, however, at least learn
the description of what may seem like such a distant goal today. We
can always make a beginning, provided we also realize that patience,
energy, and perseverance are required.

To many, the first stage, study, initially seems somewhat dry and
pedantic. But, in this case, study has nothing to do with erudition in
the usual sense. We do not need to be scholars to be initiates. Spiritual
knowledge and scholarship are not closely connected. "Study" in this
sense means something quite different, but absolutely essential. No
true Rosicrucian teacher will guide the student to higher stages if
the student has no aptitude for the requirements of this first stage. It
requires the student to develop a kind of thinking that is thoroughly
sensible and logical. This is necessary, otherwise students lose the
ground under their feet at higher stages.

Right from the beginning it must be made clear that, unless all
tendencies toward fantasy and illusion are overcome, it is entirely
too easy to make mistakes while working to enter spiritual realms.
Those inclined to see things in a fanciful, unreal light are of no use to
the spiritual world. That is one reason for "study." Another is that,
although we are born from the astral world — the spiritual world
adjacent to the physical — just as much as we are from the physical world, what we experience there is completely different from
anything we see with physical sight or hear with physical ears. But
one thing is the same in all three worlds — whether the physical, astral (spiritual), or devachanic (heavenly) world — and that is logical
thinking. Precisely because it is the same in all three worlds, such
thinking can be learned in the physical world, thus providing us with

a firm support when we enter the other worlds. If our thoughts are like will-o'-the-wisps, so that no distinction is made between appearances and reality, then we are not qualified to ascend to higher worlds. This happens, for example, in contemporary physics when the atom, which no one has even seen, is discussed as though it were a material reality.

What I am speaking of now is not what is usually meant by thinking. Ordinary thinking combines physical facts. But here we are concerned with thinking that has become free of the senses. Today, there are educated people, including philosophers, who deny that such thinking exists. Well-known modern philosophers tell us that human beings cannot think pure thoughts, but only thoughts that reflect something physical. Such a statement merely shows that such a person is incapable of thinking pure thoughts. In fact, however, it is the height of arrogance when people maintain that something is impossible just because they cannot accomplish it themselves.

On this path, we must become able to formulate thoughts that are independent of what is seen or heard physically. We must be able to find ourselves in a world of pure thought once our attention is fully withdrawn from outer reality. In spiritual science, as well as in Rosicrucianism, this is known as "self-created thinking." Those who resolve to train their thinking in this way can turn to books on spiritual science. They will not find thinking there that combines physical facts. They will find thoughts derived from higher worlds — thoughts that present self-sustaining, continuous thinking. And since anyone can follow this thinking, the reader becomes able to rise above his or her ordinary, trivial ways of thinking.

To make the elementary stages of Rosicrucianism accessible it became necessary, in print and through lectures, to make available material that had been guarded for centuries in closed circles.[6] What has been released in recent decades, however, are only the rudiments of an immeasurable, far-reaching universal knowledge. With time, more and more will flow out to humanity. Students train their thinking by studying this material. My books *Truth and Knowledge* and *Intuitive Thinking as a Spiritual Path: A Philosophy of Freedom* are particularly suitable for those who want an even stricter training. Those two books are not written like other books; no sentence can be placed anywhere but where it is. Each of those books represents not a collection of thoughts but a "thought organism." Thought has not been added to thought, but each grows organically from the one preceding, just as growth occurs in an organism. The thoughts must develop in a similar way in the reader. In this way, readers create their own thinking with the characteristic that it is self-generating. The higher stages of Rosicrucianism cannot be attained without this kind of thinking. Nevertheless, thinking can also be trained through a study of basic spiritual scientific literature; the more thorough training is not absolutely necessary to accomplish the first stage of Rosicrucian training.

The second stage is the acquisition of "Imagination" or "imaginal" thinking.[7] This should be attempted only when the stage of study has been completed so that one possesses an inner foundation of knowledge and has caused one's own thoughts that follow one another through inner lawfulness. Without such a foundation it is all too easy to lose the ground under one's feet. But what is meant by "imaginal" thinking?

Goethe, who in his poem "The Mysteries" demonstrated his profound knowledge of Rosicrucianism, hinted at what Imagination thinking is in the words spoken by the Chorus Mysticus in the second part of *Faust:* "All things transitory are but symbols."[8] The knowledge that everything transitory is only a symbol was cultivated systematically wherever Rosicrucian training was pursued. Rosicrucians had to acquire the insight that recognizes something spiritual and eternal in everything. In addition to the ordinary knowledge of what they encountered on their journey through life, therefore, Rosicrucians had to acquire Imagination as well.

When someone meets you with a smiling face, you do not stop short at the characteristic set of his features; you see beyond the physical expression and recognize that the smile reveals that person's inner life. Likewise you recognize tears as an expression of inner pain and sorrow. In other words, the outer expresses the inner: through the countenance you perceive the soul's depths. A Rosicrucian has to learn this fundamental gesture with regard to all of nature. The human face or hand gesture expresses a person's soul life; similarly, for the Rosicrucian, everything that happens in nature expresses soul and spirit. Every stone, plant, and animal, every current of air, the stars, all express soul and spirit just as shining eyes do, or a wrinkled brow or tears. If you go beyond today's materialism, which interprets words of the Earth Spirit in Goethe's *Faust* as poetic fantasy, and if you recognize that it depicts reality, then you know what is meant by Imagination or imaginal knowledge.

In the tides of life, in the storm of action,
A rolling wave,
A shuttle free,
Birth and the grave,
An eternal sea.
Weaving, flowing Life, all glowing —
Thus, at time's humming loom, my hand prepares
The garment of life that the Deity wears.

If these words of the Earth Spirit depict spiritual reality for you, you will know that you possess a deeper logic and can calmly accept being called a fool by materialists who think that it is only they who understand. Just as the human countenance expresses our soul life, so too the earth's countenance expresses the life of the Earth Spirit. When you begin to read in nature and it reveals its mysteries, and when various plants convey to you the Earth Spirit's cheer or sorrow, then you will begin to understand Imagination — imaginal knowledge. Then, too, you will also see that this is presented in the ideal of the Holy Grail as the purest and most beautiful expression of efforts toward imaginal knowledge in both Rosicrucianism and what preceded it.

Let us look for a moment, then, at the true nature of the Holy Grail. This ideal is always found in every Rosicrucian school. I will describe its form in terms of a conversation that never took place in reality, because what I will summarize could be attained only through lengthy training and development. But what I will say conveys what is seen as the quest of the Holy Grail.

Observe the way a plant grows out of the earth. Its stem works upward; its roots are sunk into the ground, pointing toward the earth's center. The opening blossom contains its reproductive organs, which bear the seeds through which the plant continues beyond itself. Darwin, the famous natural scientist, is not the first to point out that, when a human being is compared to a plant, the root, not the blossom, corresponds to the human head. This was said also by esoteric Rosicrucianism. The calyx, which chastely strives toward the Sun, corresponds to the reproductive organs that, in human beings, are oriented downward. Human beings are inverted plants. A person turns downward and covers in shame the same organs that the plant chastely turns upward to the light.

To recognize that the human being is an inverted plant is basic to Rosicrucianism — as it is, indeed, to all esoteric knowledge. Human beings turn their reproductive organs toward the center of the earth; in the plant they turn toward the Sun. The plant's root points toward the center of the earth; human beings lift their heads freely toward sunlit spaces. The animal occupies a position between these two. The three directions indicated by plant, animal and human are known as the cross.

The animal represents the crossbeam, the plant the lower part of the vertical beam, the human being the upper part. Plato, the great philosopher of antiquity, stated that the universal soul is crucified on the universal body.[9] He meant that human beings represent the highest development of the universal soul, which passes through the three kingdoms of plant, animal, and human.[10] The universal soul is crucified on the cross of the plant, animal, and human kingdoms. Plato's words are spoken completely in the sense of spiritual science and present a wonderful and deeply significant picture.

Students in the Rosicrucian school had to bring this picture repeatedly before their minds: the plant with its head downward and its reproductive organs stretching toward the Sun's rays. The sunbeam was called the "holy lance of love," which must penetrate the plant and enable its seeds to mature and grow. The student was told to contemplate the human being in relation to the plant, to compare our own substance with that of the plant. Human beings — inverted plants — have permeated their substance, their flesh, with physical desires, passions, and sensuality. The plant stretches its reproductive organs purely and chastely toward the fertilizing, sacred lance of love. Individuals reach this stage once they have completely purified all desires. In the future, when earthly evolution will have reached its height, human beings will attain this ideal. When no impure desires permeate the lower organs, then human beings will become as chaste and pure as the plant is now. Such individuals will stretch a lance of spiritual love — completely spiritualized productive force — toward a calyx that opens, just as that of the plant now opens to the sunbeam's holy lance of love.

Thus, our development as human beings takes us through the kingdoms of nature. We purify our being until we develop productive organs that are only indicated at this point. The beginning of a future productive power will be seen once human beings create something that is sacred and noble — a force we will possess fully once our lower nature is purified. A new organ will develop then; the calyx will arise on a higher level and open to the lance of Amfortas, as the plant calyx opens to the Sun's spiritual lance of love.[11]

What Rosicrucian students imagined to themselves therefore represents, on a lower level, the great future ideal of humankind, attainable when our lower nature has been purified and chastely offers itself to the spiritualized Sun of the future. Human nature (which in one sense is higher, in another lower than that of the plant) will then have developed within itself the innocence and purity of the plant calyx.

Rosicrucian students understood all of this in terms of its spiritual significance. They understood it as the mystery of the Holy Grail, humanity's highest ideal. They saw all of nature permeated and glowing with spiritual meaning. Once everything is seen in this way as symbolic of spirit, we are on the way to attaining imaginal knowledge — color and sound separate from objects and become independent. Space becomes a world of color and sound in which spiritual beings announce their presence. The student rises from imaginal knowledge to direct knowledge of the spirit realm. This is the path of Rosicrucian students at the second stage of training.

The third stage is knowledge of the esoteric script. This is not ordinary writing but related to the secrets of nature. Let me immediately make clear how to view this. A widely used sign is the so-called vortex, which might be thought of as two intertwined number sixes.

This sign is used to indicate and characterize a certain type of event that can occur both physically and spiritually. For example, a developing plant will finally produce seeds from which new plants similar to the old one can develop. To think that anything material passes from the old plant to the new is unfounded, materialistic bias and will eventually be proved wrong. What pass to the new plant are formative forces. As far as matter is concerned, the old plant dies completely; materially its offspring is a completely new creation. This dying and new becoming of the plant is indicated by drawing two intertwining spirals — a vortex — which is drawn so that the two spirals do not touch.

Many events, both physical and spiritual, correspond to such a vortex. For example, spiritual research shows us that the transition from the ancient Atlantean culture to the first post-Atlantean culture was such a vortex.[12] Natural science knows only the most elementary aspects of that event. Spiritual science tells us that the space between Europe and America, now the Atlantic Ocean, was filled with a continent, upon which an ancient civilization developed, a continent that was submerged by the Flood. This confirms that Plato's references to the disappearance of the Island of Poseidon are based on facts; that island was part of the ancient Atlantean continent.[13] The spiritual aspect of that ancient culture vanished, and a new culture arose. The vortex is a sign for that event; the inward-turning spiral signifies the old civilization and the outward-turning spiral the new.

During the transition from the old culture to the new, the Sun rose in spring in the constellation of Cancer; as you know the Sun moves forward through the course of the year. Later, it rose in early spring in the constellation of Gemini, then in Taurus, and later still in Aries. People have always felt that what reaches them from the vault of heaven in the beams of early spring sunlight was especially beneficial. This is why people venerated the ram when the spring Sun rose in the constellation of Aries; this is also the reason for legends such as the Golden Fleece. Before that, the Sun rose in spring in the constellation of Taurus, and in ancient Egypt we find the cult of the bull Apis. But the transition from Atlantis to post-Atlantis took place under the constellation of Cancer, whose sign is the intertwining spirals — a sign you will find depicted in calendars.

There are hundreds and thousands of such signs that the student gradually learns. Such signs are not arbitrary, but enable those who understand them to immerse themselves in things and experience their essential nature directly. Studying trains the faculty of reason; imagination trains the life of feelings; and knowledge of the esoteric script takes hold of the will. It is the path into the realm of creativity. If study brings knowledge, and imagination brings spiritual vision, knowledge of the esoteric script brings magic. It brings direct insight into the laws of nature that lie dormant in things — their very essence.

You can find many who use esoteric signs, even people like Eliphas Levi. This can provide an idea of what the signs look like, but not much can be learned if one is not already familiar with them. What one finds in books on the subject is usually wrong. Such signs used to be considered sacred, at least by the initiates. If we go back far enough, we find that strict rules were imposed concerning their secrecy, incurring severe punishment when broken, to ensure they were not used for unworthy purposes.

The fourth stage is known as "the preparation of the philosophers' stone" (the Stone of the Wise). What is written about this is mostly completely misleading; often it is such exaggerated nonsense that, if it were true, anyone would have a right to be scornful. What I am going to say will give you a great deal of insight into the truth of the matter.

At the end of the eighteenth century, a notice concerning the philosophers' stone appeared in an earnest periodical. It was clear from the wording of the notice that its author had some knowledge of the matter, yet it gave the impression that he did not fully understand. The notice read: "The philosophers' stone is something that all are acquainted with, something they often handle, and is found all over the world. It is just that people do not know that it is the philosophers' stone." It is a peculiar description of what the philosophers' stone was supposed to be, yet word for word quite correct.

Consider the process of human breathing for a moment. The regulation of the breath is connected with the discovery, or preparation, of the philosophers' stone. At present, human beings inhale oxygen and exhale carbon dioxide. In other words, what we exhale is a compound of oxygen and carbon. We inhale oxygen — life-giving air — and exhale carbon dioxide, which is poisonous to both human and animal. If the earth were populated only by animals, who breathe like human beings, they would have poisoned the air, and neither they nor humans would be able to breathe today. So how does it happen that they are still able to breathe? It is because plants absorb the carbon dioxide, retain the carbon and give back the oxygen for human and animal to use again.

Thus, a beautiful reciprocal process takes place between the breathing of humans and animals and the breathing (or rather assimilation) by the plant world. Consider someone who earns five dollars and spends two each day. A surplus is created, and such a person is in a different situation than someone who earns two dollars but spends five. Something like this applies to breathing. The significant point, however, is that this exchange takes place between human beings and the vegetable kingdom.

The process of breathing is quite amazing. Consider it in greater detail. Oxygen enters the human body; carbon dioxide is expelled. Carbon dioxide consists of oxygen and carbon; the plant retains the carbon and gives a person back the oxygen. Plants that grew millions of years ago are now dug from the earth as coal. Looking at this coal we see the carbon that was once inhaled by plants. Thus, the ordinary breath, just described, shows how necessary the plant is to a person's life. It also shows that humans accomplish only half the process when they breathe; to complete it, they need the plant, which has something humans lack for transforming carbon into oxygen.

The Rosicrucians introduce a certain rhythm into breathing. The details of this can be given directly only by word of mouth. Nevertheless, certain aspects can be mentioned without going into details.

Rosicrucian students receive specific instruction concerning rhythmic breathing. Such breathing is accompanied by thoughts of a special nature. The effect must be thought of as comparable to the persistent drip of water that wears away the stone. By breathing in the Rosicrucian way, even the most highly developed individual will not attain a complete transformation of the inner life processes overnight. The gradual change that takes place in the human body, however, leads eventually to a specific goal. At some time in the future, individuals will be able to transform carbon dioxide into oxygen within their own being. Consequently, what the plant now does for human beings — transforming the carbon in carbon dioxide — will be done by human beings, once the effect of the changed breath has become great enough. This will take place in an organ we will then possess, about which physiology and anatomy still know nothing, but which is now developing. We will accomplish the transformation ourselves. Instead of exhaling carbon, we will use it in our own being; with what we formerly had to give over to the plant, we will build up our own body.

We must consider all of this in conjunction with what was said about the Holy Grail — that the purity and chastity of the plant will pass over into human nature. Once our lower nature has reached the highest level of spirituality, it will be once again at the level of what is plant today. One day we will be able to accomplish in our own being the process that takes place in the plant. We will increasingly transform the substance of our present body into the ideal of a plant body, which will bear a much higher and more spiritual consciousness. Thus, Rosicrucian students learn the alchemy that will eventually enable people to transform the fluids and substances of the human body into carbon. What the plant does today — building its body from carbon — we humans will also accomplish one day. We will build a structure from carbon that will be our future body. A great mystery is therefore hidden in the rhythm of our breathing.

Now you can understand the notice alluded to earlier about the philosophers' stone. But what will human beings learn about building up the human body in the future? We will learn to create ordinary coal, which is also what diamonds consist of, and from that we will build our bodies. Human beings will then possess a higher and more comprehensive consciousness. They will be able to use the carbon from themselves within their own being. They will form their own substance — that is, plant substance made of carbon. That is the alchemy that builds the philosophers' stone. The human body itself is the retort transformed as described.

What is alluded to as the "search for the philosophers' stone" lies hidden behind the rhythm of the breath — but what is usually said about it is pure nonsense. The information given here has only recently reached the public from the school of the Rosicrucians; you will not find this in any book. What I have told you now represents only a small part of the fourth stage, the quest for the philosophers' stone.

The fifth stage, or knowledge of the microcosm, indicates something that Paracelsus said, which I have often mentioned: namely, that if we could draw an extract from all that surrounds us, it would be like an extract of humankind. The substances and forces within us are like a miniature recapitulation of all that exists in the rest of nature. As we observe the world around us, we can say that inwardly we are a "copy" of the great archetype that exists outside. Consider, for example, what light has created in human beings — the eyes. Without eyes we would not see light; the world would remain dark for us, and likewise for the animals. Those animals in Kentucky that wandered into dark caves to live lost their ability to see. If light did not exist we would not have eyes. The light enticed the organs of sight out of the organism. As Goethe said, the eye is created by light for the light, the ear by sound for the sound.

Everything is born from the microcosm. Consequently, there is the mystery that, given certain instruction and guidance, it is possible to enter deeply into the body and investigate not only what pertains to the body, but also the spiritual realm as well as the world of nature around us. Those who, under certain conditions, learn to immerse themselves meditatively in the inner eye with certain thoughts will learn the true nature of light. Another area of great significance is between the eyebrows, at the root of the nose. By sinking into this point meditatively, one learns of important spiritual events that took place as this part of the head was formed from the surrounding world; one learns the spiritual construction of the human being. We are completely formed and built up by spiritual beings and forces. That is why, by delving into our own form, we can learn about the beings and forces that built up our organism.

Something further should be said about delving into our inner being. We should not penetrate down from the I into the bodily nature (or undertake the other exercises) until after the appropriate preparation. Before beginning, we must strengthen the powers of intellect and reason. This is why training our thinking is required in Rosicrucian schools. Furthermore, students must be morally strong inwardly; this is essential, otherwise we can easily stumble. As students, when we learn to sink meditatively into every part of the body, other worlds dawn in us.

The deeper aspects of the Old Testament cannot be understood if it does not sink into our inner being. But this must be done according to certain directions provided by spiritual scientific training. Everything that is said here about this is derived from the spiritual world, and it can be understood fully only when we are able to discover it again within ourselves. We are born out of the macrocosm. We must rediscover its forces and laws within ourselves as microcosms. We learn about our own being not through anatomy but by looking into our being and perceiving inwardly that the various areas give out light and sound. The soul looking inward discovers that each organ has a unique color and tone.

People will attain direct knowledge of the macrocosm once they learn, through a Rosicrucian training, to recognize what in their own being is created from the universe. Once people recognize their inner being by sinking meditatively into the eye, or into the point on the forehead just above the nose, they will know the macrocosmic laws spiritually. Then, through their own insight, they will come to understand what it is that an inspired genius describes in the Old Testament.[14] An individual looks into the akashic record and is able to follow humanity's evolution through millions of years.[15]

This insight can be attained through Rosicrucian instruction, which is different from the usual sort of training. Genuine self-knowledge is reached neither by aimlessly brooding within oneself nor by believing that through introspection one's "inner god" will speak, as is often taught today. The power to recognize the great, universal self is attained through immersion within the organs. True, the call "Know Thyself" has sounded throughout the ages, but it is equally true that the higher self cannot be found within one's own being. As Goethe pointed out, one's spirit must expand until it encompasses the world.

This reality can be attained by those who patiently follow the Rosicrucian path and reach the sixth stage. Then they become one with the macrocosm. Immersion in one's inner being is not a comfortable path. Catch phrases and vague truisms are not enough. One must, in concrete reality, plunge into every being and phenomenon and lovingly accept it all as part of oneself. This involves concrete and intimate knowledge, far removed from mere indulgence in phrases such as "being in harmony" with the world, or "one with the universal soul," or "merging with the cosmos." Such phrases are simply worthless compared to Rosicrucian training, where the goal is to strengthen and invigorate human soul forces rather than to chatter about being in tune with the infinite.

Once we have attained this expansion of the self, the seventh stage is within reach. Knowledge now becomes feeling. What lives in the soul is transformed into spiritual perception. We no longer feel that we live only within ourselves. We begin to experience ourselves in all beings — a stone, a plant, an animal, and everything in which we immerse ourselves. These reveal to us their essential nature, not as words or concepts but in our innermost feelings. We reach a point when universal sympathy unites us with all beings; we feel with them and share in their existence. Living within all beings in this way is the seventh stage — godliness, the blessed rest within all things: when human beings no longer feel confined within their skin and feel united with all other beings and participate in their existence, and when our being encompasses the whole universe so that we can say to everything, "Thou are that."[16] Then we will also find meaning in the words of Rosicrucian knowledge that Goethe expresses in his poem "The Mysteries:" "Who added the wreath of roses to the Cross?"

These words, however, can be spoken not only from the highest point, but from the moment we make what is expressed in "the Cross wreathed in roses" our ideal and watchword. This is the symbol of overcoming our lower self — the self in which we merely brood. It stands for our ascension out of that lower self and into the higher self that leads us to the blissful experience of life and being in all things. As Goethe put it:

> And until you truly have
> This "dying and becoming,"
> You are but a troubled guest
> Roaming over dark Earth.

Unless one grasps what it means to overcome the lower, narrow self and what it means to rise to the higher self, it is impossible to understand the Cross as symbol of dying and becoming — the wood as the withering of lower self and the flowering roses as the becoming of higher self. Nor can we understand the words with which we shall close our discussion of Rosicrucianism. These words were also said by Goethe, and as a watchword they belong above the Cross wreathed in Seven Roses, symbolizing the sevenfold human being:

> Those who overcome themselves are free
> of the force that binds all humankind.

— three —

Rosicrucian Practice

The next lectures allow us to enter further into Steiner's understanding of Rosicrucianism as the appropriate path for human beings today. Against a background of evolution viewed from a Rosicrucian perspective, Steiner describes the stages of Rosicrucian training. He introduces the Rosicrucian approach to spiritual practice as being for the sake of the world rather than for individual salvation. What we do and how we act has a consequence — that is, comes back to us metamorphosed, as a future aspect of earth evolution. The impulse that entered Europe in the fourteenth century as Rosicrucianism, therefore, anticipates and prepares for future stages of evolution.

— ◆ —

Part 1
June 28, 1907, Kassel

My task today and tomorrow will be to describe the path to higher worlds that is best suited to our present circumstances. This path has been fostered in so-called esoteric schools since the fourteenth and fifteenth centuries. For a better understanding of what this path involves, let us consider first the future evolution of the human being.

We have already talked about human evolution during the Saturn, Sun, Moon, and Earth stages of the earth's development. People who think only in terms of the present have difficulty imagining how anyone can possibly know anything about the future. First of all, you must realize that certain great laws will continue to work in the future just as they work in the present. Anyone familiar with these laws

---

For all unidentified sources see p. 260.

60

can see into the future. In the field of material reality, no one doubts that the timing of solar and lunar eclipses or of other configurations of heavenly bodies can be calculated far into the future. And everyone knows that scientists can predict what will happen when specific substances are mixed in a test tube. This type of prediction, which refers to material, sense-perceptible facts, is possible because we know the laws governing the actions of matter. Similarly, in spiritual science we learn the laws that govern human life and can therefore know what will happen in the future.

At this point, admittedly, an objection may come up that has been raised by philosophers throughout the ages, namely, that if we can predict what will happen in the future, there can be no talk of human freedom. People who raise this argument, however, are confusing prediction with predetermination. With the single exception of Jakob Boehme, philosophers have been unable to make this distinction, so you find all kinds of strange claims in their works.[1] Here is an example that will help clarify the situation.

Let me use space as an analogy for time. Imagine that two people are standing outside on the street and that you are standing inside observing them from a distance. Does that mean, then, that you determine what they do? No, you simply observe what they are doing, while they act in complete freedom. The fact that you see them in no way determines what they do. Similarly, when clairvoyants see what happens in the future, they simply observe future events without influencing them in any way. If these events were predetermined or predestined by the present, clairvoyant vision would not be simply a matter of seeing into the future. This distinction becomes clear only after we have spent a long time pondering the difference between predetermination and prediction.

My intention today is not to describe the earth's outward appearance during the future Jupiter and Venus stages of Earth evolution but to sketch the future of human evolution. Let me describe a teaching that originated in the oldest Christian mysteries — in the school of the true Dionysius[2] — and has always been expounded in Christian esoteric schools. The presentation of this teaching always began somewhat as follows: "As I speak to you, you hear my words. Thus, you hear my thoughts, which existed initially in my soul and which I could conceal from you if I did not transform them into words. I transform these thoughts into sounds. If there were no air between you and me, you would not hear my words, but as soon as I begin

speaking, the air in this space moves. Each time I say a word, I induce a specific state of vibration in this space. The whole body of air
vibrates in ways that correspond to how my words are pronounced."

Let us now take this thought further. Imagine that we can transform air into a liquid and then into a solid. Already today, it is
possible to solidify air. You know that steam, the gaseous form of
water, liquefies when it cools and is transformed into solid ice when
it freezes. Now imagine that I pronounce the word "god" in air-
filled space. If you could solidify the air at the very instant these
sound waves are present, a shape — perhaps a shell-like shape, for
example — would fall to earth. The word "world" would produce a
different shape. You would be able to capture my words, and each
word would correspond to a shape made out of crystallized air.

This analogy was used in the Christian schools. Each object first
exists as a thought concealed within a being, a thought that is then
spoken and solidified. Christians imagined that the creation of the
universe began with thoughts of things, which were then pronounced
by the divinity and sent forth into space. The plants and minerals
you see are divine words that have solidified. You can imagine that
they were once dissolved in the sound vibrations of the divine cosmic
word. Each thing we see — so said the early Christians — is a divine
word become solid.

Therefore they distinguished between the Father, who remains hidden and has not yet expressed himself, the Son or Word that resounds
through space, and the solidified word, or Revelation. In this way we
can understand the deeper meaning of the beginning of the Gospel
According to John: "In the beginning was the Word, and the Word
was with God, and a God was the Word. The Word was with God at
the beginning, and through it all things came to be; no single thing
was created without it." Everything that came into existence emerged
from the Word. When we take these statements as literally as possible,
it is easy to acknowledge the creative power of the Word, or logos.
Logos must not be translated as anything except *word*, because this
passage means that the unspoken creative word underlies all external
creation. The resounding word is the source of everything that exists. If we went back through the ages, we would hear all the objects
and beings we now know as animals, plants, minerals, and humans
resounding through cosmic space, just as you hear my words today,
because the air had not yet cooled enough for them to precipitate as
solid forms.

If you bear all this in mind, you realize that the word was once a creative force. Today, we human beings are still mere beginners at what our forefathers once did. These superior divine beings once pronounced words and sent them out into space, and their creative activity became the creation that surrounds us. Today's sexual procreation, whether by plants, animals, or humans, is simply a transformation of the divine creative word of former times. Human beings include a higher and a lower nature. Our most nearly finished aspect is sexuality, while the beginning of a new means of procreation exists in the human larynx. Sending forth words is a first token of what we will later be able to produce. We are in the earliest stages of what the gods once did. In the future, the old means of procreating will be replaced. The larynx we now use to produce words will become an organ of procreation that brings forth increasingly denser and more exalted creations. In the future, what is now air will be the substance of beings. When the earth will be transformed and enter into the Jupiter stage, the human word will be creative in the mineral realm; during the Venus stage, the human larynx will bring forth plants, and so on, until it can reproduce its own kind. Our larynx acquired the form we know today when it was first possible to expel air from the lungs in the form of sound. In future evolutionary stages of the earth, what we can now only say will emerge in forms that endure. Ultimately, the larynx will become the organ through which human beings chastely reproduce their own kind without resorting to sexuality. We will transform the larynx into an organ of procreation.

Thus we recognize the potential of our larynx when we see into the future. The mysterious phenomenon of the breaking voice in adolescent males suggests that the activity of the larynx is indeed related to specific developmental stages. The larynx is at the beginning of its evolution, while sexuality is at its end. This is one of the subtle interrelationships typical of natural phenomena. Sexual activity is declining, and in the future the word, the larynx, will become our reproductive organ. Much more could be said about such organs, which we have incorporated into our respiratory system here on Earth but which actually belong to the heart system. They are present in the body as mere potentials now, but will gradually evolve further.

We will now see how the esoteric [Rosicrucian] training that was introduced in Europe during the fourteenth century anticipates future stages of human evolution and accelerates our inner development in comparison to its natural rate of evolution.

Rosicrucian training, although it has a bad reputation among those who have heard about it only in passing, is the method best suited to modern human beings. If what scholars know about from books were true, Rosicrucianism would be nothing more than the fraud it is reputed to be. Today, however, we will consider the real Rosicrucianism, which came about through the individuality concealed behind the name Christian Rosenkreutz, who provided the impetus for the founding of the Rosicrucian movement in 1459.

I wish to state explicitly at this point that everything I say today on this subject will consist only of selected examples. . . .

Having said this, let me immediately present the seven main steps in Rosicrucian training. These steps apply to everyone undertaking such a training, although not all individuals take them in the order listed. The first step is what we call "study." "Acquiring imaginative cognition" is the second step, and the third is "learning to read the occult or esoteric script." The fourth is "preparing the philosophers' stone." The fifth is called "the correspondence between the microcosm, or little world, and the macrocosm, or greater world." The sixth is "finding our way into the macrocosm," the seventh "beatitude."

While the Rosicrucian path is the safest, most profound way to understand Christianity, the Christian path is more suitable for steadfast believers who can mobilize the inner feelings I described in presenting this path yesterday. The Rosicrucian path, on the other hand, is for people capable of forging a union between Christian truths and the truths of the outer world, thus making Christianity impervious to any attack from outside. No matter how wise we are, we can never understand Christianity adequately. No level of understanding is advanced enough to allow us to completely grasp the significance of Christianity for the wisest of the wise, but the Rosicrucian path is still the most suitable path for modern individuals.

We "study" in the Rosicrucian sense when we have thoughts that no longer have anything to do with the world of our senses. The Western world is familiar with thinking free thoughts only in geometry. Gnostic Christian schools gave the name *mathesis* to thoughts related to higher truths, to God, and to the higher worlds, because such insight, like mathematical understanding, must be acquired independently of any sense perceptions. A circle drawn with chalk is highly imperfect. A true circle is possible only in thought, and everything you learn about a circle exists only in your thoughts. In mathematics, we learn to think without depending on sense perception about the circle we construct in our thoughts and about the mental triangle whose angles add up to 180 degrees. It is somewhat uncomfortable to learn to think without reference to material, sense-perceptible objects, and for most people, theosophy is the only field of study that requires such thinking. . . .

Adding machines, which teach people to think in ways that are not sense-free, were invented only in our materialistic age. Because it is important for children to learn about mathematical subjects without reference to sensory perception, the influence of spiritual science on education will be tremendously valuable. Spiritual science is also a good training in sense-free thinking. You cannot see what I told you about Saturn and the Sun or about the members of the human constitution. Such subjects can be understood only through sense-free thinking, but no one should believe that any self-training is possible in this field without first understanding the contents on a theoretical level. It is fortunate that these contents simply do not exist as far as sense perception is concerned, because this forces us to think in ways that transcend sense perception. For this purpose, it is enough for some people to expose themselves to what theosophy has to say about ideas that we cannot grasp with our senses. These ideas are essentially the same as the thoughts presented in Rosicrucian schools, and there, too, it was important for people to learn them.

When you are ready to go further, good ways of learning pure thinking can be found in my books *Truth and Knowledge* and *Intuitive Thinking as a Spiritual Path*.[3] These books exercise our sense-free thinking. In any other book, shifting the position of one thought generally does not alter the meaning significantly. The thoughts in these two books, however, cannot be moved around. When I wrote these books, my personality simply presented the opportunity for their inherent thought structure to appear in the sense-perceptible world. Such thoughts create themselves and the links among them, and we must accept their inherent order. Delving into the subject in depth may take six months and is by no means easy, but it is well worth the effort. When you read one of these books to the end, a force is realized that formerly lay hidden within you.

The second step toward Rosicrucian initiation is Imagination, or symbolic cognition, typified by Goethe's saying, "Everything transitory is but a symbol." Actually, only those who have achieved certainty in their thinking should attempt this stage, for without this certainty it is easy to succumb to figments of the imagination. Achieving clear-headedness is a prerequisite to attempting this step, because unclear thinking or faulty logic encourages errors while clear thinking prevents them.

In the broadest sense, Imagination could be described as seeing what we see in human beings in everything else we look at. When you see lines form and disappear on a human face, you do not simply describe the shapes they make; you call them smiles or frowns. We do not simply draw conclusions about a person's inner life from external appearances; the externalities are direct signs of inner activity. A human smile reveals a cheerful mood of soul, and when you see tears welling up, instead of simply observing that tears obey the law of gravity, as a physicist might do, you know that they express the sadness in a person's soul. Every outer manifestation expresses an inner soul mood. For those undergoing a Rosicrucian training, everything they see in the outer world becomes an expression of the spirit of the earth, so to speak. A plant such as the autumn crocus expresses the sorrow of earthly existence, while other plants express its joy. Just as a smiling face reveals a cheerful soul mood, flowers reveal the sad or cheerful mood of the earth. Goethe does not intend it as a superficial image when he has the Earth Spirit say, "I create a living garment for the divine."[4]

To students of Rosicrucianism, the Earth Spirit gradually comes to mean everything that is alive in the earth, and Rosicrucians develop a soul-spiritual relationship to their natural environment. Let me illustrate one particular mood of this natural environment. Imagine Rosicrucians-in-training walking over the meadows and seeing the tiny pearl-like drops of dew hanging from all the plants. The droplets recall ancient Nebelheim [literally, "mist home"] — *Niflheim* of Norse mythology[5] — where the air was filled with dew and fog and human beings related to nature very differently from today. Walking over the dewy meadows recalls the saturated atmosphere of Nebelheim, and a deep-seated memory of Atlantean times rises up in the students.

Imagination was highly developed among the students of medieval Rosicrucian schools and the schools of the Holy Grail. Let me restate some of their instruction for you. The teacher said, "Consider how the plant emerges from the ground and how its calyx,[6] which contains the organs of reproduction, opens upward. See how the Sun's rays descend, allowing the blossom to open and the fruit to ripen." Students of Rosicrucianism or of the Holy Grail were required to call this idea or image to mind. Even materialistic science compares plants to humans. When we do so, however, we must compare the plant's root to the human head and the flower to the human organs of reproduction, which we hide in shame. The human being is an inverted plant, while the animal is a semi-inverted plant. That is why the Rosicrucians told their students to look at the plant, with its root in the ground and its organs of reproduction stretched chastely toward the Sun; at the animal, with its horizontal backbone; and at the completed transformation in the human being. The evolutionary journey from plant to animal to human is symbolized by the cross. The cross is plant plus animal plus human being. Now we understand what Plato meant when he said that the world soul is bound to the cross of the earth. The all-pervading world soul is bound to the plant, the animal, and the human being.

Next the teacher said to the students of Rosicrucianism, "Look at the plant. Although it exists on a lower level than you in that it does not possess consciousness and thinking, its substance is pure and chaste. It lifts its calyx to the Sun; free of desire and lust, it raises its organ of reproduction to the Sun's rays, to the holy lance of love. Today matter is imbued with desire, but imagine, as the ideal for the future, that matter will be purified again and produced purely and chastely."

Rosicrucian teachers pointed to the larynx as the organ through which human beings will again achieve the purity and chastity of a plant's calyx. They said, "Imagine the calyx of a plant, which is still free of desire. In the higher kingdoms of nature, procreation passes through the evolutionary stage of desire, but it will become pure and chaste once again by allowing itself to be fructified by the Sun's rays transformed into spirit, by the holy lance of love. The lance that pierced the heart of Christ Jesus on the Cross presages this holy lance of love."

Yesterday we heard that the blood from the Redeemer's wound banished egoism from the earth. Thus the lance presages the higher lance of the Sun's rays transformed into spirit, and the Holy Grail points to the calyx or chalice of humankind, which will evolve out of the larynx in the future to become a purified organ of reproduction such as plants have now.

This deeper meaning of the Holy Grail was made clear to the students of Rosicrucianism — the Holy Grail on the level of Imagination. To see the difference between Imagination, whose images encompass entire cosmic processes, and mere rational thinking, compare these images — plant calyx, sexuality steeped in desire, the Holy Grail, the chalice free of desire — to the dry, rational concepts provided by modern science. It is important to realize, as people in ancient times understood, that merely rational concepts such as we have today are not creative unless they are supplemented with such images.

This fact must also be considered in educating children. Let me give a timely example. It is so easy for us to laugh at earlier generations for teaching us the silly story of the stork. Today we think we have to tell children the facts of the matter. But what if our descendants treat us the way we treat our ancestors? They will laugh to think that we believed human beings came into existence through the interaction of material substances. They will look back to a time when people explained the underlying spiritual process to children. In ancient times, when the story of the stork first appeared, the adults who told it believed it. They knew very well that at birth the person's soul descends from the spiritual world, and they always associated this descent with a winged creature. You can still find this truth in children's songs. For example:

> Fly, ladybug, fly!
> Your father's gone to war.
> Your mother's gone to Pommerland.
> Pommerland is burning down.
> Fly, ladybug fly!

"Flying" symbolizes the human soul, because in those days people had premonitions of flying bodies that enter the physical world from astral space. And what is "Pommerland"? *Pommer* is the same as *Pummerle,* a little baby, and Pummerland or Pommerland is where a mother goes to get a child. We must simply interpret the entire song in terms of the spiritual world.

When you recall that the stork that brings babies is actually a symbol of the spiritual process of reincarnation, you will realize how very important it is for people to first learn about such processes in image form. Because the minds of children work differently from those of adults, it is important to use images when we describe spiritual processes to children, so that they will then be able to hear about the physical process with reverence.

You, too, can believe in the stork again when you know that it symbolizes the descending soul! The children will sense the aura of your understanding of the truth, and your instruction will give wings to their creative fantasy. If we use Imaginations, we can teach children anything. When they ask what life after death is like, you can show them the pupa of a butterfly and tell them that a soul leaving its body is like a butterfly leaving its pupa, only we cannot see the soul. But your teaching will be convincing only if you yourself believe it when you say that the emergence of a butterfly exemplifies on a lower level what happens with the soul on a higher level. When images become alive in our hearts as a result of reimmersing ourselves in an understanding of the spiritual world through spiritual science, our teaching will be transformed, and we will no longer give children dry, rational truths that coarsen their psyches. We must not use grotesque or comical images, however. We must acknowledge the crucial importance of what underlies these images.

The third step on the Rosicrucian path is "learning to read the occult script." This script is nothing like the one we learn in ordinary life, although many of our written letters are derived from occult images. Through learning to read the occult script, we find our way into the truly great forces at work in the world. Leaps between evolutionary stages are characteristic of these forces. Take a plant, for example. Each plant has seeds, and each seed is the point of departure for a new plant. But if you could examine the process carefully enough, you would realize that no material element of the old plant is carried over into the new. In reality, the old plant disintegrates completely on the material level and the new plant is built up anew. Only a movement process of sorts is transmitted from the old plant to the new. This phenomenon is similar to sealing wax and a seal — when you press the seal into the sealing wax, its form is transmitted but not its substance. The same is true of any evolutionary process. Old matter disintegrates and simply provides a point of attachment for a new form to arise. This phenomenon is symbolized by two spirals that intertwine but do not connect. This sign also describes transitions such as the one at the end of Atlantean culture. The Atlantean stage disappeared and a new stage emerged in Indian culture. I told you that around the year 800, the Sun rose in the sign of Aries. Earlier still, the Sun rose in Taurus, and before that in Gemini and Cancer. The Greco-Latin culture that held the seeds of our own corresponded to the time when the Sun rose in the sign of Aries, while the previous cultural epoch of the Chaldeans, Assyrians, Babylonians, and Egyptians happened when the Sun was in Taurus. Earlier still was the Persian culture, when the Sun rose in Gemini, and ancient Indian culture developed when the Sun was in Cancer. The symbol for Cancer or the Crab, which consists of two intertwined spirals, was first written during ancient Indian culture.

Similarly, I could explain each sign of the zodiac in terms of its true meaning. These signs were derived from nature and are expressions of natural forces and laws. When we learn to read the characters of the occult script, we begin to transcend ourselves and delve into the hidden foundations of nature.

Today I have given you a brief sketch of the first three levels of the Rosicrucian path — study, imaginative cognition, and learning to read the occult script. Tomorrow we will discuss the remaining levels, beginning with "preparing the philosophers' stone."

Part 2
June 29, 1907, Kassel

Yesterday I described so-called Rosicrucian initiation up through the third stage, learning to read the occult script derived from natural laws. We also learned what the Rosicrucians meant by "study" and "acquiring imaginative cognition." We will now move on to the fourth stage, or "preparing the philosophers' stone." Please disregard anything you may have read previously about the philosophers' stone. Only in recent times has it become possible to report accurately on what the Rosicrucians meant when they named this fourth stage of their initiation method. Ever since Rosicrucianism was founded in 1459, "the philosophers' stone" has been the name used to describe a specific set of instructions on entering the higher worlds. You must realize that the Rosicrucian movement was kept secret and handled with the utmost care until some of its secrets were betrayed and made public in the wrong way in the late eighteenth and early nineteenth centuries. It is clear from the different descriptions of Rosicrucian secrets that were published at that time that the writers had heard something about these secrets but failed to understand what they heard. They did pick up a few authentic words about the "philosophers' stone," however. A major newspaper published a series of articles on an organization whose self-assigned task was to "prepare the philosophers' stone." One of these articles contains a statement that is comprehensible only to those who already know what is being described. It reads, "Yes, the philosophers' stone does indeed exist. Most people know about it and most have even had it in their hands, but they do not know that it is not at all difficult to find."

The meaning that was then attached to the philosophers' stone was that it gradually made people aware of the human being's immortal aspect and led them into higher worlds. It was said that when we realize that this aspect of our being cannot succumb to death, we acquire eternal life by possessing the philosophers' stone. By extension, it was said that the possessor of this stone would never die. Although the actual meaning was that the philosophers' stone would teach us about the world in which we live after death, it was seen as an elixir of life. All this made the philosophers' stone extremely desirable.

Anyone who knows the real facts of the matter must admit that these descriptions are indeed true in a strange way. However, those who do not know the secret are left none the wiser.

Let me now tell you briefly what the Rosicrucians actually meant. To understand this, you must understand one very simple scientific phenomenon, namely, the relationship between human beings and the plant kingdom. Human beings and other creatures with human-like respiration would never be able to exist without plants. Let's look at the process that takes place between us and plants. We breathe in air because we need its oxygen. Without oxygen, we would be unable to live. We inhale air, process the oxygen in our bodies, and exhale carbon dioxide, a carbon-oxygen compound. So you see, we constantly take in oxygen to maintain our bodies, and we create and breathe out carbon dioxide, a poison that would kill us. Thus we are constantly filling our surroundings with a toxin. Now what do plants do? In a certain respect, they do the exact opposite. They take in carbon dioxide, retain the carbon, and give off the oxygen, which they cannot use. We give plants what they need, and the plants give us oxygen in return. The amount of oxygen plants give off after taking in carbon dioxide far outweighs the amount of oxygen they take in. So what do plants do with the carbon they retain? It is one of the substances they use to build up their own bodies. We make it possible, as it were, for plants to construct their carbonaceous bodies in the appropriate way. The anthracite we mine is the carbon from plants that died thousands of years ago.

Plants provide the oxygen that we take in, while we give the plants carbon dioxide. The plants keep the carbon and give the oxygen back to us in a miraculous cycle. This is the current state of affairs. Human beings are still evolving, however, and in future each human body will also have an organ that transforms carbon dioxide into oxygen and retains carbon for the body to use.

This statement points to a future stage in human evolution, but in a different way than what I described yesterday with regard to Rosicrucian esoteric schooling. In the future, the human body will be desire-free, but on a higher level than we find in plants. We will be able to build up our bodies as the plants do, but on a higher level. The organ that is now the human heart will be transformed into an organ that does what plants do now. Today the plant and human kingdoms are interdependent; the one could not exist without the other. If there were no plants, all oxygen-breathers would soon die, because plants provide our oxygen. We cannot imagine ourselves existing without plants. What plants do outside us today will be done in the future by the organ that develops when the human heart is transformed into a voluntary muscle. We will spread our consciousness out over the plant kingdom and grow together with it, internalizing a function that plants now perform outside us. At that point in time, we will also retain the carbon that we now exhale and will use it to build up our own bodies. We will become like plants, but on a higher level of consciousness.

Ever since ancient times, esotericism has clothed the facts I have just recounted in the Golden Legend, one of the wonderful images presented to esoteric students and used to preserve truths for thousands of years. The Golden Legend goes something like this:

On entering Paradise for the first time, Seth, the son God gave Adam and Eve to replace the murdered Abel, discovered that the Tree of Knowledge and the Tree of Life had grown together, with their branches intertwining. At the bidding of his angelic guide, Seth took three seeds from this tree. He saved them and, when Adam died, placed the three seeds in Adam's mouth. A tree grew up out of Adam's grave, and to those who knew how to see it, the tree revealed, in flaming letters, the words *"ehjeh asher ehjeh"* — I am who was, is, and will be. Seth took wood from the tree. Many things were made from it, including Moses' magical staff. The gate of Solomon's temple was made of wood from the offspring of this tree, and later, after experiencing various other destinies, it formed the Cross on which the Redeemer hung.

Thus the legend associates the wood of the Cross on Golgotha with the tree that grew out of Adam's grave from the seeds of the Tree of Paradise.

This legend conceals the same secret that I sketched for you today. The legend meant that in ancient times the human race had not yet sunk to the level of fleshly desire but was chaste and pure like the plants extending their calyces to the Sun. Then came the Fall, and human flesh was filled with passion. But everything we once possessed in the state of innocence will be ours again when we have traveled the path of knowledge and created bodies that are as free of desire as human bodies were before we ate from the Tree of Knowledge, which, as you recall, was the source of the I. Because we no longer have desire-free bodies, we have become red-blooded lung breathers. The human form we know at present depends on respiration and circulation, which make possible the type of cognition we possess today.

Now let's shift our attention to the present-day human body and create an image of how oxygen flows in, stimulating the red blood that runs throughout the entire body like the branching of a tree, and how the blue blood then flows back, filled with carbon dioxide. We each contain two trees, the trees of red and blue blood. Without them, the human being could not support an I. Our present form of cognition requires us to incorporate red blood, to which death is also linked because we transform red blood into the blue blood that is saturated with carbon dioxide. That is why the esoteric teachers of the Old Testament said, "Look at yourself and at the tree of red blood within you. If you had not received this tree, you would never have become a thinking being. You ate from the Tree of Knowledge, but at the same time you lost the ability to give yourself life from within."

The former Tree of Life became a Tree of Death. In our present stage of evolution, our internal tree of blue blood is the Tree of Death. Initiates, however, can perceive a future stage in which human beings internalize the plant kingdom through the heart organ, which transforms blue blood back into red blood. At this stage, we will transform the Tree of Death into a Tree of Life, and human beings will become immortal. What we once were on a lower level, we will then be on a higher level. We will incorporate the process that exists today in plants. Thus, Paradise is humankind's final stage of evolution. Seth's mission was to see the balancing of the two principles within the human being that will occur at the end of time. Thus the Tree of Life and the Tree of Knowledge are intertwined in Paradise; they will be found inside human beings only when we take refuge in the plant kingdom. But how do we learn to make the trees intertwine? By developing the three higher members of the human constitution.

We have learned that the human being consists of the physical body, the ether body, the astral body, and the I. We also learned that the I works on the astral body to develop the first higher member, on the ether body to achieve the second, and on the physical body to realize the third. In the future, the human being will be a sevenfold being who will incorporate the spirit self, the life spirit, and the spirit body. Having thus transformed our lower nature, we will take the Tree of Knowledge and the Tree of Life into ourselves. At the very outset of our evolution, we received the potential for the I as the prerequisite for developing the three higher members of our constitution.

Seth took three seeds, and Adam, the first I-being, made them grow into a tree. This tree contains the aspect of the human being that passes through all the various incarnations. Your I was present at a very low level of evolution in your first incarnation and achieved ever higher levels in subsequent incarnations. The tree growing out of Adam's grave symbolizes the eternal aspect of the human being, which will achieve perfection at the end of the Earth stage of evolution. We can achieve this degree of perfection only by uniting with the highest good that we encounter on the path to the spirit. Everything that has led humanity further along this path — the staff of Moses, the temple of Solomon, and finally the Cross on Golgotha — helps us to bring the higher human trinity to full expression. The Cross on Golgotha pointed the way to the ultimate degree of human perfection. There is no more beautiful way of expressing this fact than the legend I have retold here. The Cross began as the seed placed in Adam's mouth, the seed that grew into the tree that yielded its wood to Seth. The legend represents our journey through all time. In the future, we will struggle to achieve the transformation of our own being and the ability to produce carbon for our own use, as plants do today. We too will learn to master the alchemy of plants.

The alchemical preparation of the substance I have described is accomplished when candidates for Rosicrucian initiation follow specific instructions on how to regulate their respiratory processes. We can understand this only on the basis of the principle that constant dripping wears away stone — that is, it cannot happen quickly, but students of Rosicrucianism continue to work at it. Just as drops of water slowly wear a tiny hollow in the stone, the human body is progressively transformed at a similar pace as a result of regulating the breathing process. The instructions that Rosicrucian students must follow allow them to set out on the path toward preparing the I to acquire the ability to build up subsequent bodies in a different way. Their practice is related to the fact that phenomena which will appear only later in your physical surroundings already exist in the spiritual world. The slow process of Rosicrucian instruction anticipates a future evolutionary stage, but already now its students learn to see this stage in the higher worlds. Thus, students of Rosicrucianism do two things: they work for the future of humanity, and they acquire for themselves the ability to see into the spiritual world, to see what will later descend into physical reality.

At this point, you can understand something that the man who wrote the newspaper article did not, namely, that the philosophers' stone is ordinary black carbon. The progress of humanity lies in learning to process carbon through our own inner strength. Today's coal is a precursor of the substance that will be most important for human beings of the future, although that future substance will look quite different. Remember that a brilliant diamond is also only carbon! This inner human development is what the Rosicrucian worldview calls "preparing the philosophers' stone." This term conceals a process of human transformation and a challenge to work toward future evolutionary stages of humanity. All who work in this way work on behalf of the human bodies of the future, for the kind of bodies that souls will need in the future....

This fourth, tremendously profound stage of Rosicrucian schooling thus incorporates "preparing the philosophers' stone" into humanity's evolution.

The fifth stage is "the correspondence between microcosm and macrocosm." The complicated human body that exists today underwent a very specific evolution. In earlier lectures, I guided you through its Saturn, Sun, Moon, and Earth stages in the evolution of our Earth. During the Saturn stage, only the first traces of sensory organs were present, embedded in the great mass of Saturn-like crystals embedded in a mountain today. Your eyes were like quartz crystals in a mountain. On the Sun, your most highly developed organs — all glands — covered the Sun's surface. On the Moon, the organs that now comprise your nervous system were spread out over the Moon's surface. The Moon had a nervous system, and individual animal-humans were blessed with a nervous system for the first time. On Earth, human beings received their skeletal system, for there was no mineral kingdom on the Moon.

As you see, constructing the human body was an elaborate process. What is now the human eye was spread out over the entire mass of Saturn. Before taking their place in the human body, organs existed first in the entire cosmos. Esoteric science can teach us how individual organs relate to the cosmos. It can tell us what corresponds to the human liver, spleen, heart, and so on in the world outside us and what had to happen in the greater world so that these organs could be formed. Rosicrucian epistemology provides methods of concentration that focus on our eyes or ears and enable us to acquire a clairvoyant view of these organs' development.

I took you back to a time in the Atlantean evolutionary period when the ether body was still so far removed from the physical body that it was not yet linked to the point on the head above the root of the nose. We heard how the ether body then slipped inside the physical body so that the physical body acquired its present form. There is a method of concentration — its very specific formula is communicated only from person to person — which focuses our attention on this point of connection between the head and the corresponding part of the ether body. This meditative method makes it possible to perceive what the earth looked like at the time when this portion of the etheric head slipped inside the physical human head. Similar methods for each organ of the human microcosm teach us about the other macrocosmic forces that the great cosmic architects inserted into the human body. Under esoteric guidance, therefore, we can learn about the macrocosm, because everything out there in the cosmos corresponds to some organ in the microcosm. The human body is a highly complicated creation, but just as reading a telegram allows you to guess who sent the message, meditating on individual organs makes it possible to draw conclusions about their creators.

By now we have already touched on the sixth stage, which is called "immersing oneself in the macrocosm." By learning to recognize the relationship of your own microcosm to the macrocosm, you expand your knowledge to include the entire universe. This truth is concealed in the old injunction, "Know thyself!" A great deal of damage has been done, however, by theosophists who say that each individual encompasses all of God or all of the Most High, and that in order to understand the entire universe we simply need to look into ourselves. This type of brooding on oneself is utter nonsense. It teaches you only about the lower I that you already possess; it cannot teach you about anything you do not already have. True self-knowledge, which is also knowledge of the universe, is acquired only in the complicated way I described. Real theosophy cannot make the path to such knowledge so easy for people. Instead, it must tell us that we can learn about the most complicated of all beings only through quiet, serious contemplation. The only way to learn about the Divine is to recognize it in the cosmos, bit by bit. This process requires patience and persistence. Our understanding of the greater world grows quietly and slowly. Theosophy cannot provide a universal formula that will reveal all knowledge at once. It can only point out the path that leads to self-knowledge and thus also to knowledge of the cosmos and knowledge of the Divine.

The knowledge we acquire at this sixth stage of initiation is not dry and rational; it forges an intimate connection between ourselves and the greater world. Those who achieve this knowledge are intimately related to everything in the world in a way that modern human beings know only in the mysterious relationship of love between man and woman, which is based on a secret recognition of the being of the other person. Looking at the macrocosm through such a relationship, you not only understand but also feel connected with all beings, just as lovers feel connected. You have an intimate, loving relationship to each plant and stone, to all the beings of the world. Our love becomes specialized with regard to each being, which then gives us information it ceased to provide when we descended to modern forms of cognition. Animals eat what is good for them and leave what is harmful; they have a sympathetic relationship to some foods and an antipathetic relationship to others. To develop modern cognition, we humans had to relinquish such direct relationships, but in future we will regain them on a higher level. How do modern esotericists know that a plant's flower affects human beings differently than its root? How do they know that the effect of an ordinary root is different from that of a carrot? They know because things speak to them just as they also speak to animals. At lower levels, such intimate relationships are incompatible with rational consciousness, but at the highest levels we will enter into such relationships consciously.

Once we have reached this stage, the seventh stage sets in as a natural consequence. As you may have deduced, this stage involves an understanding of feelings and emotional impressions. There is nothing here that will not touch your heart vividly, so it would be wrong to distinguish between ideational, intellectual, and spiritual knowledge. The intention of esotericists is not to move you or to tell you all kinds of beautiful things, but simply to recount the facts of the spiritual world, and they would consider it shameless to appeal directly to your feelings. But they know that the facts speak for themselves, and that the facts alone should arouse feelings. For Rosicrucians, therefore, the personality of the teacher is not an issue. The teachings have nothing to do with the person; teachers are there simply to allow the facts to speak to others. The more esoteric teachers allow themselves to serve simply as a means of expression for the perspectives of the higher world, the more correctly they speak. Anyone who still has personal beliefs and opinions and views is not suited to be an esoteric teacher, because if feelings rather than objectivity were the deciding factor, you might say that two times two is five!

Thus you see how various aspects of inner development gradually allow Rosicrucians to rise to knowledge of the higher worlds. Guidance is necessary for this development, but it always appears at the right time if you seek it seriously.

It is not correct to say that such personal guidance always recommends completing these seven stages sequentially. The teacher selects aspects that are especially suitable for each student. I also wanted to describe the preparatory levels, but let me just select two examples to demonstrate the need to develop other qualities before proceeding to the more rigorous exercises. Concentration, or focusing our thinking, is one ability we need to practice from the very beginning. Just consider how your thoughts dance around from morning till night! They come from all directions and tear you away with them. As a student of Rosicrucianism, you must set aside a time when you master your thoughts and focus on a single thought that is as uninteresting as possible. You will notice that this has a tremendously beneficial effect. How long it takes is not important, but it does require energy, patience, and persistence.

The other quality is what we call "positivity," an attitude toward life that is best characterized by a Persian legend about Christ Jesus. Once when Christ Jesus was walking along a road with his disciples, they came upon a dead dog by the side of the road. The dog was already in a very advanced stage of decay, and the disciples, whose attitudes were not as highly developed as those of Christ Jesus, turned away from the ugly sight. Only the Christ Jesus stopped to look at the dog carefully and said, "What beautiful teeth the animal has!" Every ugly thing we encounter contains an element of beauty, every untruth a kernel of truth, and every evil a grain of goodness. This does not mean that we must become absolutely uncritical! Positivity is often interpreted to mean that we can no longer dislike anything, but in fact it simply means that there is always a kernel of beauty in the ugly and a bit of good in every example of evil. This attitude encourages the soul's higher forces and is part of the preparation for esoteric schooling.

I also wanted to give you an idea of the spirit of gnostic Christian esoteric schooling. The deepest, truest Christianity is found in Rosicrucian schooling, which allows you to be a Christian in the truest sense of the word in spite of all the obstacles of modern life. It was more possible to be a Christian in the old style as long as there was more opportunity to withdraw from the world, before we became so imbued with the scientific ideas that make it difficult to accept Christianity in its original form. Our greatest thinkers say that they can no longer reconcile such thoughts with Christianity. While it is true that the spiritual world is omnipresent, it is also true that the thought forms of our materialistic age are active in us and constantly leave their mark on us. If we are conscientious, we are forced to realize that we need some means of maintaining ourselves in the face of all these ideas storming in on us. Spiritual science provides this means. Those who reject it, who refuse to make it their own, are egoists. Proponents of spiritual science feel that it is up to them to implement the intentions of medieval theosophy. Spiritual science, however, can be grasped by people familiar with all the justified counterarguments of natural science. In modern Rosicrucian theosophy, anyone will be able to find a path that leads to understanding the greater world, to peace of soul, and to certainty in life. Rosicrucian theosophy is not merely theoretical knowledge that is subject to arguments and counterarguments. This type of knowledge must find its way into our entire culture....

– four –

Stages of Rosicrucian Initiation

Düsseldorf, December 15, 1907

It might seem, in these first lectures, as though Steiner is overworking the "stages" involved in Rosicrucian spiritual practice, repeating them too often. Therefore, we considered selecting some and omitting others because of the apparent repetition or redundancy they contain. But then we realized that though the content is doubtless somewhat the "same," the context is always different — and we discovered that it is the difference of context that makes different our understanding. Each time we understood more and deeper. And this is intentional on Steiner's part, for, though he gave these lectures in different places, students followed him around and would therefore have heard the "same" lecture a number of times. But, in fact, it was never the same: the perspective, the mood, the framing was always different. This is very true of the following lecture.

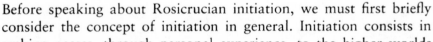

Before speaking about Rosicrucian initiation, we must first briefly consider the concept of initiation in general. Initiation consists in seeking access, through personal experience, to the higher worlds that underlie our sense-perceptible world. Initiates, clairvoyants, and adepts relate to these higher worlds in three different ways. In today's discussion of how to achieve direct personal experience of the suprasensible worlds, we will disregard these three different approaches, but we will bear in mind that we are discussing one particular method of initiation.

The fact that there are different methods of initiation is not at all confusing when we realize that individuals set out on their search for the path to higher worlds from different starting points. Once we have reached a mountaintop, we have a clear view in all directions, but to get there, we can set out from any number of different places and take different routes. It would make no sense to walk all the way around the mountain before heading for the peak instead of taking the path that lies right in front of us.

Applying this principle to initiation, we see that different points of departure exist to accommodate the different natures of individual human beings. The materialistic sciences cannot truly study such subtle differences between individuals. Our physiologists and anatomists with their crude instruments and methods cannot discern these differences. To those who possess esoteric knowledge, however, there is a tremendous difference between a person born in the Orient and one born in Europe or America. This difference is evident right down into the person's physical nature. There is also a tremendous difference between a person who still feels and experiences the Christ directly and vividly and someone who is totally estranged from the original Christian sensibilities and bases his or her worldview entirely on the accomplishments of modern science. Not only are the latter's feelings and thoughts different from those of a convinced Christian, but the difference can also be observed even in the person's physical makeup. These differences are so subtle and affect such fine bodily structures that they elude physiology and biology.

Because of such differences, however, individual natures must be considered when recommending paths of higher development. The same path to the higher world is not appropriate for all.

To understand this statement, we must go back in time to earlier stages of humankind's long evolution. In so-called Atlantean times, our forebears — that is, our own souls — lived in very different bodies in ancient Atlantis, which was located to the west between the present continents of Europe and the Americas. Then the great floods, told about in the Biblical story of the Deluge and other legends, caused the downfall of ancient Atlantis. The Atlantean age was followed by post-Atlantean developments, of which we have already passed through four eras and are now experiencing the fifth.

The first of these eras encompassed ancient Indian culture, when people were personally taught by the holy Rishis, individuals who were inspired to an extent unimaginable to modern human beings. The Indian era was followed by the second, or Persian, culture with its Zoroastrian religion. The third culture was that of Babylon, Assyria, Chaldea, and Egypt, out of which the Hebrew culture gradually evolved. The fourth era included the Greco-Roman cultural stream. There Christianity emerged, drawing elements from the Jewish people that had evolved organically out of the third culture. Now we are living in the fifth cultural era and approaching the sixth.

Not only human thinking but also our astral, etheric, and physical bodies have changed in the long time that has passed since the Atlantean catastrophe. We must not imagine, however, that all individuals in this fifth cultural stream are at the same level of evolution. Stages that developed sequentially still persist alongside each other.

Because human beings experienced different cultural streams that caused changes in their entire makeup, the methods their spiritual leaders presented for initiating people into the higher worlds had to change accordingly. In Atlantean times, human beings still possessed astral clairvoyance. They lived in the presence of their gods and spirits just as they lived surrounded by material plants, minerals, animals, and humans. In post-Atlantean times, people no longer had such easy access to the higher worlds. They could no longer enter such worlds through direct perception of the divine spirit and had to resort to artificial means of entering a state in which they again become the companions of the gods. These artificial means formed the basis of Indian yoga initiation, which consisted of subduing the consciousness and physical perception that human beings had achieved in post-Atlantean times and reverting to earlier states of clairvoyant consciousness such as the Atlanteans had possessed.

If we continue to trace the evolution of humankind through the Persian and Chaldean cultural streams, we arrive at the Christian cultural era and the emergence of Christian initiation, which can only be attained through a direct relationship to Christ Jesus. This initiation is based on the Gospel of St. John and the Book of Revelation.

This period of Christian initiation was followed by the first dawning of materialistic culture in the thirteenth and fourteenth centuries, when enlightened souls recognized the approaching age of materialism. The materialism that peaked and achieved its most extreme form in the nineteenth century had been developing for a long time. Now we find materialism not only in the sphere of outer activity but in all other spheres as well.

Very different perceptions and feelings persisted until the thirteenth or fourteenth century, but then the shift occurred in all spheres, even the seemingly most remote. For example, the great change in human feeling is evident in painting. To today's materialists, Cimabuë's choice of a gold background for his paintings seems totally arbitrary. This painter, however, still possessed the tradition of the perception of the higher world. Seeing into the highest regions of the astral world shows us that the gold background is indeed a reality. Similar paintings were later produced in imitation of the old masters who had still possessed traditional knowledge of the reality of the astral world, but these later artists seem like barbarians in contrast to those who still had an authentic relationship to the astral world. Giotto, for example, painted out of superficial tradition rather than out of a personal experience of truth. In Giotto's day it was quite natural to make the transition to materialistic art, which is restricted to what can be seen only on the physical plane. Only the greatest painters preserved the reality of the tradition. In Raphael's *Disputa,* we can see that the change in background colors from below to above accurately depicts, at least to some extent, the experience of a person ascending into higher worlds. The experience of moving step-by-step from lower to higher worlds, until finally we see the guardian spirits emerging from the gold background, is an inescapable part of the spiritual path.

Those who are aware of spiritual truths know that deeper phenomena lie concealed behind physical facts. They know that modern people are materialists because they are subject to outer materialistic influences. The esoteric perspective makes us aware that these influences are not simply a matter of outer perception and are due to other reasons. Thoughts and feelings are realities that radiate out into the world, and we live totally surrounded by the buzzing of materialistic thoughts. Even peasants who live too far out in the country to be reached by books or magazines espousing materialistic views are surrounded by the buzz of materialistic thoughts. This type of influence is all-important.

How were people received into life in times when something of the existence of esoteric powers was still a matter of common knowledge? In researching this question, we discover that in China, for example, great care was taken to surround a person's entry into the physical world with people who were filled with spiritual thoughts. This is a very different situation from being received by a materialistic physician in an environment filled with materialistic thoughts. The surroundings we encounter now are very different from the environment filled with spiritual thoughts that received us in former times. The reason for people's materialistic attitude is that ever since the thirteenth or fourteenth century they have been immersed in a materialistic atmosphere from the moment of their birth. This state of affairs was unavoidable, but it meant that for those who wanted to ascend to higher worlds, a method had to be created that would allow them to become strong enough to do so in spite of outer materialistic circumstances.

This method of initiation is the Rosicrucian method, which emerged in the late thirteenth or early fourteenth century and was first inaugurated by Christian Rosenkreutz, one of the great leaders of humanity. Since that time, this method has been practiced for centuries in strict isolation from the outer world, known only to a narrow circle of people. It was most strictly isolated during the nineteenth century, that most materialistic of centuries. Only in the last third of the nineteenth century did it become necessary to reveal, in the form of theosophy, at least some elementary aspects of the teachings of Rosicrucian schools.

In 1459, Christian Rosenkreutz, the actual founder of the Rosicrucian movement, achieved the level of development that gave him the power to influence the world by introducing a method of initiation. Since that time, the individuality of Christian Rosenkreutz has been continuously present as the leader of this movement, living throughout the centuries "in the same body."

How are we to understand this expression "in the same body"? If we observe a physical human body, we discover that although the substance that comprised it ten years ago is no longer there, the person's consciousness remains the same. Every seven or eight years we replace all the physical substance in our body, but continuity of consciousness survives this ongoing exchange of substance and persists for a lifetime. This happens to all of us between birth and death, but initiates are able to extend the process so that when they die they are quickly reincarnated in new bodies, as babies, and their consciousness survives from one incarnation to the next. They undergo reincarnation in complete consciousness. Even their new bodies are physically similar to the old, because their souls developed these bodies consciously on the basis of their experience in the previous incarnation. The highest leader of the Rosicrucian school lived for centuries in this way.

It has only recently become possible to communicate some of the principle aspects of the Rosicrucian view. Previously, nothing had been made public, with the exception of one incident.

The Rosicrucian method of ascending into higher worlds consists of the following seven steps: First, study; second, acquiring imaginative cognition; third, learning to read the occult script; fourth, preparing the philosophers' stone; fifth, the correspondence between microcosm and macrocosm; sixth, merging into the macrocosm; seventh, "beatitude." I do not mean to imply that these seven steps must always be undertaken sequentially. The instruction given to each student who approaches a Rosicrucian teacher corresponds to that student's individuality. From the seven stages, the teacher selects what is best suited to a particular student. One person may begin with the first and second steps and then proceed to the fourth and fifth. Only the stage we call "study" is the same for everyone and always comes first.

"Study" in this sense means something different, however, than what we understand by the term in everyday life. Here it means acquiring sense-free ideas and concepts. In ordinary people, all thinking is bound up with outer sense perception. Try to observe everything you experience in a day, imagining away everything that you have seen and heard. For most people, nothing or only very little is left. If we want to find our way to the higher worlds, however, we must learn to be able to think even without linking our thoughts to the world outside us. We must learn to derive our thoughts exclusively from what lies within us.

Mathematics is the only type of sense-free thinking that is known in the West. Although children first learn that two times two is four in terms of outer perception, by counting fingers or beans or using those awful adding machines, we do not achieve satisfying results in mathematics as long as we depend on outer perception as the basis of our thoughts. We can never see a circle in external reality. Circles drawn on the board are merely sequences of little lumps of chalk. Only our mental image of a circle is precise. We must construct circles in the spirit; we must think the circle.

Today we find sense-free human thinking only in the domain of number and geometry. This field is not accessible to most people, however, so I mention it only for purposes of comparison. Theosophy itself is the best means of developing sense-free thinking, because in theosophy we hear about beings and events that we have not seen. When we learn how the human being consists of physical, etheric, and astral bodies, or how the earth itself evolved through different stages, we hear about things we cannot see. By exerting our thinking to grasp the inherent logic of this information, however, we can use ordinary logic to understand such beings and events, if in fact we want to base ourselves solely on the comprehensive foundations of logic. When people say that they cannot understand such ideas, it is not because they are not clairvoyant but because they are unwilling to apply logic in their attempts at understanding. Clairvoyant discoveries can be understood by means of ordinary logic; actual clairvoyance is required only for conducting the research. Only the contents of theosophy are truly logical with regard to both theoretical and practical activity. In contrast, materialistic statements about suprasensible phenomena are illogical. The contributions of spiritual science are truly concrete and productive.

Let's compare how the theosophical worldview and the materialistic approach view education. The former provides information about the developing human being that we cannot confirm through sense perception. Nonetheless, this information is real, true, and concrete. Our modern worldview does not understand the developing child. We understand the nature of the human being in the context of the whole world only when we consider it in its fullness instead of observing it superficially.

Those who discover the teachings of the theosophical worldview also discover a means of learning sense-free thinking. True theosophy will always aim to develop sense-free thinking to the greatest possible extent by describing states that we cannot see. For example, in considering the origin and evolution of our Earth, we describe the planetary stage of the old Moon, where everything was different from our present Earth. At that stage, Earth had no solid, mineral crust that people could walk around on; the entire planet was plant-like. In this vegetative mass, which could be compared to spinach or other greens, any solid components that existed resembled the bark of today's trees. There was no mineral element at all yet.

When people find fault with these statements from the materialistic perspective because they can only imagine plants growing in mineral soil, we must admit that under present circumstances, that is indeed the only way plants can grow. In those times, however, totally different circumstances prevailed. Materialists cannot imagine this possibility because they relate everything to present-day circumstances. In images of earlier evolutionary stages, however, we can free ourselves from what we see around us. What is nonsense today makes sense when we consider circumstances in the distant past. Thus we train ourselves to let go of our sense-perceptible surroundings by calling to mind images of unfamiliar circumstances, raising our thinking above the level of today's possibilities. If we relate our thinking only to today's possibilities, we cling to them and cannot let them go. For "study" in the Rosicrucian sense, it is important to practice thinking in images of circumstances that are no longer present. To develop one concept out of another in completely sense-free thinking is a means of achieving the stage called "studying."

This stage can also be achieved by studying a book such as *Intuitive Thinking as a Spiritual Path: A Philosophy of Freedom*. Its author simply provided an opportunity for the thoughts to think themselves. Because each individual thought in this book develops sequentially, on the basis of the preceding thought, no thought can be removed and inserted in a different location, just as we cannot remove a hand from the human body and reattach it in a different location. Such is the path of sense-free thinking.

Many people are burning with desire to find their way into higher worlds, but this desire is unhealthy. A healthy striving consists of cultivating inherently sound logic based on thinking that is free of all sense perception.

Those who truly know about the higher world understand that perceptions there are totally different from perceptions in the physical world. One thing, however, does remain the same in the physical and astral worlds and in devachan, namely, logical thinking. This reliable guide protects us from all flighty and illusory thoughts. Without it, we never learn to distinguish illusion from reality and mistake every illusion for an astral reality. Here in the physical world it is easy to distinguish deceptions from realities, because the material facts correct us when we go astray. For example, if you walk down the wrong street, you cannot arrive at the right place. In the higher worlds, we must use our own spiritual strength to find the right path. We will wander into ever more complex labyrinths if we have not learned to distinguish illusion from reality, as we can learn through Rosicrucian training.

The second stage of Rosicrucian schooling is imaginative cognition or understanding through images. This is the first stage of lifting ourselves out of the physical world into a spiritual world. In the final words of part 2 of *Faust,* Goethe provided a leitmotiv for this stage when he said that everything transitory is but a semblance. When we begin to see everything around us as images of spirit, we know that we are making our way upward into the world of Imagination.

Teachers in Rosicrucian schools and earlier esoteric schools attempted to convey to their students the principle of evolving through the different kingdoms of nature. Today, both the materialistic school of thought and theosophy talk about evolution, but while ordinarily only our reason is involved in understanding the principle of evolution, theosophy attempts to raise the concept to the level of

Imagination by transforming it into an image. Imagination is achieved when the student's soul is transformed over the course of many weeks or months by the teacher's instructions. This process is best reproduced in the form of a dialogue, although in fact it never took place in that way. The teacher says something like, "Look at how the plant strives toward the Sun with its leaves and flowers and sinks its roots into the ground in the direction of the earth's center. When you compare the plant to the human being, it is wrong to compare the flower to the head and the root to the organs of reproduction." Darwin made the correct association, pointing out that the plant's root corresponds to the human head. The human being is an inverted plant. The root that the plant sinks into the earth corresponds to the human head, while the flowers and organs of pollination that the plant chastely extends toward the Sun correspond to organs the human being turns toward the earth. Totally inverting the plant yields the human being, while rotating it only ninety degrees results in the animal with its horizontal backbone.

Calling such imaginations to mind leads not only our thoughts but also our sensations and feelings deep into the surrounding world. We learn to see the intrinsic connection between plants and humans. We recognize the pure, chaste nature of plants, which has not been imbued with desires and passions, and the nature of the human being, in which chaste plant substance has been transformed into flesh filled with desires and passions. This transformation, however, made it possible for the higher element of clear day-consciousness to enter human nature. Plants sleep, but human beings acquire consciousness by incarnating into flesh that is filled with desires, passions, and instincts. This transformation requires a complete inversion. Animals occupy a position between plants and humans in that they possess desires and passions but have not yet achieved clear day-consciousness.

The teacher says to the student, "When you sense this relationship, you learn to understand what Plato meant when he said that the world soul is crucified on the world body." Plant, animal, and human being — that is the most profound meaning of the sign of the cross. Universal soul nature, the world soul that pervades the kingdoms of nature, is symbolized by the cross. Esoteric schools teach this deepest meaning of the sign of the cross.

Then the teacher says to the student, "See how chastely the plant raises its calyx to the Sun, and how the Sun kisses the flower." This touch was called the chaste kiss of the Sun's rays, of the holy lance of love. It points to an ideal state of the future when human organs will evolve to regain plantlike chastity. Human beings have evolved to the stage of being filled with desires, but we will continue to evolve to a level where we will transform our desires and will once again be kissed by the spiritual rays of the Sun. Our powers of reproduction will be spiritualized, and we will bring forth our own kind on a higher level. Esoteric schools called this spiritualization of reproduction "the Holy Grail." The true ideal of the Holy Grail is an organ that human beings will have when our powers of reproduction have been spiritualized. We see the chaste nature of plants in the past; human beings imbued with desire in the present; and in the future, human beings with the purified body, the chalice of the Holy Grail, as a further evolutionary stage of the plant calyx that receives the spiritual rays of the Sun.

Imaginative cognition is not abstract thinking. It is a state in which we do not merely think about each evolutionary level of development but feel it. Sensing evolution in this way, we gradually rise to the level of receiving the images of imaginative cognition. When we liberate such images from sensory appearances and receive them from the higher world, the image of the Holy Grail confronts us.

When we allow such images — which have been determined by esoteric schools to depict specific processes in the spiritual world — to work on us, we are "reading the occult script." This is the third step in Rosicrucian training.

We saw other such images at the Munich congress in the seals and columns depicting the Apocalypse and the beginning and end of humanity's evolution. In very ancient times, human beings lived on an Earth that was glowing hot and fluid. We achieved our present bodies only gradually, through many incarnations, and we will continue to evolve through many further incarnations. Above all, the human larynx and heart will be transformed. They are our future organs of reproduction. Today our thoughts, feelings, and sensations are embodied only in words, which allow the stirring of our souls to move on waves through space to the ears of others, where they awaken similar thoughts and sensations in other souls. Later, we will create warmth and, ultimately, light, just as we now imprint our thoughts on the air in the form of words. In the past, we descended from a sphere of light and warmth. In the future, we ourselves will create warmth and light.

The first apocalyptic seal depicts this process. The fiery river of metal at the feet of the human being represents the initial stage of

humanity's evolution, when Earth was still in a fluid state of glowing heat. The fiery sword emerging from the human being's mouth
represents the future state. Such images, which reveal nature's great
forces, work not only on our imagination but also on our will, because the same primeval force that is active in human will is also
active in the entire world outside us. When we train our own will,
the world-will lives in us; our own will becomes one with the will
that flows through all of nature. We learn to do this through selfless
devotion to the characters of the occult script.

The fourth stage of Rosicrucian schooling is "preparing the philosophers' stone." This is an exalted mystery whose secrecy was very
closely guarded. At the end of the eighteenth century, certain aspects
of this mystery were betrayed. For example, a newspaper in central Germany published certain remarks by someone who had heard
something about preparing the philosophers' stone. The newspaper
article said that the philosophers' stone really does exist, that there
are very few people who are not aware of it, and that many have
even held it in their hands but do not know it is the philosophers'
stone. The wording of this description is quite correct and not merely
allegorical. We must simply understand its meaning.

Rosicrucians work in the real world, right down into human physiology. They work at transforming the earth and the human being, not merely on the level of moral improvement, ennobling behavior, and so on, but right down into the physical body. Let's look first at human respiration, because regulating the breathing process plays an important part in esoteric development. When we human beings inhale, we use oxygen, which is combined with carbon inside us and exhaled as carbon dioxide. If this were the only process taking place, the earth's atmosphere would gradually become so saturated with carbon dioxide that humankind could no longer survive. Our survival depends on the existence of plants, which take in carbon dioxide, retain the carbon, and give off oxygen. Thus oxygen cycles constantly between human beings and plants. Humans, animals, and plants belong together. The one could not exist without the other.

As esoteric studies show us, further evolution of the human body will transform our heart and respiratory organs in ways that make it possible for us to perform a function that plants must now do for us, namely, producing carbon or coal. As you know, the remains of plants can still be seen in anthracite coal. One way to incorporate this plant process and perform it in full consciousness is by rhythmizing respiration in such a way that it no longer relinquishes carbon dioxide to the plants but retains carbon for use within the human body. Thus we will learn to build up our own bodies.

Comparing this to what was said earlier about the Holy Grail makes the whole concept of the Holy Grail more concrete. By rhythmizing the respiratory process, human beings learn to produce carbon within themselves. In the mineral world, carbon occurs in the form of graphite and diamonds. It is also the chaste substance upon which plant life is based. Being able to create this pure, chaste substance within ourselves is called "preparing the philosophers' stone." We must imagine this substance like a transparent diamond, but softer. Within the human being lies a powerful transformative mechanism. Through esoteric schooling, we learn that we are working to evolve our own sexuality into a higher form. Hearing this, one person of materialistic mind very characteristically remarked, "How nice! It might be possible to base a very profitable industry on that." Absolutely not. This remark demonstrates the great importance of preserving the secrecy of such communications. Such mysteries can be shared only with people who have achieved such a high moral and intellectual level that they can no longer think in egotistical terms.

The fifth stage is the correspondence between microcosm and macrocosm. For every process that takes place in the world outside us, there is a process within the human being that replicates the external process on a small scale. By reflecting on what takes place within us, we can intuit processes outside us in the cosmos. For example, a particular form of meditation and concentration that focuses on the essential nature of the human eye teaches us to recognize the nature of the Sun, because the human eye is an extract of the Sun's essential nature. Goethe once said that the eye was created by and for light. Light created the eye. Without the Sun, there would be no eye. All aspects of the nature of the Sun are repeated in some way within the eye. In Rosicrucian schooling, concentrating on the nature of the eye teaches us to understand the light of the Sun. Thus, by beginning within the human being, we can learn to understand the whole world. By concentrating on our liver, for example, we learn about very specific natural forces that influence the creation of the human being. Similarly, a specific concentration exercise that focuses on the human heart informs us about the nature of the lion in the outer world. This is no mere cliche. Because we ourselves are a miniature cosmos, we can learn to understand the whole cosmos by studying ourselves. We learn to recognize the real correspondences between microcosm and macrocosm.

When we learn to find our way into every detail of the greater universe, a feeling of oneness with the entire cosmos develops quite naturally. Patiently and step by step, we learn to find our way from every organ of our body — including the ether and astral bodies — to the corresponding aspect of the great universe. When we do so, our own organism expands into an organism that encompasses all of space; we incorporate all beings and are present in all beings. We can then experience the sensation that is called godliness, or beatitude.

The important point here is that we must escape from ourselves in order to find the path to the creative powers. The more we come out of ourselves, the more we ascend into the higher worlds. In his poem "The Mysteries," Goethe describes a traveler who wanders into a mysterious temple where he meets people who bring together different schools of thought. Goethe places the Cross entwined with roses at the temple's entrance. "Who brought the roses together with the Cross?" the poem asks. This question can only be asked by those who know that the rose-entwined Cross signifies evolving to a higher stage of humanity. Goethe expressed it in these words:

> And until you truly have
> This "dying and becoming,"
> You are but a troubled guest
> Roaming over the dark Earth.

We must draw ever closer to the stage of evolution that will permit us to rise, inwardly renewed, from the dying aspect of our being. Just as the bark dies off on the outside while the tree produces new sprouts from within, we must renew ourselves inwardly while surrounding ourselves outwardly with death. For this reason, the initiates known as druids were compared to the oak tree. "Dying and becoming" means that we constantly produce fresh life within ourselves. The dying aspects become the maintainer of new life, which is why Goethe says,

> Human beings who overcome themselves
> Free themselves of the power that binds all beings.

This means that we must overcome our ordinary life, transforming it into a vessel from which the new shoots of a higher life can emerge.

five

Goethe's Rosicrucian Poem "The Mysteries"

Cologne, December 25, 1907

The third rule of the Rosicrucians, as published in their Fama, *was that "every year upon the day C. [Christmas] they should meet together at the house* Sanctus Spiritus, *or write the cause of their absence."*

What better day, therefore, than December 25, to introduce Goethe's marvelous esoteric poem of 1782 — his "Rosicrucian fragment" as he later called it — "The Mysteries."

This is the text that poses the critical question: Who added roses to the Cross? For Goethe, the answer to this question is bound up with the figure of Humanus — the fully human — the leader, guide, and teacher of the community of twelve to which, in the poem, the hero Brother Mark finds his way.

For Steiner, too, the "roses" in some mysterious way represent the "Self," whose development Christ's incarnation makes possible for all human beings. The cross, of course, besides representing the threefold nature of the physical, the etheric, and the astral, is also the symbol of death. As Goethe says in another poem, "Die and be reborn."

This lecture bears repeated readings — not just for Goethe's poem but also for Steiner's commentary, which, too, is filled with manifold meanings and surprising secrets.

— ◆ —

If you were in the cathedral last night, you would have seen the illuminated letters: *C.M.B.* As you know, according to Christian tradition, these letters represent the names of the so-called "Three Wise Men," also called "The Three Holy Kings:" *Caspar, Melchior, and Balthasar.*

These names evoke quite special memories in Cologne. An old

legend recounts how, some time after the three kings had become bishops and died, their bones were brought here. Another legend tells how a Danish king once came to Cologne, bringing with him three crowns for the three kings. After he returned home he had a dream in which the three kings appeared to him and offered him three chalices. The first contained gold, the second frankincense, and the third myrrh. When the Danish king awoke, the three kings had vanished, but the chalices remained — they stood before him, the three gifts that he had retained from his dream.

There is profound meaning in this legend. By it, we understand that in his dream the king attained a certain insight into the spiritual world by which he learned the symbolic meaning of the three kings, the three wise men from the East who brought offerings of gold, frankincense, and myrrh at the birth of Christ Jesus. From his realization the king retained a lasting possession. He understood the three human virtues symbolized by gold, frankincense, and myrrh — by gold, self-knowledge; by frankincense, piety, the piety of the innermost self (which we can call self-surrender); and by myrrh, self-perfection, self-completion, and self-development, or the preservation of the eternal in the self.

The king could receive these three virtues as gifts from another world because he had tried with his whole soul to penetrate the profound symbol hidden in the three kings who brought their offerings to Christ Jesus.

Many features in this legend lead us a long way toward understanding the Christ principle and what it will do in the world. The adoration and the offering by the three Magi, the three Oriental kings, are among its profoundest features. Only with the deepest understanding may we approach this fundamental symbolism of the Christian tradition.

Later it began to be thought that the first king represented the people of Asia, the second, the European peoples, and the third, the people of Africa. Wherever people sought to understand Christianity as the religion of earthly harmony, they saw in the three kings and their homage a union of the different streams of thinking and religious movements in the world into one principle, the Christian principle. At the time the legend received this form, those who had penetrated the principles of esoteric Christianity saw in Christianity more than a force that had affected the course of human development, for they saw in the being embodied in Jesus of Nazareth a cosmic world-force — a force far transcending the merely human that prevails in this present age. They saw in the Christ principle a force that indeed represents for humankind an ideal lying in a far-distant future, an ideal that can only be approached by our understanding the whole world more and more in the spirit. They saw in the human being, in the first place, a miniature being, a miniature world, a microcosm, an image of the macrocosm, the great, all-embracing world. This macrocosm comprises all that the human being can perceive with the external senses, see with the eyes, hear with the ears, but comprises, besides, all that the spirit can perceive, from the perceptions of the least-developed human spirit up to perceptions in the spiritual world. This was how the esoteric Christians of the earliest times regarded the world. All they saw in the firmament or on our Earth, all they saw as thunder and lightning, as storm and rain, as sunshine, as the course of the stars, as sunrise and sunset, as moonrise and the setting of the Moon — all this was for them a gesture, something like a mime, an external expression of inner spiritual processes.

Esoteric Christians looked on the universe as they looked on the human body. When they looked on the human body they saw it as consisting of different limbs: the head, arms, hands, and so on. When they looked on the human body and saw the movements of hand, eye, and so on, they saw these as the expression of inner spiritual and soul experiences. Just as they looked through the human limbs (and their movements) into what is eternal and spiritual in human beings, esoteric Christians regarded the movements of the stars — the light streaming down from the stars, the rising and setting of the Sun and the Moon — as the external expression of divine-spiritual beings pervading all space. For the early esoteric Christians, all these natural phenomena were the deeds and gestures of the gods, the silent expressions of divine spiritual beings — as also was everything that occurred among human beings when they established social communities and submitted to moral commandments and regulated their dealings through laws and created tools from the forces of nature. All that human beings did more or less unconsciously was, for esoteric Christians, the outer expression of inner divine spiritual influences.

But esoteric Christians did not confine themselves only to such general forms. They pointed to quite specific individual gestures — single parts of the physiognomy of the universe, of the universal dance — and sought to see in these single parts quite definite expressions of the spiritual. When they pointed to the Sun, they said: "The Sun is not merely an external, physical body; this external, physical solar body is the body of a soul-spiritual being, one of those soul-spiritual beings who are the rulers, the leaders of all earthly destiny, the leaders of all natural occurrences on the earth, but also of all that happens in human social life, in the relationships between people as determined by laws." When esoteric Christians looked up to the Sun they revered Christ's outer revelation in it. Christ was for them in the first place the soul of the Sun. So esoteric Christians said: "From the beginning the Sun was the body of the Christ, but people on Earth and Earth itself were not yet mature enough to receive the spiritual light, the Christ light, which streams from the Sun. Therefore, people had to be prepared for the Christ light!"

Esoteric Christians looked up at the Moon, too, and saw that the Moon reflects the light of the Sun, but more feebly than the Sun's light itself; and they said to themselves: "If I look with my physical eyes into the Sun I am dazzled by its shining light. If I look into the Moon I am not dazzled; it reflects in a feebler degree the shining light of the Sun." In this subdued sunlight — in this moonlight pouring down on the earth — esoteric Christians saw the physiognomic expression of the old Jehovah (Jahve) principle, the expression of the religion of the old Law.

They said: "Before the Christ principle, the Sun of Righteousness, could appear on Earth, the Jahve principle had to send down on Earth this light of righteousness, toned down in the Law, to prepare the way." And so what lay in the old Jehovah principle, in the old Law — the spiritual light of the Moon — was for esoteric Christians the reflected spiritual light of the higher Christ principle.

As had the pupils of the ancient Mysteries, esoteric Christians, until late into the Middle Ages, saw in the Sun the expression of the spiritual light ruling the earth, the Christ light, and in the Moon the expression of the reflected Christ light, whose full strength would blind us. In the earth itself, esoteric Christians saw — as the pupils of the ancient Mysteries had done — something that sometimes disguised and veiled the spirit's blinding sunlight. For esoteric Christians, the earth was just as much the physical expression of a spirit as every other bodily form was an expression of something spiritual. When the Sun visibly looked down on the earth, when it sent down its rays, beginning in the spring and continuing through the summer, and called forth from the earth all the budding and sprouting life, and when it had culminated in the long summer days — then esoteric Christians imagined that the Sun cherished and maintained the external, up-shooting life, the physical life. Esoteric Christians saw the same principle, in an external, physical form, in the plants springing from the soil, in the animals unfolding their fertility in these seasons, as they saw it in the beings whose external expression was the Sun. But when the days became shorter, when autumn and winter approached, they said: "The Sun withdraws its physical power more and more from the earth. But to the same degree as the Sun's physical power is withdrawn from the earth, its spiritual power increases and flows to the earth most intensively when the shortest days come, with the long nights, in the season later fixed by the Christmas festival."

Human beings cannot see this spiritual power of the Sun. They would see it, however, said the esoteric Christians, if they possessed the inner power of spiritual vision. Thus, the esoteric Christians still had a consciousness of what was a fundamental conviction and experience of the Mystery pupils from the earliest times into the more modern age.

During those nights, now fixed by the festival of Christmas, the Mystery pupils were prepared for the experience of inner spiritual vision, so that they could see inwardly, spiritually, that which during this very time withdrew its physical power from the earth most completely. In the long winter Christmas night the novice could have advanced enough to have a vision at midnight. Then the earth was no longer a veil for the Sun, which stood behind the earth. The earth became transparent for the novice. Through the transparent Earth he or she saw the spiritual light of the Sun, the Christ light. This fact, which marked a profound experience for the Mystery novice, was recorded in the expression, "To see the Sun at midnight."

There are places where the churches, otherwise open all day, are closed at noon. This is a fact that connects Christianity with the traditions of ancient religious faiths. In ancient religious faiths the Mystery pupils said, on the strength of their experience, "At noon, when the Sun stands highest, when it unfolds the strongest physical power, the gods are asleep. They sleep the deepest sleep in summer, when the Sun develops its strongest physical power. They are widest awake on Christmas night, when the external physical power of the Sun is weakest, but when, on a summer noon, the Sun's physical light pours most lavishly onto Earth, its spiritual power is weakest."

In winter midnight, however, when the Sun shines down the least physical power to Earth, one can see the Sun's spirit through the earth, which has become transparent. Esoteric Christians felt that through absorption in Christian esotericism they increasingly approached that power of inward vision through which they could imbue their feeling, thinking, and will impulses in gazing into this spiritual Sun.

Then the Mystery novice was led to a vision of the greatest importance:

As long as Earth is opaque, the separate parts appear inhabited by people of different faiths, but the unifying bond is not there. Human races are as scattered as the climates. Human opinions are scattered all over the earth and there is no connecting link. But to the degree that people begin to look through Earth into the Sun by their inner power of vision, to the degree that the "star" appears to them through Earth, their faiths will flow together into one great, united brotherhood.

Those who guided the great separated masses of humans in the truth of the higher planes, toward their initiation into the higher worlds, were known as "Magi." They were three in number, as powers express themselves in the various parts of the earth. Humanity had, therefore, to be led in different ways. But the star rising beyond the earth appears as a unifying power. It brings scattered individuals together, and then they bring offerings to the physical embodiment of the solar star, appearing as the star of peace. Thus the religion of peace, of harmony, of universal peace, of human brotherhood, was connected cosmically and humanly with the ancient Magi, who laid the best gifts they had in store for humanity before the cradle of the Son of Man incarnate.

The legend has retained this beautifully, for it says that the Danish king attained an understanding of the Wise Men, of the three kings, and because he had attained it they bestowed on him their three gifts: first the gift of wisdom, in self-knowledge; second, the gift of pious devotion, in self-surrender; and, third, the gift of the victory of life over death, in the power and development of the eternal in the self.

All those who have understood Christianity in this way have seen in it the profound idea, contained in spiritual science, of the unification of religions. For they have had the firm conviction that whoever understands Christianity thus can rise to the highest grade of human development.

One of the last to understand Christianity in this way was Goethe, who laid down for us this kind of Christianity, this kind of religious reconciliation, this kind of theosophy, in his profound poem "The Mysteries." This poem, indeed, remained a fragment, but one that shows us in a deeply significant way the inner spiritual development of an individual who is penetrated and convinced by the feelings and ideas I have just described.

Goethe invites us first to follow the pilgrim path of such an individual. He indicates that this pilgrim path may lead us far astray, that
it is not easy to find it, and that one must have patience and devotion
to reach the goal. Whoever possesses these will find the light that he
or she seeks.

Let us hear the beginning of the poem:

> I have made a wonderful song for you —
> Hear it gladly! Call everyone to listen!
> The way leads you through mountains and valleys.
> Now your view is restricted, now it is free again.
> If the path gently disappears into the bushes,
> Don't think it's a mistake —
> When the time is right, when we have climbed enough,
> We shall approach our goal.
>
> Let no one think, no matter how deeply they reflect,
> That they will unravel all the wonders hidden here.
> Nevertheless, many people will gain many things on this way
> For Mother Earth produces many flowers.
> Some may leave with downcast eyes,
> But others, with cheerful gestures, will stay:
> This way will bring everyone a different pleasure.
> For the spring flows for many pilgrims.

This is the situation to which we are introduced. Then, we are
shown "Brother Mark," a pilgrim who, if we were to ask him, would
not be able to express formally what we have just seen to be the
esoteric Christian idea, but in whose heart and soul these ideas live,
transformed into feeling. It is not easy to discover everything that has
been secreted into this poem called "The Mysteries." In it, Goethe
has clearly indicated a process occurring in human life in which the
highest ideas, thoughts, and conceptions are transformed into feelings
and perceptions.

How does this transformation take place?

We live through many embodiments, from incarnation to incarnation. In each, we learn many things, each full of opportunities for
gathering new experiences. We cannot carry over everything in every
detail from one incarnation to another. When we are born again it is
not necessary for everything that we have once learned to come to life
in every detail. But if we have learned a great deal in one incarnation
and then die and are born anew, although there is no need for all our

ideas to live again, we come to life with the fruits of our former life, with the fruits of what we have learned. Our powers of perception and feeling are in accord with our earlier incarnations.

In this poem, we have a wonderful phenomenon: an individual who, in the simplest words — as a child might speak, not in definite intellectual or abstract terms — shows us the highest wisdom, which is a fruit of former knowledge. He has transformed this knowledge into feeling and experience and is thereby qualified to lead others who have perhaps learned more in the form of concepts.

In "Brother Mark" we have before us such a pilgrim with a ripe soul that has transformed into direct feeling and experience much of the knowledge it gathered in earlier incarnations. As a member of a secret brotherhood, Brother Mark is sent out on an important mission to another secret brotherhood. He wanders through many different places. Finally, when he is getting tired he comes to a mountain. He journeys up the path (every feature in this poem has a deep significance), and when he has climbed the mountain he finds himself before a monastery. This monastery indicates the other brotherhood to which he has been sent. Over the gate of the monastery he sees something unusual. He sees the Cross, but in unusual guise; the Cross is garlanded with roses! And at this point he utters something significant that can be understood only by one who knows how again and again this motto has been spoken in secret brotherhoods: *"Who added to the Cross the wreath of Roses?"*

Around the Cross he sees the Triangle shining, radiating beams like the Sun. There is no need for him to understand in ideas the meaning of this profound symbol. The experience and understanding of it already live in his soul, in his ripe soul. His ripe soul knows its inner meaning.

What is the meaning of the Cross? He knows that the Cross is a symbol for many things, among others, for the threefold lower nature of the human being: the physical body, the etheric body, and the astral body. Within this the I, the Self, is born. In the Rose Cross we have the fourfold human being: in the Cross the physical, the etheric, and the astral bodies, and in the roses the self.

Why roses for the self? Esoteric Christians added roses to the Cross because they felt called upon by the Christ principle to develop the self more and more from the state in which it is born in the three bodies to an ever higher self. In the Christ principle they saw the power for higher and higher development of this self. The Cross is the symbol of death in a quite particular sense. This, too, Goethe expresses in another beautiful passage when he says:

> And until you truly have
> This "dying and becoming,"
> You are but a troubled guest
> Roaming over the dark Earth.

"Die and be reborn" — overcome what you have first been given in the three lower bodies; deaden it, not out of a desire for death, but purify what is in these three bodies so as to attain in your self the power to receive an ever greater perfection. If you overcome what is given you in the three lower bodies, the power of consummation will live in the self. The Christian must absorb this power in the Christ principle into the self, must absorb this power of consummation down to the very blood. Right into the blood this power must work.

Blood is the expression of the self, the I. In the red roses esoteric Christians saw the power of the Christ principle purifying and cleansing the blood, purifying the self, and so guiding us upward to our higher being. They saw the power that transforms the astral body into "spirit self," the etheric body into "life spirit," the physical body into "spirit body."

Thus the Rose Cross, with the Triangle, shows us the Christ principle in a profound symbolism. Brother Mark, the pilgrim who arrives here, knows he is at a place where the most profound meaning of Christianity is understood.

> Wearied by a day of traveling,
> Undertaken with the highest motive,
> Staff in hand, like a pious pilgrim,
> Brother Mark came one evening
> To a valley off the beaten track,
> Longing for a little food and drink,
> Full of hope that in the valley's wooded gorges
> He would find a friendly roof to spend the night.
>
> In the steep mountainside now before him
> He thought he saw the traces of a way.
> He followed the path. It wound as it went.
> As it climbed, it hugged the cliffs.
> He rose high above the valley.
> The Sun again seemed warm and friendly.

Soon, with heartfelt, deep delight,
He saw the summit come within his sight.

Beside the peak, the magnificent setting Sun
Sat, enthroned in the clouds in the darkening sky.
He gathered his strength for the final ascent,
Hoping his weariness would be rewarded there.
Now, he said to himself, perhaps I shall see
Something human in the vicinity.
He climbed, he listened, he was as if new born!
The chime of bells rang in his ears.

As he stood atop the summit
Nearby he saw a gently sloping valley.
His quiet gaze glowed with pleasure —
Suddenly, he saw, before the forest,
Lit by the last rays of the Sun,
A beautiful building in a green field.
He hurried through fields damp with dew:
Before him stood a monastery, its lights shone toward him.

Now he stood before that quiet spot.
It filled his spirit with peace and hope.
On the arch, above the closed gate,
He noticed a mysterious image.
He stood and thought, he whispered soft words
Of prayer that rose up in his heart;
He stood and thought: *What does this mean?*
The Sun set, the chiming died away.

He saw raised up there majestically the sign
That brings hope and comfort to all human souls,
The sign to which many thousands pledge themselves,
To which many thousand hearts ardently confess —
The sign that overcame the power of bitter death
Fluttering in so many victorious flags:
A refreshing stream filled his heavy limbs
He saw the Cross and dropped his eyes.

He felt again the salvation that sprang from thence,
He felt the faith of half the earth;
But, as he saw the image before his eyes,
He felt himself inspired by new, unknown meaning —

The Cross stood densely hung about with roses!
Who added roses to the Cross?
The garland of roses swelled, spread on all sides
To surround the hard wood with softness.

Light silvery clouds soared,
Rose upward with Cross and roses,
And from the center sprang holy life —
A threefold ray from a single point.
But not a word surrounded the image
To give the mystery sense and clarity.
In the gathering dusk growing gray and grayer,
The pilgrim stood, pondered, and felt himself raised up.

The spirit of the deepest Christianity that pervades this building is expressed by the Cross entwined by roses. As the pilgrim enters, he is actually received in this deepest Christian spirit. When he enters he becomes aware that in this house no one religion holds sway but that the higher oneness of all the world religions rules here. Once in this house, then, he tells an old member of the brotherhood at whose behest and on what mission he has come.

He is made welcome and hears that in this house a brotherhood of twelve brothers lives in perfect seclusion. These twelve brothers are representatives of different human races from all over the earth. Every one of the brothers is the representative of a different religious faith. None is accepted here in the immaturity of youth, but only when he has explored the world, when he has struggled with the joys and sorrows of the world — when he has worked and been active in the world and won his way to a free view beyond his narrowly confined domain. Only then is he accepted in the circle of the twelve. And these twelve, each representing one of the world religions, live here together in peace and harmony. They are led by a thirteenth who surpasses them all in the perfection of his human self. The thirteenth surpasses them all in his broad view of human circumstances.

How does Goethe indicate that this thirteenth is the representative of true esotericism? He indicates by the words the brother speaks that the thirteenth is the bearer of the religion of the Rose Cross: "He was among us; now we are in deepest sorrow because he is about to leave us; he wishes to part from us. But he finds it right to part from us even now; he desires to rise to higher regions, where he no longer needs to reveal himself in an earthly body."

He is worthy to rise. For he has risen to the point that Goethe describes with the words, "In every religion there is the possibility of attaining the highest purity."

When each of the twelve religions is ripe to form a basis of harmony, the thirteenth, who has before brought about this harmony externally, can pass away. And we are beautifully told how we can achieve this consummation of the self. First, the life story of the thirteenth is related; but the brother who has received Brother Mark knows many details, which the great leader of the twelve cannot tell. Several features of profound esoteric significance are now recounted by one of the twelve to Brother Mark. He learns that when the thirteenth was born a star appeared to herald his life on Earth. Here there is a direct connection with the star that guided the Three Holy Kings, and with its inner meaning. This star has an enduring significance: it shows the way to self-knowledge, self-surrender and self-consummation. It is the star that opens the mind for the gifts the Danish king received from the vision in his dream, the star that appears at the birth of anyone ripe enough to absorb the Christ principle.

And there were other signs. There were signs showing that the thirteenth had developed to the height of religious harmony that brings the peace and harmony of the soul. Profoundly symbolic in this sense, too, is the vulture that swoops down at the birth of the thirteenth. Instead of destruction, this vulture spreads peace around it among the doves. We are told still more. While his little sister is lying in the cradle, a viper winds itself around her. The thirteenth, still a child, kills the viper. In this way it is wonderfully indicated how a ripe soul — for only a ripe soul can achieve such a thing after many incarnations — kills the viper in early childhood, which is to say he overcomes the lower astral nature. The viper is the symbol for the lower astral nature; the sister is his own etheric body, around which the astral body winds itself. He kills the viper to save his sister. Then we are told how he submitted obediently to every demand of his parents. He obeyed his stern father. The soul transforms its knowledge into ideas and thoughts; then healing powers develop in the soul and can bring healing into the world.

Miraculous powers develop, represented by the sword with which he strikes a spring out of the rock. We are here definitely shown how his soul follows the path of the Scriptures. Gradually the higher human, the representative of humanity, the chosen one, develops — the one who works as the thirteenth here, in the society of the twelve, the great secret brotherhood which, under the sign of the Rose Cross,

has taken upon itself for all humankind the mission of harmonizing
the religions scattered in the world. This is how we are made acquainted, in a profound manner, with the soul nature of the one who
until now has guided the brotherhood of the twelve.

At last he knocked. Overhead, the stars already
Looked down with shining eyes.
The gate swung open. The brothers welcomed
Him with open arms and ready hands.
The traveler spoke of whence he came, from what distant place
The command of higher Beings had sent him here.
They listened amazed. They knew to treat stranger
As a guest but now they honored the one who had been sent.

They crowded around to listen, their inmost being
Moved by a mysterious power. They held their breath
So as not to disturb the special guest
Whose every word echoed in their hearts.
What flowed from his lips moved his hearers.
It was deep childlike wisdom teaching:
In his openness, in the innocence of his gestures,
He seemed like a human being from another world.

At last an old brother cried: "If your mission
Brings comfort and hope — welcome!
You see us: we all stand here filled with worry.
Although the sight of you stirs our souls,
Our greatest joy is being taken from us!
Care and fear move us.
Thus you come as a stranger within our walls
To share an important time of sadness and mourning:
Alas! He who united everyone here,
Whom we know as father, friend, and leader,
Who kindled light and courage within us,
Is about to leave us.
He himself announced it a short while ago.
Yet he will not tell us how or when:
And so our quite certain parting from him
Is full of mystery and bitter pain.

You see that all of us here have gray hair,
How nature herself prescribes rest for us all:
We do not admit anyone here who, young in years,

Desires to flee from worldly joy and zest.
Only after we experienced life's pleasures and burdens
And the wind no more blew in our sails
Were we allowed to land here with honors,
Confident that we had found a safe harbor.

The noble man who led us here —
The peace of God dwells within his breast —
I walked with him on the path of life.
I remember all the times we spent together;
But now the hours that he prepares himself in solitude
Announce to us the approaching loss.
What is a human being? Why cannot a lesser one give
A life so that a greater one might live!

That is now my only wish!
Why must I renounce my longing?
How many have already gone before me!
Now I must most bitterly lament him!
With what friendship he would have received you!
He gave us only this house —
No one can appoint himself successor —
And yet he is already in the spirit, parted from us.

Every day he comes to us for only a moment.
He speaks, and is more moved than before:
We hear from his own mouth
How wondrously Providence guided him;
We take note, so that the smallest thing
May be kept certain for posterity
And take care that one of us writes swiftly
So that his memory shall live both true and pure.

Much I would rather have told myself
That now I can only quietly listen to;
I cannot forget the smallest circumstance;
All is still alive within my mind.
I listen and can scarcely conceal
How unhappy I always am.
One day I shall speak of all these things;
They will fall splendidly from my lips.

As the third, I told more and freely,
How an angel made a promise to his mother
And how a star at his baptismal feast
Showed itself shining in the evening sky,
And how with mighty wings a vulture swooped down
Into the yard among the doves —
Not to pounce on them to harm them,
But to invite them gently into unity.

He modestly concealed from us
How as a child he destroyed a viper
That he found snuggled around his sister's arm,
His sister sleeping peacefully.
The nurse had fled and left the baby alone.
He killed the snake with a firm blow;
His mother came and saw with thrill and joy
Her son's deed and her daughter freed.

He was silent, too, about a spring that sprang
From the barren rock before his sword,
Powerful as a brook, with rippling waves,
It poured down the mountainside into the depths;
It bubbled forth so strongly, so silver-bright,
When it first flowed toward him!
And travelers who saw the wonder
Could hardly trust themselves to drink.

For when a person is raised above nature,
It is no wonder that he can achieve much;
We must praise in him the Creator's power
That brings such honor to human weakness;
But when someone in all the trials of life,
Even the hardest, controls himself,
Then with joy we can point him out to others,
Saying:" This is he, this is his alone!"

For all power presses forward into space
To live and act and be effective here and there,
While the stream of the world hampers and hinders
Us on every side and pulls us along;
Within this inner storm and outer struggle
Our spirit hears a word it can scarce comprehend:

One who overcomes himself can free himself
From the power that binds all beings.

This person who had overcome himself — that is, who has overcome that I which is humanity's portion in the beginning — has
become the head of the chosen brotherhood. Therefore, he leads the
twelve. He has led them to a point at which they are mature enough
for him to leave them. Our Brother Mark is then led into the rooms
where the twelve work.

How do they work? Their activity is of an unusual kind. We are
told that it is activity in the spiritual world. Someone whose eyes observe only physically, whose senses experience only the physical plane
and only what is done by people in the physical world, has difficulty
imagining that there is still another task that may be even more vital
and important than what is done externally on the physical plane.
Work from the higher planes is far more important for humankind.
Naturally, those who wish to work on the higher planes can do so
only on condition that they have first completed their tasks on the
physical plane. The twelve had done this. Therefore, their combined
activity is of great importance as a service to humanity.

Our Brother Mark is led into the hall where the twelve were accustomed to assemble. There he sees in deeply symbolic guise the nature
of their combined activity. The individual contribution of each of the
brothers to this combined activity is expressed by an individual symbol above his. Symbols of many kinds are to be seen there, expressing
profoundly and in very different ways the contribution of each to the
common task — which consists in spiritual activity — so that these
streams flow together into a current of spiritual life that then flows
through the world and invigorates the rest of humanity. There are
such brotherhoods, such centers from which streams emanate and
have their effect on the rest of humanity.

Above the seat of the thirteenth, Brother Mark again sees the
sign — the Cross entwined with roses: the Cross, which is a symbol
of the fourfold nature of the human being, and the red roses, which
are the symbol of the purified blood or I principle, the principle of
the higher human being. And then we see what is to be overcome by
this sign of the Rose Cross, portrayed in a symbol of its own, to the
right and left of the seat of the thirteenth.

On the right, Mark sees the fiery-colored dragon, representing the
human astral nature. It was well known in Christian esotericism that

the human soul can surrender to the three lower bodies. If it suc-
cumbs to them it is dominated by the lower life of the threefold
bodily nature. This is expressed in astral experience by the dragon.
The dragon is not just a symbol, but a very real sign that represents
what must be overcome first. In the passions, in those forces of astral fire that are part of human physical nature — in other words, the
dragon — Christian esotericism, which inspired this poem and which
spread through Europe, saw what humankind received from the tor-
rid zone, the South. It is the South that has bestowed on humankind
the fierce passions that tend chiefly toward the lower senses. The
first impulse to fight and overcome it was divined in the influences
streaming from the cooler North. The influence of the cooler North,
the descent of the I into the threefold human physical nature, is expressed according to the old symbol taken from the constellation of
the Bear: it shows a hand thrust into the jaws of a bear. The lower
physical nature expressed by the fiery dragon is overcome, and what
has been preserved, represented by the higher rank of animal life,
was expressed in the bear; and the I — which has developed beyond
the dragon nature — was represented with profound appropriateness
by the thrusting of a human hand into the bear's jaws. What must
be overcome by the Rose Cross appears on both sides of it, and it is
the Rose Cross that calls upon us to purify and raise ourselves more
and more.

Thus the poem really describes the principle of Christianity in the
profoundest way. Above all, it shows us what we ought to have before
our mind's eye, particularly at a festival such as Christmas.

The eldest of the brothers living here and belonging to the Brotherhood expressly tells Pilgrim Mark that their combined activity is of
the spirit — is spiritual life. This work for humankind on the spiritual plane has a particular meaning. The brothers have experienced
life's joys and sorrows; they have passed through conflicts outside
these walls; they have accomplished tasks in the world; now they are
here, but that does not mean that their work is at an end; the further development of humankind is their unending task. Mark is told:
"You have seen as much now as can be shown to a novice to whom
the first door is opened. You have been shown in profound symbols
what humanity's ascent should be. But the second door hides greater
mysteries still: those of the influence of higher worlds on humankind.
You can only learn these greater mysteries after lengthy preparation;
only then can you enter through the other gate."

Profound secrets are expressed in this poem.

"How early his heart taught him
What, in him, I may hardly even call virtues:
He honored his father's powerful word,
And was willing, when his father fiercely
Burdened his leisure hours with duties,
To carry them out joyfully,
Like some poor boy who, friendless and astray,
Is happy to work for trifling pay.

He had to join the warriors in the field.
In storm and sunshine, at first on foot,
He tended the horses, prepared the meals,
And well and faithfully served old soldiers.
Often as a messenger swift and keen
He hastened through the woods by day and night;
And so used was he to live for others
That weariness seemed to give him only happiness and joy.

And brave and cheerful in the strife
He sought the arrows scattered on the ground;
Then hastily he gathered curing herbs,
With which he cooled and bound the burning wounds.
As if his very touch were healing,
The sufferers soon were strong and sound.
All regarded him with joy and pride!
Only his father seemed dissatisfied.

Like a sailing ship that feels its cargo
As no great load and speeds from port to port,
He bore the burden of his parents' teaching lightly:
He was obedient to their every word —
As pleasure is to boys, and to youths reputation,
For him, his father's will was all prevailing:
Whatever he demanded,
Each task he soon fulfilled, each trial he stood.

At last the father yielded and acknowledged
His son's merit in word and deed;
Of a sudden all his sternness vanished,
And he gave his son a swift and precious steed.
Now a sword replaced his shorter dagger,
And from his lesser duties he was freed:

Thus, destined by his birth and well acquitted,
He was now admitted into an Order.

I could report for many days
Amazing things to every one who hears;
And higher than the most delightful tales
His life will be esteemed in coming years;
For what in poetry and fiction charms,
And yet to our mind incredible appears,
Will with greater pleasure still be heard,
Because it has really happened!

The name of him whom Providence has chosen
That he should achieve wondrous things on Earth,
Whom I may praise, though insufficiently,
Whose destiny we scarcely can believe,
Is *Humanus,* Saint and Sage,
The best of men whom I ever saw:
By origin, another name he bears,
Which he shares with illustrious ancestors.
The aged brother would have spoken on.
Filled with the miracles he knew,
He could have gladdened us for weeks
With all the stirring facts he still could show;
But he was interrupted, just as
His heart was pouring forth in fervent flow.
The others had passed softly in and out
And thought it time to intervene at last.

When Mark had bowed before his hosts and prayed
In gratitude for the sustaining meal,
He requested a crystal bowl of water.
They brought what he asked with friendly zeal,
Then led him to their festive hall,
To show him an unusual sight.
And what he saw you soon will know,
For I shall describe everything with care.

No ornament was there to lead the eye astray.
A cross-arched vault rose sternly from the ground.
He saw thirteen chairs against the walls
Like a pious chorus ranged around,
By clever hands full delicately carven;

In front of each a little desk he found.
Devotion seemed to fill the very air,
Fraternity and restfulness and prayer.

Above each chair was hung a special shield,
Thirteen in all the number he could see.
They seemed to be important, purposeful,
No boast of ancestors in shallow pride.
And Brother Mark, with longing all aglow,
Desired to learn what secret they did hide:
In the middle, he saw that mystic sign
For a second time: *a Cross with sprays of Roses.*

Souls can here find much inspiration
One object draws one, another another;
Some places are adorned by swords and lances,
While helmets hang above those other shields;
Here battered weapons are to be discovered,
Such as one may collect on battlefields:
There spears and banners, come from distant lands,
And even fetters here and iron bands!

Each brother sank down before his chair,
Rested profoundly wrapped in silent prayer;
Then softly chanted fervent hymns of thanks
In which cheerfulness and piety mingled;
With mutual blessing they retired to sleep,
A short repose, by fancies unmolested:
But Mark remains, surrounded by a few,
Still wishing more attentively to view.

Though tired in body, full awake his mind,
Preoccupied by many hidden things:
For here, his thirst in raging flames appeasing,
A dragon is enthroned with fiery wings;
And here between his jaws a bear is holding
An arm from which the blood it loses springs.
Both shields, in distance corresponding quite,
Hung next the Rosy-Cross to left and right.
"The paths were wonderful that led thee here,"
The aged brother says to his guest:
"Oh let these symbols bid thee stay until
The many heroes' deeds we manifest;

Our mysteries we will confide to thee,
For what is here concealed, can ne'er be guessed;
Although thou wilt divine what here was done,

Do not believe that the brother spoke
Only of times gone by. Here wonders never fail;
And more and ever more you shall behold,
Until the shrouding veil is withdrawn.
You have gone through only one gate:
And if you feel the call, O friend, prevail!
You have attained only the first court,
But you worthy art to gain entrance to the inmost core."

After a short sleep, our Brother Mark next learns to divine at least something of the inner mysteries. In the powerful symbols he has let the ascent of the human self work upon his soul, and when he is awakened from his short rest by a sign he comes to a window, a kind of lattice, and hears a strange threefold harmony sounding three times, and the whole as if intermingled with the playing of a flute. He cannot look in. He cannot see what is happening there in the room. We do not need to be told more than these few words as an indication of what awaits the individual who approaches the spiritual worlds when he is so purified and perfected by his endeavors in developing his self that he has passed through the astral world and now approaches the higher worlds where the spiritual archetypes of the things here on Earth are to be found.

When he approaches what is called in esoteric Christianity the world of "heaven," he approaches it through a world of flowing color. He enters a world of sound, the harmony of the universe, the music of the spheres. The spiritual world is a world of sound. A person who has developed the higher self to the level of the higher worlds must become at home in this spiritual world. Goethe clearly expressed the higher experience of a world of spiritual sound in *Faust* when he lets Faust be carried up to heaven, and the world of heaven is revealed to him through sound.

> The orb of the Sun sings, in emulation
> Amid brother-spheres, his ancient
> round . . .

The physical Sun does not sing, but the spiritual Sun sings. Goethe retains this image when, after long wanderings, Faust is exalted into the spiritual worlds:

> Sounding loud to spirit-hearing,
> See the newborn day appearing.
> Pealing rays and trumpet-blazes —
> Eye is blinded, ear amazes:
> The Unheard can no one hear![1]

If we evolve higher, passing through the symbolic world of the astral, we approach the world of the harmony of the spheres, the *devachanic* domain, the spiritual music. Only softly, softly, does Brother Mark, after passing through the first portal, the astral portal, hear floating out to him the sound of the inner world behind our external world — the world that transforms the lower astral world into that higher world pervaded by the triple harmony. In reaching the higher world, human lower nature is transformed into the higher triad: the astral body is changed into spirit self, the etheric body into life spirit, the physical body into spirit body.

In the music of the spheres one first senses the triple harmony of the higher nature. And, becoming one with this music of the spheres, one has a first glimpse of the human rejuvenation that occurs when we enter into union with the spiritual world. One who has risen in this way sees, as in a dream, rejuvenated humankind floating through the garden in the form of the three youths bearing three torches.

This is the moment when Mark's soul has awakened in the morning from darkness, and when some darkness still remains; his soul has not yet penetrated it. But precisely at such a time the soul can gradually look into the spiritual world. It can look into the spiritual worlds as it can look when the summer noon is past, when the Sun is losing power and winter has come. Then, at cosmic midnight, the Christ principle shines through the earth in the night of Christmas. Through the Christ principle humanity is exalted to the higher trinity, represented for Brother Mark by the three youths who are the rejuvenated human soul. This is the meaning of Goethe's lines:

> And until you truly have
> This "dying and becoming,"
> You are but a troubled guest
> Roaming over the dark Earth.

Every year anew Christmas will indicate to the one who understands esoteric Christianity that what happens in the external world is the "imitation," the gestures, of inner spiritual processes. The outer power of the Sun lives in the spring and summer sunshine. In the

Scriptures this outer power of the Sun — which is only the forerunner of the inner spiritual power of the Sun — is represented by John the Baptist. The inner, spiritual power of course is represented by Christ. And while the physical power of the Sun slowly abates, the spiritual power rises and grows in strength until it reaches its zenith at Christmastime. This is the meaning underlying the words in the Gospel of St. John, "He must increase, but I must decrease." He increases until he appears where the Sun force has again attained the outer physical power.

In order to revere and worship the spiritual power of the Sun in this external physical power, we must learn the meaning of the Christmas festival. For those who do not know this meaning, the new power of the Sun is nothing but the old physical power returning. But those who have become familiar with the impulses that esoteric Christianity, and especially the Christmas festival, should give them will see in the growing power of the solar body the external body of the inner Christ that shines through the earth and gives it life and fruitfulness, so that the earth itself becomes the bearer of the Christ power, of the Earth Spirit. Thus what is born every Christmas night will be born for us each time anew. Through Christ we shall experience inwardly the microcosm in the macrocosm, and this realization will lead us higher and higher.

The festivals, which have long ago become something external to humankind, will again appear in their deep significance once human beings are led by this profound esotericism to the knowledge that the occurrences of outer nature — such as thunder and lightning, sunrise and sunset, moonrise and moonset — are the gestures and physiognomy of spiritual existence. And we should realize that the turning points marked by our festivals are also times of important happenings in the spiritual world. Then we will be led on to the rejuvenating spiritual power represented by the three youths, which the I can win only by devoting itself to the outer world and not egotistically shutting itself away from it. But there is no devotion to the outer world if this outer world is not permeated by the spirit. That this spirit appears every year anew for all people, even for the feeblest, as light in the darkness, must be written every year afresh in our hearts and souls.

This is what Goethe wished to express in this poem "The Mysteries." It is at once a Christmas poem and an Easter poem. It indicates profound secrets of esoteric Christianity.

If what Goethe wished to indicate of the deep mysteries of Rosicrucian Christianity is allowed to work upon our souls, if we absorb its power even in part, then for some few at least in our environment we will become missionaries; we will succeed in fashioning this festival once more into something filled with spirit and with life.

> When after a short repose within his cell
> A deep resounding bell awakes our guest,
> His soul is filled with a longing for devotion,
> He rises quickly with unwearied zest
> And hastens to the church, with all his heart
> Responding to the gladly heard behest,
> Obedient, peaceful and by prayer bestirred;
> But alas! The door is locked. He stands deterred.
>
> But hark! A blow on dull resounding ore
> Three times in equal intervals renewed,
> No chime it seems to be of clock or bells,
> From time to time with tones of flute imbued;
> The floating music fills the heart with joy,
> It is mysterious and scarce to be understood,
> It sounds like singing, solemn and entrancing,
> To which couples interlace in dancing.
>
> Bewildered and by strange emotion moved,
> He hastens to the window there to gaze;
> The day is dawning in the distant east,
> The sky transfused by lucent streaks of haze.
> May he trust his eyes? A mystic light
> Is fleeting through the garden's winding ways;
> Three youths with torches in their hands he sees
> Who hasten along the paths between the trees.
>
> He clearly sees their wonderful apparel,
> The white resplendent garments which they wear,
> Their girdles made of intertwining roses,
> The wreaths of flowers in their curly hair;
> They seem to come from some nocturnal dances,
> With joy of movement thrilled, enlived and fair.
> But as the stars will fade, when day is near,
> Extinguishing their torches, they disappear.

six

Rosicrucian Symbols

We end this section with a deeper look at Rosicrucian training and the worldview that underlies it.

... We are able to have physical sense organs (eyes, for example) only by allowing the elemental world into ourselves and then holding it back. We can have a nervous system only by admitting the world of spirit into ourselves and then holding it back; we can have a brain and reasoning faculty only by allowing the world of "reason" into ourselves and then holding it back, thus forming the brain. To form higher organs, therefore, we must be able to hold back an even higher world. We must be able to send something toward it, just as in our brain we send what holds back the world of reason. In other words, if we wish to develop in a true way, we must do something. To develop to a higher stage in the true sense, we must derive forces from a higher world. That is, we must do something to hold back the forces of the world of archetypal images that would otherwise simply pass through us. We ourselves must create a reflecting apparatus for that purpose.

The method of spiritual science, beginning with Imagination knowledge, creates such an apparatus in the way we today are able to do this properly.

What we normally perceive and know is the outer, physical world. To attain higher knowledge, we must do something to create higher organs for ourselves. We must halt within ourselves a world that is higher than the world of reason, and this we can do by developing a new kind of activity that can confront the world of archetypal images

Macrocosm and Microcosm, lecture 8, March 28, 1910 (*Makrokosmos und Mikrokosmos: Die grosse und die klein Welt: Seelenfragen, Lebensfragen, Geistesfragen,* GA 119), revised translation by Dorothy Osmond and Charles Davy.

and begin to hold it back. We engender this new activity by learning to undergo extraordinary inner experiences. A typical experience of this is described in chapter five of *An Outline of Esoteric Science*. It comes about by picturing the Rose Cross.[1] How should we proceed to have this mental picture of the Rose Cross as a true experience within us?

A student who aspires to be led to higher stages of knowledge would be initially told by a teacher to contemplate the way a plant grows out of the soil and how it forms its stem, leaves, flowers, and fruit. Green sap flows through the whole structure. Then he or she would be asked to compare that plant with a human being. Blood flows through the human being and is the outer expression of impulses, appetites, and passions. Also, because we are endowed with an I, we see ourselves as higher beings than plants. Only a bizarre mind (and there are many) would believe that a plant's consciousness is similar to our own and could reflect impressions inwardly. Consciousness arises not by exercising activity, but because an impression is reflected inwardly, and we (not the plant) are able to do this. Thus, in a certain respect we have reached a higher stage of development than the plant, but the cost is the possibility of error. The plant is not liable to error, nor does it have a higher and a lower nature. It is without the impulses and appetites that would degrade it. We may be impressed by the chastity of the plant compared to human impulses, desires, and passions. Having red blood, we exist as beings who, in terms of our consciousness, have developed to a higher stage than the plant, but at the cost of a certain deterioration.

All this would be made clear to those who aspire to higher knowledge. The teacher would say that now we must attain what the plant reveals to us at a lower stage; we must master our appetites, impulses, and so on. We achieve this mastery once our higher nature has won the victory over the lower, when our red blood has become as chaste as the plant's sap as it reddens in the rose. And so the red rose can be a symbol for us of what human blood will become once our lower nature has been mastered. We see the rose as an emblem, or symbol, of the purified blood.

And if we associate the wreath of roses with the dead, black, wooden cross — what the plant leaves behind once it dies — then for us the Rose Cross symbolizes the victory of our higher, purified nature over the lower. In the human being, unlike the plant, lower nature must be overcome. For us, the red rose can symbolize the purified red blood. But the rest of the plant cannot be emblematic in this

sense, since there we would have to imagine that the sap and green-
ness of the plant have become woody. Thus, in the black wooden
cross we have an emblem of the vanquished lower nature and in the
roses an emblem of developed higher nature. The Rose Cross signifies
human development as it advances in the world. This is not an abstract concept; it can be felt and experienced as real development. The
soul can glow with warmth at the image of development presented
by the symbol of the Rose Cross.

This shows that we can have mental images that do not correspond
to any outer reality. Those who merely desire ordinary consciousness
in which the mental pictures always represent some outer reality will
mock the Rose Cross symbol and insist that mental pictures are false
unless they represent external facts. Such people ask, Where is there
anything like the Rose Cross? Do red roses ever grow on dead wood?
The whole point, however, is that we acquire a soul faculty that is
lacking in ordinary consciousness; we should gain the capacity to
elaborate mental images and concepts that bear a certain relationship
to the outer world but do not replicate it. The Rose Cross is related
in a certain way to the outer world, but we ourselves must create the
nature of this relationship. We have contemplated the plant and the
ascendancy attained by humankind, and we imagine this to ourselves
in the image of the Rose Cross. We then inscribe this symbol into our
world of mental pictures and ideas. The same could be done with
other symbols.

I will speak of another symbol, so that we can understand one
another fully. Let us consider the entire life of an ordinary person.
Day alternates with night, waking and sleeping. The day brings a
number of experiences, and during the night, without being aware
of it, forces are drawn from the spiritual world. Just as we have
experiences in conscious life, during the night we have experiences
in the subconscious region of our being. Now, with the object of
gaining knowledge, we can take stock of our inner life from time to
time and ask ourselves, What sort of progress have "I" made? Has
each experience during the day in fact taken me forward another
step? We have reason to feel satisfied if we make only a slight advance
every day, having had our daily experiences and gaining new strength
each night. We must, of course, experience a great deal every day if
we are to become more mature. In this sense, ask yourselves what
sort of progress you have made in a single day. You will find that
in many cases, despite innumerable experiences, the I advances very
slowly from one day to the next and that a great many experiences go

unnoticed. If, on the other hand, we look back to the most agreeable period of our life, childhood, we can see how rapidly children advance compared to what we achieve in later life. It is reasonable to say that even if you devote your whole energy to world travel in order to acquire knowledge and make personal progress, you will not advance to the degree that children do through what they learn from their first caregivers.

The progress of the human I may be indicated by a double spiral of two serpent forms, one light and one dark, winding around a vertical staff. The light one represents the experiences of the day, the dark one the forces active during the night. The vertical line indicates progress. Here we have a different symbol representing human life.

We can make complicated and simple symbols. An example of a simple one would arise by concentrating on the growth of a plant, observing it until the seed forms and the plant gradually diminishes, until only the seed remains. We can visualize this as a very simple symbol of growth and decay.

In the Rose Cross we have a symbol of human development from one's present stage to purification. In the Staff of Mercury we have a symbol of human development through one's experiences of day and night and the progress of the I. Symbol after symbol can be created in this way.

None of them reflects any outer reality. But by surrendering ourselves through inner contemplation to what these symbols mean, the soul becomes familiar with activities it would not otherwise exercise. Such activities finally engender an inner force that enables us to hold back the world of archetypes, or archetypal images, just as we hold back the other worlds.

We do not need to limit symbols to images; they may also involve words that concentrate profound cosmic truths. When cosmic truths are concentrated into symbolic sentences, we have access to a force through which we can mold our soul substance. By working on ourselves in this way, we consciously build up what the outer world has already accomplished in us without our help in forming the brain from the world of reason, the nervous system from the world of spirit, and the sensory organs from the elemental world. We ourselves build the organs higher than the brain, ones that are not externally visible to ordinary consciousness because they are beyond the physical realm. Just as the eyes were formed out of the elemental world, the nerves out of the world of spirit, and the brain out of the world of reason, higher spiritual organs are formed and shaped out of the world of archetypal images. These organs gradually enable us to penetrate the higher world and to see into it. Such organs simply represent a development and continuation of the activity that took place at a lower level. These higher organs of perception appear in the shape of spiritual flowers, which bud from the human being and are consequently called lotus flowers (spiritual "wheels," or chakras).

In those who practice such exercises, new organs may become visible to clairvoyant consciousness. For example, one of them unfolds like a wheel, or flower, at the center of the forehead. This is the two-petaled lotus flower, a spiritual sensory organ. The purpose of these spiritual sensory organs is to make us aware of the world that cannot be seen with ordinary physical eyes, just as a physical sensory organ exists to make us aware of the surrounding world. These so-called lotus flowers are forces and systems of forces that bud from the human soul.

A second organ of this kind may form in the area of the larynx, another near the heart, and so on. Through the patient and vigorous practice of immersing oneself in symbolic mental pictures, we can cultivate these spiritual sensory organs (the word inevitably implies a contradiction, but there is no better expression in our modern language designed for the physical world). Such symbolic mental pictures do not depict anything in the outer world, and in this respect they differ from the mental pictures of ordinary consciousness, since they do not reflect anything outer but work in the soul to produce forces that can hold back the world of archetypal images, just as eyes, nerves, and brain hold back the other worlds around us.

To arrive at this point, however, is not enough. Anyone who possesses the faculty of clairvoyant vision can perceive these higher human sensory organs. But these organs themselves must now be developed further. Thus far they have been formed from a world higher than those from which our human constitution has been built up. Now comes the second stage — a preparation for real vision. For those aware of having attained imaginative cognition by developing the lotus flowers, the preparatory process now becomes somewhat more difficult; it moves to a higher stage of inner work.

So that the higher sensory organs may be developed with patience and endurance, the first stage involves the elaboration of symbolic mental images, which are given in all schools of real spiritual training and vary according to the individual. At the next stage, as soon as we have acquired a certain skill in picturing the symbols, we must then reach a point where we can exclude those pictures from consciousness, concentrating only on the inner force that created them. By forming the picture of the Rose Cross, we considered the plant and human being, and only then did we build up the symbol itself. Now we eliminate from consciousness this symbol as well as that of the Staff of Mercury, concentrating instead on the activity we ourselves have exercised in building up the pictures. This means that we focus attention on our own activity and ignore its product, which is more difficult. After creating a symbol, we ask, How did I do this? Most people will have to make numerous attempts to progress from the symbol itself to the activity that created it. The process takes a very long time. It will be necessary to repeatedly create the symbols until we are able to dismiss them, thus enabling us to experience something very new without visualizing anything external — that is, the activity that created those images.

After practicing this for a long time, if we feel a kind of inner churning and swirling, progress has been made. We can then, in fact, experience the moment when we do not merely possess higher organs or lotus flowers but see a new realm flashing before us, which we never suspected previously. Now we have reached the stage at which we have a new field of vision, and we have our first insight into the world of spirit.

This is what we experience: We have left the ordinary outer world, we have lived in a world of symbols, and now we eliminate those symbols and pictures. Then we are surrounded by a black darkness. Consciousness does not cease but churns and swirls, stirred by our own activity. At an earlier stage we held back the world of archetypal images; now we hold back the world of reason as well, but not as we did before — we hold it back from the opposite side. We hold back what would otherwise flow into us. Previously we saw only the shadow images of the world of reason in our own intellectual activity; now we see this world of reason from the other side; we see the beings known as the hierarchies. Little by little everything becomes filled with life.

This is our first step, but there is more. Another step involves acquiring the power to suppress our own activity. First the pictures were suppressed, now our own activity. If we really make the attempt, we begin to realize how difficult this is. This is a longer process, because we will usually fall asleep. Nevertheless, if any consciousness at all is left to us, we will advance to the point where we not only hold back the world of reason but the world of spirit also. Now from the other side we see the world of spirit as well as the spiritual realities and beings in that world. The previous stage of knowledge (when the activity creating the symbols is held back) is known as Inspiration, or knowledge through Inspiration. This next stage, when we eliminate our own activity, is called Intuition. Through Intuition we glimpse the true configuration of the world of spirit, which we otherwise see only in shadow images — the laws of nature. Now we become aware of the beings and their activities, which express themselves outwardly in the realities and laws of nature.

We have described a path of knowledge that is somewhat different from the one when we merely become aware of, for instance, entering or leaving the world of spirit as we go to sleep or awake. This method first creates the organs by holding back the world of archetypal images and using its forces to create the organs we need. Then, through Imagination and Inspiration knowledge, we are led into the world of spirit, into which we are now able to see. But when we have reached the stage of Intuitive knowledge, we can also grow into the elemental world in such a way that we enter fully prepared, seeing it before us as a final experience. Certainly this path is a hard one for many, because it demands much renunciation. First, we must practice for a long time with symbols and wait for the requisite organs to form. To begin with, however, we cannot see with these organs.

It is very often the case today that people do not want to go along a certain path, but above all would rather see something quickly through rapid success. Success will surely come, but it must be achieved by practicing a certain renunciation. First we must work on ourselves for a long time to find entry little by little into higher worlds. In fact, what we first see of the world of reason and in the world of spirit is a very colorless sight. But once we return from those realms to the elemental world — once we are very advanced in Intuitive knowledge — only then does everything acquire color and vividness, because then it has been permeated by the elemental world and its effects. These things can be described only from the vantage point of Intuitive knowledge.

Moreover, only when we have joy in building up the symbols, when we work with patience and perseverance to develop the organs, can we become aware of any progress. Although initially we see only a little of the higher worlds, it is a sure path and one that protects us from illusions. The reward comes later, but it is a path that safeguards against idle fantasy. If we have worked our way to the stage of Imaginative knowledge, we stand in the world immediately above our own, and we feel that we have made something from a higher world a part of ourselves. Then we gradually rise to higher and higher stages and finally attain real understanding of the higher worlds.

You will find an outline of this process of development in my book *How to Know Higher Worlds* and in chapter five of *An Outline of Esoteric Science*. The accounts there are somewhat condensed, since they are intended for a somewhat broader public. Today, however, I wanted to speak of more intimate matters that elaborate on what is contained in those books on the path to higher knowledge. I have tried to make it clear that in the microcosm, the nervous system, and the brain, human beings are mirror images of the activities and beings of the macrocosm. It has been shown that other work has already been applied to our development as human beings even before we begin to work on ourselves to unfold higher qualities. We have realized that we are really simply continuing the work that has been applied to us. Just as our physical constitution has been built from higher worlds, so we ourselves build our "spirit human being." We transcend our ordinary selves by advancing our development. No one who takes the concept of evolution seriously can doubt that such development is possible. Those who believe that what actually exists arose from previous stages of existence must also admit that development can move forward. But because we have become conscious beings, we must also assume responsibility for our own conscious development. And in full consciousness we can take the path of development that has been described. If we need a teacher, we no longer need the kind that existed when the old methods were used — teachers who take something from their followers or allow something to stream to them. In such circumstances, those who were guided by teachers were not free. Today we have been learning of a path entirely appropriate for the consciousness of modern humanity. Those who take this path entrust themselves to someone else in the same sense that students might entrust themselves to a tutor in mathematics. We go to tutors because we assume that they know more about a subject than we do. In this sense, we entrust ourselves to a leader or teacher who simply gives us suggestions. At every step we remain our own master, while scrupulously following the suggestions offered. We follow indications from the teacher as we would those given by a tutor in mathematics, but in this case our whole soul is engaged. It is not simply a matter of applying the intellect to solve a mathematical problem. Rather, it is the essence of this new method of initiation that it considers first and foremost human independence; a "guru" is no longer a guru in the old sense, but in the sense that we are given advice on how to advance.

The successive epochs change, and humankind passes constantly through new stages of existence. Consequently, the methods for development must also change. Earlier times required different methods. The so-called Rosicrucian method (so named after its most important symbol) is most appropriate and fitting for today's human souls. We see how, in addition to the older methods, there is an appropriate modern method that leads us in the way indicated into higher worlds.

Part 2

THE MISSION OF CHRISTIAN ROSENKREUTZ

— s e v e n —

Who Was Christian Rosenkreutz?

The next four lectures unfold Rudolf Steiner's understanding of the being or individuality of Christian Rosenkreutz. As we enter this domain, we see the depth and radical originality of Steiner's spiritual vision. Rosicrucianism, for Steiner, is not just a question of theory or of history or even of practice simply as such, it has above all and primarily to do with spiritual facts, realities — that is, with encountering and knowing spiritual beings, in this case, the being of Christian Rosenkreutz himself. Interestingly, there is for Steiner no contradiction here with the earthly, historical facts — or lack of them.

Steiner takes the account of the life and mission of Christian Rosenkreutz as narrated in the Fama *as a true description of both the historical and the spiritual facts. Indeed, for Steiner, history, theory, and practice, if correctly*

Esoteric Christianity and the Mission of Christian Rosenkreutz, Neuchâtel, September 27, 1911 (*Das esoterische Christentum und die geistige Führung der Menschheit*, GA 130), translated by Pauline Wehrle, revised.

*pursued, lead to and are infused by beings — and in the case of Rosicru-
cianism specifically with the being of Christian Rosenkreutz. This is what
distinguishes Rudolf Steiner's Rosicrucianism from that of others.*

*With this section, too, we enter more deeply into the milieu of Steiner's
own spiritual research. That is, we learn not only of inner realities surrounding the events described in the* Fama, *but we also become privy to
happenings not recorded at all by exoteric history. Steiner opens his story
with happenings in the thirteenth, not the fourteenth century. He tells of
an incarnation before the one by which the name of Christian Rosenkreutz
became known. During this incarnation, we see the* twelve, *who represent
the full wisdom of humanity (Eastern and Western), pouring their wisdom
into the thirteenth, who thus becomes the new* Humanus *(as in Goethe's
poem) and the bearer of the universal and ecumenical impulse that, by this
account, is true Rosicrucianism. We also learn something of Steiner's view
of the transmission of Rosicrucianism, as well as of the central role of a
mysterious "boundary substance," which has something of the character of
"soul," in Rosicrucian teaching.*

— ◆ —

It gives me great joy to be here for the first time in this newly established group bearing the great name of Christian Rosenkreutz. It
is my first opportunity to speak at any length about him. What is
the mystery of Christian Rosenkreutz? I cannot tell you everything
about this person in one evening. Today we will discuss Christian
Rosenkreutz himself; tomorrow, his work.

To speak of Christian Rosenkreutz presupposes great confidence in
the mysteries of spiritual life — confidence not only in a person, but
also in the great secrets of the life of spirit. To establish a new group
always assumes faith in spiritual life. As for Christian Rosenkreutz,
he is an individual who is active both when he is physically incarnated
and when he is not; he works not only as a physical being through
physical forces but, above all, spiritually through higher forces.

As we know, human beings live not only for themselves but also
in relation to human evolution as a whole. Usually when we pass
through death, the etheric body dissolves into the cosmos. But a part
of this dissolving etheric body always remains intact, and so we are
always surrounded by remaining portions of the etheric bodies of
those who have died, both for our good and to our detriment. They
affect us for good or ill according to whether we are good or bad
ourselves. Far-reaching effects also emanate from the etheric bodies
of great individuals. The great forces that emanate from the etheric

body of Christian Rosenkreutz can work into our soul and spirit. It is our task to become acquainted with these forces, because as Rosicrucians we work with them.[1]

Strictly speaking the Rosicrucian movement began in the thirteenth century. At that time these forces worked with extraordinary strength, and the spiritual stream of Christian Rosenkreutz has been active in spiritual life ever since. There is a law that this powerful spiritual stream becomes especially strong every hundred years or so (this may be seen at the present in the theosophical movement). Christian Rosenkreutz suggested this in his final exoteric statements.[2]

In 1785, the collected esoteric revelations of the Rosicrucians were published in a work called *The Secret Symbols of the Rosicrucians* by Hinricus Madathanus Theosophus.[3] In a limited sense, this publication refers to the Rosicrucian stream that was active during the previous century, expressed for the first time in the works collected by Hinricus Madathanus Theosophus. A hundred years later, we see the influence of the Rosicrucian stream being expressed again in the work of H. P. Blavatsky, especially in her book *Isis Unveiled*. Much of the meaning of that image was put into words by Madame Blavatsky. A considerable amount of Western esoteric wisdom is contained in the book and is still a long way from being improved upon, although the composition is sometimes very confused.

It is interesting to compare *The Secret Symbols of the Rosicrucians* by Theosophus with the works of H. P. Blavatsky. We must think especially of the first part of her publication, which is written in symbols. In the second part Blavatsky deviates somewhat from the Rosicrucian stream and departs entirely from it in her later works. Consequently, we must be able to distinguish between her earlier and her later publications, though something of H. P. Blavatsky's uncritical spirit does appear in the early ones. It can only be the wish of H. P. Blavatsky, who is not incarnated now, that this be said.

When we look at the characteristics of human consciousness in the thirteenth century, we see that original clairvoyance, which in earlier times everyone possessed, had gradually disappeared. During the mid-thirteenth century this loss reached its lowest point. Suddenly there was no more clairvoyance. Everyone experienced a "spiritual eclipse." Even the most enlightened and highly developed personalities, including initiates, no longer had access to the spiritual worlds. When they spoke of spiritual worlds they had to limit themselves to what they remembered. People knew about the spiritual world only from tradition or from initiates who awakened their memories of what they had previously experienced. For a short while, however, even those souls could not see directly into the spiritual world.

This brief period of darkness was necessary to prepare for the nature of our own age, that of intellectual, rational development [the consciousness soul], which is the central reality in our own fifth post-Atlantean cultural epoch.[4] During the previous Greco-Roman cultural epoch, human intellectual development was not what it is today. Direct perception was the vital factor, not intellectual thinking. People identified with what they saw and heard — also, indeed, even with what they thought. They did not produce thoughts from themselves then as we do today — appropriately so, for this is the task of the fifth post-Atlantean cultural epoch.

Human clairvoyance, then, having disappeared, gradually began again, and we can develop future clairvoyance.

As I said, the Rosicrucian stream began in the thirteenth century. During that century those suited for initiation had to be specially chosen. Initiation itself, however, could take place only after that brief period of darkness had run its course.

In a place in Europe that cannot be named yet (though this will be possible before long) a very spiritual lodge was formed made up of a council of twelve who had received into themselves the whole of ancient and contemporary spiritual wisdom. Thus we are concerned with twelve human beings who lived in that dark era, twelve outstanding individualities who united to help humanity progress. None of them could see directly into the spiritual world, but they could awaken memories within themselves of what they had experienced during earlier initiations. Human karma brought it about that all that humanity had retained of the ancient Atlantean epoch was incarnated in seven of those twelve.

In my *Outline of Esoteric Science* I wrote that everything left over from the Atlantean epoch was preserved in the seven teachers of the ancient Indian cultural epoch — the seven holy Rishis. These seven men now incarnated again in the thirteenth century, and were part of the council of twelve. These seven were able to look back into the seven streams of the ancient Atlantean cultural epoch of humanity and into the continuing course of these streams. Each of these seven was able to bring one stream to life for their time and for the present time. The other four were unable to look back into ancient times, but they could look back to the esoteric wisdom humankind had acquired during the four post-Atlantean epochs. The first of these could look back to the ancient Indian period, the second to the ancient Persian cultural period, the third to the cultural period of Egypt, Chaldea, Assyria, and Babylonia, and the fourth to the Greco-Roman culture. These four joined the seven to form a council of wise men in the thirteenth century. The twelfth individual had the least amount of memories, so to speak, but he was the most intellectual of them all, and it was his particular task to nurture natural science. These twelve individuals not only lived in the experiences of Western esotericism, but these twelve different streams of wisdom interacted to make a whole. We find a remarkable reference to this in Goethe's poem "The Mysteries."

The mid-thirteenth century saw the beginning of a new culture. As I said, a certain low point in spiritual life had been reached at the time — even the most highly developed could not approach the spiritual worlds. It was then that this council of spiritual elite assembled. These twelve, who represented the sum of all the spiritual knowledge of their age and the twelve tendencies of thought, assembled in Europe in a place that cannot yet be named.[5]

This council of the twelve possessed only clairvoyant memory and intellectual wisdom. The seven successors of the seven Rishis remembered their ancient wisdom, and the other five represented the wisdom of the five post-Atlantean cultures. Thus the twelve represented the whole of Atlantean and post-Atlantean wisdom. The twelfth was a man who attained the intellectual wisdom of his time in the highest degree. Intellectually, he possessed all the knowledge of his time, while the others (to whom direct spiritual wisdom was also denied then) acquired their knowledge by recalling their earlier incarnations.

The beginning of a new culture was possible only because a thirteenth joined the twelve. The thirteenth did not become a scholar in the accepted sense of the time. Previously, he had been incarnated at the time of the Mystery of Golgotha, and during the incarnations that followed he prepared for his mission through humility of soul and a life fervently devoted to God. He was a great soul, a pious and deeply mystical person, who had not acquired these qualities but was born with them.

Imagine a young man who is very pious and devotes all his time to fervent prayer to God — this gives you a picture of the thirteenth individual. He grew up entirely under the care and instruction of the twelve, and he received as much wisdom as each could give him. He was educated with the greatest care, and every precaution was taken to see that no one but those twelve influenced him. He was kept apart from the rest of the world. He was a very delicate child during that incarnation of the thirteenth century. Consequently, the education that the twelve gave him affected even his physical body.

Having deep devotion to their spiritual tasks and being permeated inwardly with Christianity, the twelve were conscious that the conventional Christianity of the Church was no more than a caricature of true Christianity. Those men were permeated with the greatness of Christianity, though the outside world treated them as its enemies. Each worked his way into one particular aspect of Christianity. They endeavored to unite the various religions into one great whole. They were convinced that all spiritual life was fully contained in their twelve streams, and each of them influenced their student to the best of his ability. Their goal was to synthesize all religions, but they knew that this was not to be achieved by means of any theory, but only as the result of living a spiritual life. A suitable education of the thirteenth was essential for this goal. While the spiritual forces of the thirteenth increased beyond measure, his physical forces drained away. It reached the point where he almost ceased to have a connection with outer life — all interest in the physical world disappeared. He lived entirely for the sake of the spiritual development being brought about within him by the twelve. The wisdom of the twelve was reflected in him. Finally, the thirteenth refused to eat and wasted away.

Then an event occurred that could happen only once in history. It was the kind of event that can take place when the forces of the macrocosm cooperate for the benefit of what they can accomplish together. After a few days the body of the thirteenth became quite transparent, and for days he lay as though dead. The twelve gathered round him at certain intervals. At such moments all knowledge and wisdom flowed from their lips. While the thirteenth lay as though dead, they let their wisdom flow toward him in short prayer-like formulae. We can best imagine them together in a circle around the thirteenth.

The situation ended when the soul of the thirteenth awakened as a new soul. He had experienced a great soul transformation. Now there was something new within his soul, a completely new birth of the twelve streams of wisdom. As a result, the twelve wise men could now learn something entirely new from the youth. He came to life physically, too, in such a way that the revival of his absolutely transparent body was astonishing. The youth could now speak of new experiences. The twelve recognized that he had experienced the event of Damascus — a recapitulation of Paul's vision on the road to Damascus. Over the course of the next few weeks, the thirteenth reproduced all the wisdom he had received from the twelve, but it was in a new form, as though given by Christ himself. The twelve called what he revealed to them true Christianity, a synthesis of all religions, and they distinguished between this true Christianity and the Christianity of their time.

The thirteenth died relatively young. The twelve then devoted themselves to the task of recording what the thirteenth had revealed to them in Imaginations, because it could have been done only in that way. Thus arose the symbolic figures and pictures such as are contained in the collection of Hinricus Madathanus Theosophus, and the communications of H. P. Blavatsky in *Isis Unveiled*. We have to see the esoteric process in such a way that the fruits of the initiation of the thirteenth remained as the residue of his etheric body, within the spiritual atmosphere of Earth. This residue inspired the twelve as well as their students who succeeded them, so that they were able to form the esoteric Rosicrucian stream. And it continued to work as an etheric body, becoming part of the new etheric body of the thirteenth when he incarnated again.

The individuality of the thirteenth reincarnated as early as the fourteenth century — roughly in the middle of the century. He lived for over a hundred years in that incarnation. He was brought up in a similar way to before, within a circle of students and successors of the twelve, but not in such a secluded way as in that previous incarnation. At the age of twenty-eight, he formed a remarkable resolution. He had to leave Europe and travel, first to Damascus, where he again experienced what Paul had experienced there. This event may be described as the fruit of what happened in the previous incarnation.

The forces of that wonderful etheric body of the thirteenth-century individuality had remained intact, a permanent etheric body in the etheric spheres. They had not dispersed after death into the general cosmic ether. Now, this same highly spiritual etheric body radiated again from the spiritual world into that new incarnation in the fourteenth century. And thus he was led to experience the event of Damascus again.

This is the individuality of Christian Rosenkreutz. He had been the thirteenth in the circle of the twelve. He was named Christian Rosenkreutz from this incarnation onward. Esoterically, he was already Christian Rosenkreutz in the thirteenth century, but in an exoteric sense he received that name in the fourteenth century. The students of this fourteenth-century individuality are the successors of the other twelve of the thirteenth century: they are the first Rosicrucians.

At that time, Christian Rosenkreutz traveled through all of the world known to Europeans. He had received all the wisdom of the twelve, fructified by the exalted being of Christ — therefore it was easy for him to receive all the wisdom of that time within the span of seven years. After seven years, when he returned to Europe, he took the most highly developed students and successors of the twelve as his pupils, and he then began the true work of the Rosicrucians. Through the grace of what radiated from the wonderful etheric body of Christian Rosenkreutz, they could develop an absolutely new view of the world.

What the Rosicrucians have developed until now is a work that has both an outer and an inner nature. The outer work was to discover what lies behind the illusion of the material world: the Rosicrucians wanted to investigate the illusion of matter. Remember: just as we have an etheric body, so the whole of the macrocosm has an "etheric macrocosm" or etheric body. Thus, there is a certain point of transition from the dense to the more subtle substances; there is a boundary between physical and etheric substance.

What lies between physical and etheric substance is like nothing else in the world. It is neither gold nor silver, lead nor copper. It cannot be compared with any other physical substance, yet it is really the essence of all of them. It is a substance contained in every other physical substance, so that the other physical substances can be considered modifications of this one substance. The Rosicrucians sought to see this substance clairvoyantly. They saw that the preparation and development of such vision requires a heightened activity of the soul's moral forces, which would enable them to see this substance. In other words, they realized that the power for this vision lay in the moral power of the soul.

This "boundary" substance was in fact seen and discovered by the Rosicrucians. They found that this substance lived in the world in a certain form, both in the macrocosm and in the human being. In the world outside human beings, they revered it as the grand garment of the macrocosm. They saw it arising in human beings whenever there is a harmonious interplay between thinking and willing. Indeed, they saw the will forces as being not only in the human being but in the macrocosm as well — in thunder and lightning, for example. They saw the forces of thought in the human being, and also outside in the world, in the rainbow and in the rosy light of dawn.

The Rosicrucians sought the strength to achieve such harmony of willing and thinking in their own soul, in the force radiating from the etheric body of the thirteenth, Christian Rosenkreutz.

It was established by the first Rosicrucians that all their discoveries had to remain their secret for a hundred years. Not until a hundred years had passed could these Rosicrucian revelations be divulged to the world — not until they had worked at them for a hundred years could they speak of them in an appropriate way.

Now, it is also very important to realize that in any century the Rosicrucian inspiration is given in such a way that the name of the one who receives the inspiration is never made public. Only the highest initiates are aware of it. Today, for example, only occurrences that happened a hundred years ago can be made public, because that is the length of time that must pass before it is permissible to speak of them in the outside world. The temptation for people to fanatically idealize a person bearing such authority is too great, which is the worst thing that can happen — it would be too much like idolatry. This silence, however, is essential if we wish not only to avoid the egoistic temptations of ambition and pride (which we could probably overcome), but above all to avoid the occult, astral attacks that would be directed constantly at an individual of that level. This is why it is essential that a fact such as this not be mentioned until after a hundred years.

Through the works of the Rosicrucians, the etheric body of Christian Rosenkreutz became increasingly strong and powerful as the centuries passed. It worked not only through Christian Rosenkreutz but also through all those who became his students. From the fourteenth century on, Christian Rosenkreutz has been incarnated repeatedly. Everything that is revealed in the name of spiritual science is made stronger by the etheric body of Christian Rosenkreutz, and those who make spiritual science known permit themselves to be overshadowed by this etheric body, which can work on them both while Christian Rosenkreutz is incarnated and while he is not physically incarnated.

The Count of Saint Germain was the exoteric reincarnation of Christian Rosenkreutz in the eighteenth century.[6] This name, however, was given to others as well; consequently, not everything said of Count Saint Germain here and there in the outer world applies to the true Christian Rosenkreutz. Christian Rosenkreutz is incarnated again today. The inspiration for H. P. Blavatsky's *Isis Unveiled* came from the strength radiating from his etheric body. It was also

Christian Rosenkreutz's influence working invisibly on Lessing that inspired him to write *The Education of the Human Race* (1780).[7] Because of the rising tide of materialism it became increasingly difficult for inspiration to occur in the Rosicrucian way. Then the high tide of materialism arrived in the nineteenth century. Many things could be presented only in a very incomplete way. In 1851 the problem of the soul's immortality was solved by Widenmann through the idea of reincarnation.[8] His text was awarded a prize. Around 1850 Drossbach wrote from a psychological point of view in favor of reincarnation.

The forces radiating from the etheric body of Christian Rosenkreutz continued during the nineteenth century. A renewal of theosophy came about because by 1899 the "little" Kali Yuga had run its course.[9] That is why the approach to the spiritual world is easier now and spiritual influence is possible to a far greater degree. The etheric body of Christian Rosenkreutz has become very strong, and, through devotion to this, humankind will be able to acquire the new clairvoyance, and high spiritual forces will come into being. But this will be possible only for those who follow the training of Christian Rosenkreutz correctly.

Until now an esoteric Rosicrucian preparation was essential, but the mission of the twentieth century is to enable this etheric body to gain enough power to work exoterically. Those who are affected by it will be granted Paul's experience on the road to Damascus.

Up until now, too, this etheric body was active only in the Rosicrucian school, but in the twentieth century increasing numbers of people will be able to experience its effect. Through this they will experience the appearance of Christ in the etheric body. It is the work of the Rosicrucians that makes possible the etheric vision of Christ. And the number of people who gain the ability to see it will continue to grow. We must attribute this reappearance to the important work of the twelve and the thirteenth during the thirteenth and fourteenth centuries. If you can become an instrument of Christian Rosenkreutz, you can be certain that the smallest detail of your soul activity will be present for eternity.

– eight –

The Teaching of Christian Rosenkreutz

At some point during this lecture, we realize that Rosicrucianism and alchemy are, in fact, central and even determinant for Rudolf Steiner's spiritual path and teaching. He clearly studied and meditated and practiced the alchemical injunctions and deep evolutionary and cosmological wisdom encrypted in medieval and Renaissance alchemical texts.

This realization comes after Steiner's subtle and even tender description of how one finds one's way to this teaching — that is, how "Christian Rosenkreutz selects his students."

Steiner then turns to a consideration of the difference between earlier Rosicrucianism (or alchemy) and its contemporary form as spiritual science. He does this by way of a profound discussion of the three great processes of nature, called by the alchemists — whom Steiner here names "medieval theosophists" — sulphur, mercury, and salt. He describes how these three processes are simultaneously laboratory processes and soul processes. It is the soul process, however, that is primary. Thus we understand that for Steiner the spiritual path is the essential thing and that to be caught up in the content is a trap.

My task today is to say something to you about the work of Christian Rosenkreutz. This work began in the thirteenth century and continues today, as it will right into eternity.

The work began as I told you yesterday with the initiation of Christian Rosenkreutz and all that took place between the council of the twelve and the thirteenth. When Christian Rosenkreutz was born again in the fourteenth century — an incarnation that lasted more than a hundred years — his main task was instructing students

Esoteric Christianity and the Mission of Christian Rosenkreutz, Neuchâtel, September 28, 1911 (*Das esoterische Christentum und die geistige Führung der Menschheit,* GA 130), translated by Pauline Wehrle, revised.

of the twelve. At the time, hardly anyone else knew of Christian Rosenkreutz besides these twelve. This should not be taken to mean that Christian Rosenkreutz did not meet other people, but that they failed to recognize him for what he was. Fundamentally this has not changed to this day. However, the etheric body of Christian Rosenkreutz has been active without ceasing within the circle of his students, with its forces working in continually growing circles, to the point where many are able to be influenced by the forces of his etheric body.

The way Christian Rosenkreutz selects his students is remarkable. Those chosen must pay close attention to a certain kind of event or events in life. Christian Rosenkreutz selects people in such a way that, for example, one arrives at a decisive turning point or a karmic crisis in life. Imagine that someone is about to do something that will lead to his or her death. These things can vary considerably from one person to another. A person unknowingly follows a path that can lead to great danger. Perhaps it leads to the edge of a precipice. Now, only a step or two from the precipice perhaps, the person hears a voice saying "Stop!" He or she feels compelled to stop without knowing why.

There could be a thousand similar situations. I should mention, of course, that this is only the outer indication of being ready for a spiritual calling. To be inwardly qualified, the chosen one must be interested in some sort of spiritual science. The external event I described is a fact of the physical world, though it does not come from a human voice. Such an event always occurs in such a way that the person knows clearly that the voice comes from the spiritual world. We may at first imagine that the voice came from someone hidden, but if the student is mature it will quickly become obvious that this intervention was not by a physical person. In other words, this event convinces the student that there are messages from the spiritual world.

Such events may occur once or many times in a person's life. We have to understand what effect this has on the soul of the student. The student thinks, I have gained another life by grace; the first was forfeited. This new life given through grace illuminates all of the rest of a student's life. One has a definite feeling that may be thought of this way: Without this Rosicrucian experience, I would have died. My life would not have the same value if this had not taken place.

It could happen, of course, that although we have already experienced this once, or even several times, we do not immediately come to spiritual science. Later, however, the memory of such an event may return. Many of you present today could examine your past lives and find that similar instances have happened to you. We give too little attention to such things today. We need to be fully aware of the great importance of occurrences we ignore as they pass. This is an indication of how the more advanced Rosicrucian students are called.

This kind of event may pass us by without being noticed at all, in which case the impression is blotted out and we attach no importance to it. On the other hand, assuming we are attentive, we come to appreciate its significance and perhaps think, I was actually confronted by a crisis then, a karmic crisis; in fact, my life should have ended at that moment. I had forfeited my life and was saved by something resembling chance. Since that hour a second life has been added to the first, as it were. Now I must begin to view this life as a gift and live accordingly.

In our time one becomes a follower of Christian Rosenkreutz once such an event awakens the inclination to view life as a gift. That is his way of calling these souls to him. And anyone who can recall such an experience can know that Christian Rosenkreutz has given a sign from the spiritual world that one belongs to his stream. We sense that Christian Rosenkreutz has added the possibility of such an experience to our karma. This is how Christian Rosenkreutz chooses his community of students. Anyone who experiences this consciously knows that a path has been shown that must be followed. One must see how far one's own forces can be used to serve Rosicrucianism. Those who have not understood the sign, however, will do so later, because those who have received the sign will never be free of it. People can have such an experience once they have encountered Christian Rosenkreutz in the spiritual world between their last death and their next birth. Christian Rosenkreutz chooses then. He places the intent in us that leads to such experiences. This is the way spiritual connections are established.

To go further, let us discuss the difference between Christian Rosenkreutz's teaching in earlier times and more recently. This teaching used to be more like natural science, but today it is more akin to spiritual science. In earlier times, for instance, people considered natural processes scientifically and called this alchemy, and the processes beyond the earth were called astrology. Today, we consider things from a more spiritual perspective. We learn about the nature of the soul's development, for example, when we consider the successive post-Atlantean cultural epochs — ancient India, ancient Persia, the cultural period of Egypt, Chaldea, Assyria, and Babylonia, and that of Greece and Rome. The Rosicrucians during the Middle Ages studied natural processes and regarded them as the earthly processes of nature. They distinguished, for example, three different natural processes that they thought of as the three great processes of nature.

The first important process is the salt process. Anything in nature that can form a deposit of hard substance from a solution was called "salt" by the Rosicrucian of the Middle Ages. When medieval Rosicrucians saw this salt formation, however, they saw it very differently than people do today. If they wanted to have a sense of understanding it, they witnessed the process in such a way that it affected the soul like prayer. Consequently, medieval Rosicrucians tried to become clear about what would have to happen in their own souls so that salt could form there as well. They arrived at this thought: Human nature perpetually destroys itself through instincts and passions. Our lives would consist merely of decomposition and putrefaction if we followed only our instincts and passions. If we really wish to protect ourselves from this process of putrefaction, we must constantly devote ourselves to noble thoughts that turn us toward spirit.

Medieval Rosicrucians knew that if they did not struggle against their passions during one incarnation, they would be born in the next with a predisposition for illness. They knew that if they purified their passions they would enter the next incarnation with a tendency toward health. The process of spiritually overcoming the forces that lead to degeneration is microcosmic salt formation.

One can understand how a natural process such as this engendered the most reverent prayer. While observing salt formation, medieval Rosicrucians would say with a feeling of deep devotion, "For thousands of years, divine spiritual forces have been active in this, just as noble thoughts work in me. I pray to the thoughts of the gods, the thoughts of divine spiritual beings behind the appearances of nature." Medieval Rosicrucians knew this and said to themselves, "When I let nature inspire me to develop such feelings within, I become like the macrocosm. But if I observe this process only outwardly, I cut myself off from the gods and fall away from the macrocosm." Such were the feelings of the medieval theosophist or Rosicrucian.

The process of dissolution gave a different experience. It was a different process of nature that could also lead the medieval Rosicrucians to prayer. Anything that can dissolve something else medieval Rosicrucians called quicksilver, or mercury. Now they would ask,

What is the human soul quality that corresponds to this? What quality works in the soul the way quicksilver works outside in nature? Medieval Rosicrucians knew that every form of love in the soul corresponds to mercury. They distinguished between lower and higher processes of dissolution, just as there are lower and higher forms of love. Thus, witnessing the process of dissolution became another reverent prayer, and medieval theosophists said to themselves, "God's love has been active out there for thousands of years, just as love is active in me."

The third important natural process for medieval theosophists was combustion, which occurs when a material substance is consumed by flames. Again, medieval Rosicrucians looked for the inner process that corresponds to combustion. The inner soul process they saw was ardent devotion to deity. They used the term sulphur to describe everything that can go up in flames. In the developmental stages of the earth they saw a gradual process of purification similar to combustion, or a sulphur process. They knew that the earth will someday be purified by fire; they also saw a combustion process in fervent devotion to the deity. In the earth's processes they saw the work of the gods who look up to more powerful gods above them. The process of combustion permeated them with great devotion and deep religious feelings, and they told themselves, "The gods are now making a sacrifice to the gods above them." And when medieval theosophists produced the combustion process in the laboratory themselves, they felt, "I am doing just as the gods do when they sacrifice themselves to higher gods." Rosicrucians considered themselves worthy of carrying out such a process of combustion in the laboratory only when they were filled with a mood of sacrifice — when they were filled with a desire to devote themselves in sacrifice to the gods. The power of the flame filled them with exalted, deeply religious feelings. They would say to themselves, "When I see flames out in the macrocosm, I see the thoughts and love of the gods and their willingness to sacrifice."

Medieval Rosicrucians produced these processes themselves in the laboratory, and then they contemplated those salt formations, solutions, and processes of combustion, all while allowing themselves to become filled with deeply religious feelings and awareness of their connection with all the macrocosmic forces. These soul processes evoked divine thoughts, divine love, and divine sacrifice in them. Then these medieval Rosicrucians discovered that when they produced a salt process, noble, purifying thoughts arose in them. A solution process inspired divine love in them. And a combustion process enkindled a desire to sacrifice — they were encouraged to sacrifice themselves on the altar of the world.

One who did these experiments had these experiences. If you had been able to attend such experiments yourself clairvoyantly, you would have perceived a change in the aura of those involved. An aura that had been a mixture of colors before the experiment — full of instincts and desires to which the person may have succumbed — became a single hue because of the experiment. First, during an experiment with salt formation, it took on a copper color, that of pure, divine thoughts; then in the experiment with a solution, the color of silver, or divine love; and finally, with combustion, the color of gold, or divine sacrifice.

Thus, the alchemists said that, out of the aura, they had made subjective copper, subjective silver, and subjective gold. And the result was that those who truly experienced this experiment inwardly were completely permeated by divine love. Such was the way these medieval theosophists became permeated with purity, love, and the will to sacrifice, and through this sacrificial service they prepared themselves for a kind of clairvoyance. This is how medieval theosophists could see through illusion into the way spiritual beings helped things to manifest and pass away. This also enabled them to recognize which forces of aspiration in human souls are beneficial and which are not. They came to know our human forces of growth and decay. The medieval theosophist Heinrich Khunrath, in a moment of enlightenment, called this process "growth and decay."[1]

By observing nature, medieval theosophists learned the law of "ascending and descending evolution." The science they acquired from this was expressed in certain signs, imaginative images, and figures. It was a kind of imaginative knowledge.

This is how the best alchemists worked between the fourteenth and nineteenth centuries. Nothing has been published about this truly moral, ethical, intellectual work. And the works printed on alchemy concern only strictly exoteric experiments, all written by those who performed alchemy as an end in itself. The "false" alchemists wanted to create substance. When they experimented with burning substances, they saw only the material results gained, whereas true alchemists attached no importance to the physical results. To them it all depended on their inner soul experiences during the formation of the substance — the thoughts and inner experiences. Consequently, there was a strict rule that those medieval theosophists who produced gold and silver from their experiments were never allowed to profit personally from it. They were allowed only to give away the metals produced in this way. People today no longer have the correct concept of those experiments. They have no idea about what the experimenter would experience. Medieval theosophists were able to experience whole dramas of the soul in the laboratory when, for example, antimony was extracted; the experimenters saw significant moral forces at work in such processes.[2]

If these things had not taken place at that time, we would not be able to practice Rosicrucianism as spiritual science today. What medieval Rosicrucians experienced while observing natural processes is a holy natural science. The mood of spiritual sacrifice and tremendous joys, the great natural events of pain and sadness, and the events that lifted them with joy were all experienced during the experiment. It worked on them in a way that liberated and redeemed. All that was planted in them then, however, is now concealed within the depths of humankind.

How do we rediscover these hidden forces that once led to clairvoyance? We will find them by investigating spiritual science and by devoting ourselves deeply to our inner soul life through serious meditation and concentration. Through this kind of inner development, working with nature will eventually become a sacrificial rite again. Before this can come about, people must pass through what we now call spiritual science. People by the thousands must devote themselves to spiritual science and cultivate the inner life, so that in the future the spiritual reality behind nature will be perceptible again; then we will once again come to understand the spirit behind appearances. In the future, though it will happen only to a small number of people initially, they will be able to experience Paul's vision on the road to Damascus and perceive the etheric Christ, who will come among humankind in an invisible form. But before this happens, we will have to return to a spiritual view of nature.

If we did not understand the whole significance of Rosicrucianism, we could think that humanity is still at the same stage as it was two thousand years ago. Until we have gone through this process — which is possible only through spiritual science — we will not attain spiritual vision. There are many good and pious people who are theosophists at heart but not adherents of spiritual science....

— n i n e —

Christian Rosenkreutz and Gautama Buddha

Here Steiner moves us to a different level, one in which we see Christian Rosenkreutz for the first time as a cosmic being — a guide and teacher of humanity, a coworker and collaborator with other great leaders of human evolution, such as the Buddha, Hermes, Zoroaster, Manes, Scythianos, and "the Master Jesus."

We turn first to consider the context of Rosicrucianism's appearance on the historical scene. The context is the birth of modern science in Copernicanism — called by Steiner "one of the last great attacks by Lucifer upon human evolution." It is "luciferic" because it is an illusion. Christian Rosenkreutz "had to save esotericism in an age when all the concepts of sciences were false." To this end, in the sixteenth century, he called a conference. His coworker in this was the Buddha. To explain this, Steiner tells how the Buddha had overlit the Luke Jesus Child, thus participating in Christ's evolutionary work; then, he speaks of a conference in the seventh/eighth century, held somewhere in the vicinity of the Black Sea. Here the Buddha taught and one of his pupils was the individuality who became St. Francis. St. Francis accomplished a tremendous amount for human evolution, but following his great work spirituality and practical life in the West came in danger of separating and in the gulf between spiritual life and everyday life, modern science arose. The inner, spiritual understanding of the world was in danger of being lost.

This was the issue Christian Rosenkreutz, with the Buddha, sought to address in the sixteenth century. How they determined to do so is a meditation in itself — for it concerns the Buddha's purification of the "Mars forces"

Esoteric Christianity and the Mission of Christian Rosenkreutz, Neuchâtel, December 18, 1912 (*Das esoterische Christentum und die geistige Führung der Menschheit*, GA 130), translated by Pauline Wehrle, revised.

in the consciousness of those pursuing modern science. This is a deep lecture that requires much meditation, one that allows us to understand the "ecumenicism" of Rosicrucianism in a new and more profound way.

Friends have asked me to speak again today on the subject of a talk I gave here a year ago. I said then that the initiation of Christian Rosenkreutz occurred in very special circumstances in the thirteenth century and that, since then, this individual has worked continuously throughout the centuries. Today, we will hear more about the character and person of Christian Rosenkreutz as we study the great task that fell to him at the dawn of the intellectual age: to provide for the future of humanity.

Anyone who makes a mark in the world as a leading esotericist, as did Christian Rosenkreutz, must deal with conditions particular to his or her time. The inherent nature of spiritual life as it exists in the present age first developed when modern natural science arrived on the scene with people such as Copernicus, Giordano Bruno, Galileo, and others. Today, people are taught about Copernicus early on in school, and the impressions they receive remain with them throughout their whole lives. In earlier times the soul experienced something different. Try to imagine to yourselves the contrast between a modern person and one who lived centuries ago. Before the time of Copernicus, everyone believed that Earth remains stationary in cosmic space while the Sun and stars revolve around it. The very ground was pulled from under human feet when Copernicus presented the image of an Earth moving with tremendous speed through the universe. We should not underestimate the effects of such a revolution in thinking, accompanied as it was by a corresponding change in the human life of feeling. All human thoughts and ideas were suddenly changed from what they had been before the time of Copernicus.

What does esotericism have to say about this revolution in thinking?

If, from an esoteric standpoint, you ask what sort of worldview can be taken from Copernican doctrines, you must admit that, although these ideas may lead to great achievements in natural science and life in general, they are unable to advance any understanding of the spiritual foundations of the world and phenomena. Never, in all of human evolution, have there been worse ideas for understanding the spiritual foundations of the world than those of Copernicus. This is because every Copernican concept is inspired by Lucifer.

Copernicanism is one of the last great attacks by Lucifer upon human evolution. In earlier, pre-Copernican thought, the outer world was indeed illusory, but much traditional wisdom and truth concerning the world and things remained alive. Since Copernicus, however, we are surrounded by illusion, not only in our material perceptions, but in our concepts and ideas as well. People take it for granted today that the Sun is firmly fixed at the center and that the planets revolve around it in ellipses. Soon, however, the realization will arise that Copernican views of the starry world are far less accurate than the earlier Ptolemaic view. The adherents of Copernicus and Kepler hold worldviews that are very convenient, but they nevertheless fail to describe the macrocosm truthfully.

Christian Rosenkreutz was confronted by a worldview that is itself an illusion, and had to come to terms with it. Christian Rosenkreutz had to save esotericism in an age when all the concepts of science were themselves false. During the mid-sixteenth century, Copernicus's *Book of the Revolutions of the Celestial Spheres* was published.[1] Thus, by the end of the sixteenth century, Rosicrucians were faced with the need to understand cosmology esoterically, because, even as a concept, the materially conceived Copernican cosmology of globes in space was an illusion.

Consequently, around the end of the sixteenth century, one of the conferences that we heard about here a year ago took place in connection with the initiation of Christian Rosenkreutz himself in the thirteenth century. That esoteric conference of leaders united Christian Rosenkreutz with the twelve of that earlier time along with certain other great individuals concerned with the direction of humanity.[2] There were not only individuals present who were currently incarnated on the physical plane, but also some who were in the spiritual worlds. The individual who had incarnated as Gautama Buddha six centuries before Christ also participated.

The esotericists of the East correctly maintain and know it to be true that the Buddha, who in his twenty-ninth year advanced from bodhisattva to buddhahood, incarnated physically then for the last time. It is absolutely true that the individuality of a bodhisattva who becomes a buddha does not physically incarnate on Earth again. This does not mean, however, that a buddha is no longer active in earthly affairs. A buddha continues to work for Earth but is never present again in a physical body. Rather, a buddha sends down influence from the spiritual world. The Gloria that the shepherds heard in the fields hinted from the spiritual world that the Buddha's forces were flowing into the astral body of the child Jesus described in the Gospel of St. Luke.[3] The words of the Gloria [Luke 2:14] came from the Buddha working in the astral body of the child Jesus. This wonderful message of peace and love is an integral part of the Buddha's contribution to Christianity. Later on, too, the Buddha influenced human actions — not physically but from the spiritual world — and he has cooperated in measures necessary for the progress of human evolution.

During the seventh and eighth centuries, for example, there was a very important center of initiation in the area of the Black Sea, where the Buddha taught in his spiritual body. In such schools there are those who teach in the physical body, but it is also possible for the more advanced students to receive instruction from one who teaches only in an etheric body. And so the Buddha taught the students there who were able to receive higher knowledge. Among the students of the Buddha at that time was one who incarnated again a few centuries later. We are speaking of a physical person who lived again in a physical body centuries later in Italy, known to us as St. Francis of Assisi. Because Francis himself was a student of the Buddha, the character of Francis of Assisi and his monks was similar to that of the Buddha's disciples.[4]

It is easy to perceive the contrast in qualities between people like Francis of Assisi who worked fervently for the spirit and those who are engrossed in a world of industry, technology, and the discoveries of modern civilization. There were many, including esotericists, who suffered deeply at the thought that two separate classes of human beings would inevitably arise in the future. They foresaw one class completely surrendered to the affairs of practical life, convinced that security depends entirely on food production, the manufacture of machines, and so on. On the other hand, they saw another class made up of people like Francis of Assisi, who withdraw completely from the practical affairs of the world for the sake of a spiritual life.

It was thus a significant moment in the sixteenth century when Christian Rosenkreutz gathered a large group of esotericists to prepare for the conference mentioned above. He described to them the two types of people who would inevitably arise in the future. First, he gathered a large group of people and later a smaller one to receive this ponderous fact. Christian Rosenkreutz held this preparatory meeting a few years beforehand, not because he doubted what would happen, but because he wanted to get people to contemplate such perspectives of the future. To stimulate their thinking, he said something like this: "Let us take a look at the future of the world. The world is moving quickly in the direction of practical activities — industry, mass transportation, and so on. People will come to be like beasts of burden. And those who reject this will, like Francis of Assisi, be impractical with regard to life, and will develop only their inner lives." Christian Rosenkreutz made it clear to his listeners that there was no earthly way of preventing the formation of these two classes of people. Despite all that might be done for people between birth and death, nothing could prevent the division of humankind into these two classes. In terms of the conditions on Earth, it is impossible to find a remedy for this class division. The only thing that would help is a kind of education that does not take place between birth and death but between death and a new birth. Thus Rosicrucians faced the task of working from the suprasensory world to influence individual human beings. To understand what had to happen, we must consider life between death and a new birth from a particular point of view.

Between birth and death we live on Earth. Between death and a new birth we have a certain connection with other planets. In my book *Theosophy* you will find *kamaloka* described.[5] This human sojourn in the soul world is a time during which we become inhabitants of the Moon. Then one after the other, we inhabit Mercury, Venus, Sun, Mars, Jupiter, and Saturn, and then we inhabit the far reaches of the cosmos. It is correct to say that between two earthly incarnations we are incarnated spiritually on other planets. Today, humankind is not yet developed enough to recall while incarnated those experiences between death and a new birth; but in the future this will become possible. Although people today cannot remember what was experienced on Mars, for example, they still contain Mars forces, though they are unaware of them. It is justifiable to say, "I am not only an inhabitant of Earth; I contain forces that also include something acquired on Mars."

Let me consider a man who lived on Earth after the Copernican worldview had become commonly accepted. Where did Copernicus, Galileo, Giordano Bruno, and others acquire their capacities for their particular incarnations? Recall that shortly before that, from 1401 until 1464, the profound individuality of Copernicus had been incarnated as Nicholas of Cusa, a mystic. Consider the completely different mood of Cusa's *Docta Ignorantia*. How did the forces that made Copernicus so very different from Nicholas of Cusa come into that individual? The forces that made him the astronomer he was came from Mars. Similarly, Galileo also received forces from Mars, which invested him with the special configuration of a modern natural scientist. Giordano Bruno, too, brought his powers with him from Mars, and so it is with the whole of humanity. People think like Copernicus or Giordano Bruno because of Mars forces acquired between death and a new birth.

The acquisition of powers that led from triumph to triumph was a result of the fact that the influence of Mars was different in those days and unlike what it had exercised previously. Mars used to radiate different forces. The Mars culture that human beings experience between death and a new birth went through a great crisis during the earth's fifteenth and sixteenth centuries. On Mars during the fifteenth and sixteenth centuries it was as decisive and catastrophic a time as it had been on Earth during the time of the Mystery of Golgotha, when the human I-being was born. And like that birth, a particular tendency was born on Mars, which is expressed in the Copernican view. As these conditions gained force on Mars, the natural consequence would have been for Mars to continue sending human beings to Earth who brought only Copernican ideas — ideas which are, in fact, merely illusion. Thus, what we are seeing is the decline of the Mars culture. Previously, Mars had sent forth beneficial forces. Now, however, Mars was increasingly sending out forces that would have led humankind deeper and deeper into illusion. The achievements inspired by Mars at that time were ingenious and clever, but they were illusion all the same.

So you see that in the fifteenth century you could have said that the salvation of both Mars and Earth depended on a fresh impulse to renew the declining culture of Mars. On Mars, it was somewhat similar to what it had been like on Earth before the Mystery of Golgotha when humanity had fallen from spiritual heights into the depths of materialism. On Earth, the Christ impulse signified an ascent. During the fifteenth century, the necessity arose on Mars for its culture to receive an upward impulse. The significant question facing Christian Rosenkreutz and his students was, How can this upward impulse be given to the Mars culture, since the salvation of Earth is also at stake? Rosicrucianism was confronted by a grand task. It had to solve the problem of what had to happen so that, for the good of Earth, Mars culture should be established once again on an ascending path.

The beings on Mars, however, were not in a position to know what would bring about their salvation, because Earth was the only place where one could know the situation on Mars. On Mars itself, they were unaware of the decline. Consequently, to find a practical solution to this problem, the conference I mentioned earlier met at the end of the sixteenth century. Christian Rosenkreutz had prepared this conference well, since his closest friend and student was Gautama Buddha, living in a spiritual body. And it was announced at the conference that the being who had incarnated as Gautama Buddha — in the spiritual form he had assumed since becoming Buddha — would move the scene of his activities to Mars. The individuality of Gautama Buddha was sent by Christian Rosenkreutz, as it were, from Earth to Mars. Thus, Gautama Buddha left his activity and went to Mars. In 1604 Gautama Buddha accomplished for Mars what the Mystery of Golgotha did for Earth.

Christian Rosenkreutz had known the effect the Buddha would have on Mars and what it would mean for the whole cosmos. He knew what the Buddha's teachings of Nirvana and liberation from Earth would mean on Mars. The teaching of Nirvana was inappropriate for a culture directed primarily toward practical life. The Buddha's student Francis of Assisi exemplified the fact that this teaching produces in its adepts complete indifference to worldly affairs. But the essence of Buddhism — which was not adapted to practical human life between birth and death — was very important for the soul between death and a new birth. Christian Rosenkreutz realized that the teachings of Buddha were the most suitable for a certain purification needed on Mars. The Christ being, the essence of divine love, had come once to Earth, to a people who were in many ways alien. And in the seventeenth century, the Buddha, the prince of peace, went to Mars — the planet of war and conflict — to accomplish his mission there. The souls on Mars were warlike and torn by strife. The Buddha performed an act of sacrifice similar to that of the bearer of divine love in the Mystery of Golgotha. To dwell on Mars as Buddha was an act of sacrifice offered to the universe. He was like a lamb offered in sacrifice on Mars, and for him to accept this environment of strife was a kind of crucifixion. Buddha performed this on Mars in the service of Christian Rosenkreutz. This is how the great beings who guide the world work together, not just on Earth but from planet to planet.

Ever since the mystery of Mars was consummated by Gautama Buddha, the forces that human beings receive from Mars between death and a new birth have been different from those that emanated during the cultural decline on Mars. Not only do we bring very different Mars forces into a new birth, but, because of the influence of the Buddha's spiritual act, forces also flow from Mars into those who meditate as a method of reaching the spiritual world. When modern students of spiritual science meditate as suggested by Christian Rosenkreutz, the forces sent to Earth by the Buddha as the redeemer of Mars flow into them.

Christian Rosenkreutz is revealed to us as the great servant of Jesus Christ; but the Buddha, as an emissary of Christian Rosenkreutz, was also destined to contribute to the work of Jesus Christ; this also had to help the work performed by Christian Rosenkreutz in service to Jesus Christ. The soul of Gautama Buddha has not since been physically incarnated on Earth, but he is completely dedicated to the work of the Christ impulse. What was that word of peace sent by the Buddha to the child Jesus as described in the Gospel of St. Luke? "Glory to God in the highest, and on Earth peace, good will toward men." And this word of peace, issuing mysteriously from Buddha, was sounded from the planet of war and conflict to human souls on Earth.

Because of all these events it was possible to avert the division of humankind into the two distinct classes, those like Francis of Assisi and those who live in a completely materialistic way. If the Buddha had remained directly connected with Earth, he would have been unable to concern himself with "practical" people, and his influence would have rendered all the others monks like Francis of Assisi. Through his act of redemption on Mars, it is possible for us, while we pass through the Mars period of existence between death and a new birth, to become followers of Francis of Assisi without causing subsequent deprivation to Earth. Though it may seem like an exaggeration, it is nonetheless true that since the seventeenth century every person has been a Buddhist and a Franciscan, a close follower of Francis of Assisi while on Mars. Francis of Assisi subsequently had only one brief incarnation on Earth as a child. He died in childhood and has not incarnated since. From that time on, he has been connected with the Buddha's work on Mars and is one of his most eminent followers.

We have presented our souls with a picture of the events that came to pass through that great conference at the end of the sixteenth century. It resembles what happened on Earth in the thirteenth century when Christian Rosenkreutz gathered his faithful around him. It fully accomplished the possibility of averting the threatened separation of humanity into two classes, and people were allowed to remain inwardly united. Those who wish to develop esoterically despite absorption in practical life can achieve their goal, because the Buddha is working from the sphere of Mars and not from the sphere of Earth.

The forces that promote a healthy esoteric life can therefore also be attributed to the work and influence of the Buddha.

In my book *How to Know Higher Worlds,* I dealt with the methods that are appropriate for meditation today. The essential point is that development in Rosicrucian training is such that people are not torn from the earthly activities demanded by their karma. Rosicrucian esoteric development can progress without causing the slightest disturbance in any of life's situations or occupations. Because Christian Rosenkreutz was able to transfer the work of the Buddha from Earth to Mars, it is now possible for Buddha to send his influences into us from beyond Earth.

Again we have heard of one of the spiritual acts of Christian Rosenkreutz; but to understand these activities of the thirteenth and sixteenth centuries, we must discover their esoteric meaning and significance. It would be beneficial if it were commonly known how entirely consistent the progress of Western theosophy has been since the beginning of the Theosophical Society's Central European section.[6] Here in Switzerland we have had lecture cycles on the four Gospels.[7] The potential for those Gospel cycles is contained in my book *Christianity as Mystical Fact,* written twelve years ago. The book *How to Know Higher Worlds* describes the Western path of development, which is compatible with all practical activities. Today I have shown that an essential aspect of these matters is the mission assigned by Christian Rosenkreutz to Gautama Buddha. I have spoken of the significant influence that this movement of Buddha to Mars allowed in our solar system. Consequently, stone upon stone fits into its proper place in our Western philosophy, since it has been built consistently and according to principle, and everything that comes later harmonizes with what went before. Inner consistency is essential in any worldview if it is to stand on the ground of truth. Those who can approach Christian Rosenkreutz will see with reverent wonder the consistent way he has accomplished the great mission entrusted to him, which in our time is the Rosicrucian, Christian path of development. The great teacher of Nirvana is currently fulfilling a mission beyond Earth on Mars, and this, too, is one of the wise and consistent acts of Christian Rosenkreutz.

In conclusion, I will add the following brief practical suggestion for those who aspire to become students of Christian Rosenkreutz.

A year ago we heard about how the knowledge of having a certain relationship to Christian Rosenkreutz may come to a person spontaneously. It is also possible to ask a question of one's own destiny: Can I make myself worthy of becoming a student of Christian Rosenkreutz? It can happen in this way: Try to present your soul with a picture of the great teacher of our modern age, Christian Rosenkreutz, in the midst of the twelve as he sends Gautama Buddha into the cosmos as his emissary at the beginning of the seventeenth century, thus consummating what came to pass in the sixth century before Christ in the sermon of Benares.[8]

We can gain quiet confidence in our aspiration to be students of Christian Rosenkreutz if this image appears vividly before the soul in all of its significance, and if we can feel something flowing from this picture that invokes words such as these in the soul: You are not merely an earthly being; you are indeed a cosmic being. This picture of the relationship between Christian Rosenkreutz and Gautama Buddha is a powerful and effective meditation.

I wanted to awaken this aspiration in you with these considerations. Ideally, we should never lose interest in worldly events; and we should find a way, through these studies, to develop our capacities for higher worlds.

Part 3

THE ROSICRUCIAN PATH OF ALCHEMY

— t e n —

On The Chemical Wedding of Christian Rosenkreutz

We now reach the heart of this collection: the essay that Steiner wrote for Alexander von Bernus. In it, Steiner magisterially delineates the crucial difference between "mysticism" and "alchemy" — which is clearly his path and the Rosicrucian path.

Alexander von Bernus (1880–1965) was a poet, an alchemist, and a patron of the arts. As a student he published a magazine in Munich to which many of the revolutionary authors living at that time in the famous Schwabing district contributed. Ricarda Huch, Else Lasker-Schuler, Franz Wedekind (who, according to Steiner, in his Karmic Relationships *volumes, was the reincarnation of an alchemist close to the great alchemist Basil Valentine), Rainer Maria Rilke, Stefan Zweig, Thomas Mann, Hermann Hesse were among the best known. Von Bernus's own first book was published in 1903. From 1907 to 1912, he ran a small theater. Then, in 1912, he met Rudolf Steiner, with whom he developed a close friendship.*

Besides many literary works, von Bernus — with Steiner's blessing and (in the early days) collaboration — dedicated himself to the practice and renewal of alchemy. In 1921, he founded his own alchemical laboratory which, after decades of work, developed more than thirty healing substances. In his alchemical work, Bernus continued the ancient Paracelsian-Rosicrucian tradition in a practical way, returning "the spiritual dimension to the natural sciences."[1]

From 1916 to 1920, von Bernus published a magazine called Das Reich *(The Realm), for which Rudolf Steiner wrote the important series of essays published here. In January 11, 1916, von Bernus had asked Steiner to write an "introduction" to the* Chemical Wedding *for his new journal, but the task took some time to come to completion. The essay was serialized, appearing between October 1917 and April 1918.*

On March 20, 1918, Steiner wrote to Bernus: "In my article I have gone as far as is possible at present. I could only go further, if from one perspective or another the spirit of my interpretation were to be shown to be wrong. In the framework I have presented it is certainly unnecessary to concern myself with exoteric Rosicrucian literature any more than I have at the end of the piece. What I have said right at the end about the relationship of Andreae to Rosicrucianism is the result of spiritual scientific research alone. This anyway will cause a few heads to shake among those who have written about this matter. But my spiritual scientific result is well-founded."

Steiner had of course had a long association with the Chemical Wedding *before turning to the writing of this commentary. Indeed, there is a history to this. In June 1786, a century or so before Steiner, Goethe had written to his friend Frau von Stein: "I have just read the* Wedding of Christian Rosenkreutz. *A good fairy tale could be made of this at the right time. But it will have to be reborn, for it cannot be enjoyed in its old skin." A few years later, therefore, Goethe metamorphosed the* Wedding's *teaching, giving it a new form in his esoteric and hermetic* Tale of the Green Snake and the Beautiful Lily. *Steiner worked with this story extensively, giving many lectures on it and writing an important essay on it for the sesquicentennial of Goethe's birth in 1899. Then Steiner, in turn, in 1910, further transformed its ethical and soul content into a mystery drama,* The Portal of Initiation. *Deep though this initiatory work may be, it represents only the tip of the iceberg that is the path of alchemy in Rudolf Steiner's life. The present essay speaks to this in many ways at many different levels and gives evidence of Steiner's profound understanding of both the theory and the practice of alchemical spiritual science. Thereby it helps us understand the depths to which the Rosicrucian-alchemical impulse penetrates in Steiner's life and philosophy.*

— ◆ —

Anyone who knows what the human soul experiences once it has opened the gates into the spiritual world need read only a few pages of *The Chemical Wedding of Christian Rosenkreutz of the Year 1459* to recognize that the descriptions it contains are based on real spiritual experiences. Subjectively created images quickly betray themselves to a reader with such real experiences, because the images we ourselves create never entirely correspond to reality either in their form or in their sequence.

The Chemical Wedding may first be considered from this perspective — as an account of real spiritual experience. That is, we may follow these experiences, as it were with our souls, investigating what may be said of them through insight into spiritual realities.

For this reason, I will not concern myself with everything that has been written about this book but will consider it only from the above point of view. I shall use only what the book itself says. Only after we have done this will we be able to speak to other questions, raised before they have a sufficient basis.

The First Day[2]

The traveler's experiences on the way to the Chemical Wedding are arranged as a seven-day labor of the soul. The first day begins with an imagination that appears before the seeker's soul, leading to his decision to undertake the journey. The nature of the description shows the special care that has been taken to differentiate between what the seeker was able to understand when the vision arose and what remained hidden from him until later. The description also distinguishes what approaches the seer from the spiritual world without the participation of his will and what occurs through his will. His first experience does not happen arbitrarily, nor does he fully understand it. It offers him the possibility of entering the spiritual world, but it does not meet him unprepared.

Seven years previously a "bodily vision" intimated that he would be called to participate in *The Chemical Wedding*. The expression "bodily vision" cannot be misunderstood by anyone who understands the spirit of the book. "Bodily vision" is not a vision of a diseased, or half-dreaming soul life, but a perception attainable by a spiritual seer. Its content has the same reality for the soul that a percept has for the physical eye.

To experience such a vision presupposes a soul state that is not that of ordinary human consciousness. Ordinary consciousness knows only the alternating conditions of sleeping and waking and, between these, dream experiences unrelated to reality. In ordinary consciousness, the soul knows itself to be related to reality through the senses. When this relation to reality through the senses ceases in sleep, the soul is no longer consciously connected with reality nor with itself and its inner experiences. What connection the soul has with reality while dreaming, it cannot at first comprehend.

At the time of the "bodily vision," the traveler to the Chemical Wedding already remembers a different state of consciousness from the ordinary one. He realizes that the soul can perceive even when, as far as the senses are concerned, it is in a condition similar to sleep. The concept of the soul living apart from the body and experiencing reality in such a state has become valid for him. He knows that the soul can strengthen itself and, separating from the body, unite with the spiritual world — just as it unites with nature through its bodily sense organs. He knows by experience — by means of "bodily vision" — that such a union is possible and awaits him. But he knows too that the actual experience of this union could not come through vision. It is this actual experience, symbolized for him by participation in the Chemical Wedding, which he awaits. In this way, the traveler is "ready" for a renewed life in the spiritual world.

This experience of renewal comes to him on "an evening before Easter Day," during an exalted mood of soul.[3] He feels as if a storm is raging around him.[4] It is clear to him that he is experiencing a reality independent of physical perception. He feels lifted out of the balance of the world forces that a human being enjoys through the physical body. That is, his soul no longer shares in the life of the physical body, but feels united with the body of formative forces that interpenetrates the physical. This formative forces body, however, does not live in the stable balance of world forces but in the mobility of the suprasensory world adjacent to the physical. We perceive this world once the gates of spiritual vision open. Only in the physical world do forces become fixed in the stable condition needed for specific form; in the spiritual world perpetual mobility rules.

The perception of a violent storm symbolizes for the traveler's consciousness the fact that he is caught up into this etheric formative movement.

Out of the indeterminate character of this perception there appears: *the manifestation of a spiritual being.*[5] This revelation occurs through a specific, formed imagination.[6] The spiritual being in question appears to the traveler in a blue mantle covered with stars. This description must be kept free from all that a dilettante esotericist would use to "explain" the image symbolically. Our concern is a nonphysical experience, one that the experiencer expresses in an image — for himself and others. The blue, star-spangled mantle is no more a symbol for the blue night sky than the idea of a rose tree is a symbol in ordinary consciousness for the glow of a sunset. In suprasensory perception, a much more animated and conscious activity of the soul is present than in that of the senses.

In the case of the wanderer to the Chemical Wedding this activity is exercised by the body of formative forces, just as in physical sight the eyes are the mediators for the physical body. This activity of the formative-forces body may be compared with the stimulation of radiating light. Such light shines on the spiritual being, who is thus revealed and radiates it back. The seer thus perceives his own radiating light and beyond and by virtue of its limits he beholds the being that limits and reflects his own light. Through this connection of the spirit being with the spiritual light of the formative forces body, "blue" appears, the stars being that part of the spirit light that is not radiated back but absorbed by the being. The spiritual being has objective reality. The picture by which this being is revealed is the change in the radiation of the formative forces body that it brings about.

This imagination must not be confused with a vision. The subjective experience of one having such an imagination is something completely different from that of the visionary. Visionaries live in their vision through inner compulsion. The person who experiences an imagination unites the imagination to the spiritual being described, or to a spiritual event; and he or she does this with the same conscious inner freedom with which one uses a word or a sentence to express an object of the senses. Anyone with no knowledge of the nature of the spiritual world might suppose that it is wholly unnecessary to clothe the imageless experiences of this spiritual world in imaginations that evoke the semblance of the visionary. To this it must be objected that in reality the imagination is not the essential thing in what is spiritually perceived, but that this is the means through which what is essential must reveal itself in the soul. A sensory color cannot be perceived without the definite activity of an eye any more than one can experience something spiritual without meeting it from within with a specific imagination.

This does not however prevent the use of pure concepts (as are customary in natural science or philosophy) to represent spiritual experiences attained through imagination. The present article indeed uses such concepts to describe the content of *The Chemical Wedding*. But in the seventeenth century, when J. V. Andreae wrote his book, it was not yet customary to use such concepts to any great extent. At that time, authors presented the unmediated imagination through which they experienced suprasensory beings and events.

The traveler to the Chemical Wedding recognized in the spiritual form that revealed itself to him the being who could give him the right impulse for the journey. Meeting this figure, he feels himself standing consciously in the spiritual world. The way he stands there indicates the specific orientation of his spiritual path of knowledge.

This traveler does not follow the way of the "mystic" in the narrower sense. He takes the path of the "alchemist." To understand the description that follows, we must eliminate from the idea of alchemy all that has been associated with it through superstition, fraud, thirst for adventure, and so on. We must think of what was striven for by the honest, unprejudiced seekers of truth who first gave form to this path. Their goal was to recognize the real relationships that exist between natural objects, and to see them as conditioned not by natural activity but by a spiritual being manifesting through nature. They sought for suprasensory forces that are active in the sense world but cannot be recognized by the senses.

The traveler to the Chemical Wedding takes the path of such investigators. In this sense, he represents the alchemical quest. As one on the alchemical path, he is convinced that the suprasensory forces of nature are hidden from ordinary consciousness. He has created in his inner being the experiences that enable the soul, through their effects, to use the body of formative forces as an organ of perception. He wants to attain a vision of the suprasensory forces of nature through this organ of perception. Above all, he wants to recognize the extra-human, suprasensory forces of nature in a spiritual form of existence that can be experienced outside the realm of sensory perception and ordinary intellectual activity. Then, equipped with the knowledge of these forces, he wants to penetrate the real nature of the human body itself. He believes that through a knowledge to be attained by the soul in union with the formative forces body (now operating apart from the physical organism), it will be possible to penetrate to the nature of our bodily being, and thereby approach the mystery accomplished by the cosmos through our physical being.

For ordinary consciousness this cosmic-physical mystery is veiled;

we live in it, but we do not see through the experience. By starting from the suprasensory knowledge of nature, the traveler to the Chemical Wedding wishes to reach a vision of human suprasensory nature in the end.

This way of investigation makes the traveler an "alchemist" rather than a "mystic" in the narrower sense of the term. Mystics also strive for a different experience of the human being than is possible with the ordinary consciousness. However, mystics do not choose the way leading to a use of the body of formative forces independently of the physical body. Mystics start from a vague feeling that a penetration of the physical body by the formative forces body, deeper than is customary in waking life, leads one from a connection with what is physical to a union with one's spiritual nature.

Alchemists, on the other hand, strive *consciously* to draw themselves out of the ordinary connection with the physical and to enter the world that is "the spiritual in nature" behind the sense-perceptible world.

Mystics seek to lead the conscious soul deeper into its connection with the bodily — to enter consciously into the realm of the corporeal that is hidden from self-awareness when the latter is filled with sense perceptions. Mystics do not always seek to give a full account of this striving. Too often they describe the path quite differently. In most instances, in fact, mystics are poor exponents of their own being. This is connected with the fact that, for the mystic, certain feelings are linked with the spiritual quest. A certain contempt for the connection of body and soul — even a contempt for the body itself — can possess the mystic's soul because, through a kind of self-induced delusion, he or she wants to overcome the connection with the body as experienced in ordinary consciousness. Therefore the mystic will not admit that mystical experience is based upon an even closer connection with the body than is usual. Mystics in fact perceive an alteration in their thinking, feeling, and willing as a result of this more intimate connection with themselves.

But they devote themselves to this changed perception without wanting to become clear about the basis of the alteration. Although the change is due to a dipping down deeper into the body, it appears to them as a spiritualization of their inner life. Indeed, they are fully justified in so regarding it. For the perceptive faculty is nothing other than the form of existence that the soul experiences when standing in the relation with the body that forms the basis of ordinary waking consciousness. If the soul connects itself more deeply with the body than is the case in this latter form of existence, then it experiences a relation of the human being to the world that is more spiritual than that produced by the senses.

The ideas that then arise condense to imaginations — which are revelations of the powers that the body of formative forces exercises on the physical body. These powers remain hidden for ordinary consciousness. But in the mystic, feeling is strengthened to such a degree that the moral and spiritual forces streaming from the cosmos and acting upon the human being are experienced as through an inner touch. With the will surrendered to a spiritual activity that incorporates the person into a suprasensory relationship with the world from which he or she is separated by the subjective will of ordinary consciousness, the mystic soul comes to know itself. Real mysticism arises only when — not driven to pathological visions or dimmed consciousness under the compulsion of the bodily organization — one brings one's fully conscious soul into closer connection with the body.

True mysticism, therefore, strives to experience the *internal* human spiritual nature that for the ordinary consciousness is submerged by sensory perception.

True alchemy, on the other hand, makes itself independent of sensory perception in order to behold the spiritual nature of the world that is *external* to humanity, but is concealed by sensory perception. Before entering the inner being of the soul, mystics must bring themselves into a state in which the soul is not exposed to the extinguished or dimmed consciousness resulting from the enhanced counterthrust of the more intimate connection with the body. Before they enter the spiritual world lying behind the physical, alchemists, too, need to strengthen the soul so that it will not lose itself in the beings and events of that world.

The mystical and the alchemical ways of investigation lie in opposite directions. Mystics enter directly into their own spiritual being. Their aim, which may be called the "Mystical Marriage," is the union of the conscious soul with their own spiritual being. Alchemists wish to wander through the spiritual realm of nature so that, by means of the forces of knowledge won in this region, they may thereafter come to behold human spiritual nature. Their aim is the "Chemical Marriage" — union with the spiritual aspect of nature. Only after this union has been achieved does the alchemist wish to experience the vision of the spiritual human being.

At the very beginning of their paths, both alchemists and mystics experience a mystery that, by its nature, cannot be penetrated by ordinary consciousness. This mystery has to do with the relationship between the human body and the human soul. As soul beings, we live in truth in the spiritual world, but at our present stage of development in world evolution we are unable to orient ourselves in the realm of spirit. We lack that capacity. Through the forces of our ordinary consciousness, we can only establish a relationship to ourselves and to the world outside us. This is because it is our body that provides the direction for our soul activity. The body is so placed in the world that it corresponds to cosmic harmony.

While the soul lives in sensory perception and ordinary intellectual activity, it is given up to the body to the precise extent that the body is able to transmit to it its own harmony with the cosmos. If the soul raises itself out of this experience — in a mystical or alchemical way — it becomes necessary to ensure that it does not lose this cosmic harmony with the universe attained through the body. Without such precaution, on the mystical path the soul is threatened with the loss of its spiritual connection with the cosmos, and on the alchemical path with the loss of the capacity for distinguishing between truth and error.

Without such care, mystics, because of their closer connection with the body, could condense the force of self-awareness to the degree that, overpowered in their own life by this force, they would no longer be able to share the experience of world life. Consequently, their consciousness could enter the realm of a different spiritual world from the one that corresponds to the human spiritual world. (In my writings on the science of spirit I have called this realm the " luciferic" world.) Alchemists, for their part, if they do not take due care, lose the power of distinguishing between truth and illusion.

In the great cosmic relationships, illusion is necessary, but at our present stage of evolution we cannot fall victim to it. The realm of sense perception is our safeguard. Were this illusion not in the back-ground of human world experience, however, we could not develop the different stages of our consciousness. Illusion is the driving force for this development of consciousness. At the present stage of the evolution of consciousness, illusion must work so that consciousness will arise, while illusion itself must remain in the unconscious. If it appeared in consciousness it would overpower the truth.

The moment the soul takes the alchemical path, it enters the region of spirit behind sense perception, and it falls into the vortex of illusion in which it can preserve its being only if it brings out of its experience in the sense world a sufficient capacity to distinguish error and truth.

If it has not taken the precaution to acquire such a capacity, then the whirl of illusion will drive it into a world where it must become lost. (In my writings, I have called this the "ahrimanic" world.)

Mystics, before starting on their path, need to bring the soul into such a condition that their own lives do not become overpowering; alchemists must reinforce their sense for truth so that they will not lose it, even when they are not supported by sense perception and the understanding connected with it.

The one who experiences what is described in *The Chemical Wedding* is aware that on his path as an alchemist he needs a strengthened capacity for distinguishing between truth and illusion. From the life connections that impel him to start upon his alchemical path, the traveler seeks the support of Christian truth. He knows that what unites him with Christ has already developed in his life in the sense world a force in his soul leading to truth — a force that does not need the support of the senses and therefore still leads to truth when this support is no longer present. In this attitude, then, the traveler's soul stands before the being in blue garments that shows him the way to the Chemical Wedding.

Initially, this being could just as well belong to the world of error and illusion as to that of truth. The traveler to the Chemical Wedding must distinguish. But the capacity for distinction would be lost, and error would overpower him if he could not, within suprasensory experience, remember what unites him with an inner force to truth in the sensory world. Out of his own soul arises what has happened within it through Christ. Over and above his own light, the Christ light also radiates from his body of formative forces, toward this being who is revealed. The right imagination is formed.

The *letter* that shows him the way to the Chemical Wedding contains the sign of Christ and the words *In hoc signo vinces*.[7] The traveler knows he is connected with a being that appears through a force that points to the truth. If the force that led him into the suprasensory world were to incline toward illusion, he would stand before a being that would injure his power to remember the Christ impulse living within him. He would then be attended only by the misleading powers that attract human beings when the suprasensory world bring forces to meet them that are injurious for their being and their will.

The letter brought to the traveler by the being that invites him to the Chemical Wedding is in a form of expression belonging to the fifteenth century. Its content is a description of his relationship with the spiritual world insofar as he can be conscious of it at the beginning of the first day of his spiritual experience.[8] The sign accompanying the words expresses how the mutual relationship between the physical body, the body of formative forces, and the soul and spirit has taken shape in him.[9] It is fully significant for him that he can perceive how this condition of his human nature stands in harmony with cosmic relationships. "By diligent reckoning and calculation" of his "annotated planets" he discovers that this condition might possibly arise in him at the moment when it now occurs. The "astrology" here will be understood neither by proponents nor by opponents of modern astrology.

The "author" of *The Chemical Wedding* added "the Year 1459" to the title of his book with good reason. He knew that the inner soul mood and the outer world would not be in harmony if the soul of the one experiencing this union of inner and outer did not correspond to a mood attained at a specific moment in world becoming. The soul that has become independent of ordinary sensory perception must meet the external suprasensory world essence harmoniously, if — through the agreement of both — the condition of consciousness is to arise that forms the Chemical Wedding. But whoever believes that the constellation of "the annotated planets" contains a mysterious force that determines the condition of human experience is like someone who supposes that the position of the hands of his watch has the power to cause him to take the walk that the circumstances of his life require him to take at a certain hour.

In the letter "three temples" are indicated. At the time he receives the letter, the one who has the experience does not understand what they mean. Anyone who perceives in the spiritual world must know that sometimes imaginations are assigned that to begin with one cannot understand. One must receive them as imaginations and let them ripen within one's soul. As they ripen, they bring forth in one's inner being the power required to understand them. When one tries to explain a vision at the moment it occurs, one usually lacks sufficient power of understanding, and one's thinking becomes distorted. In spiritual experience much depends on having the patience just to make observations — at first simply to accept them, and to wait with understanding them until the right moment arrives.

The traveler to the Chemical Wedding describes what he learns on the first day of his spiritual experiences as having been announced to him in a "bodily vision" "seven years" before. At that time he did not dare to form an intellectual opinion about the meaning of the "vision." He had to wait until the "vision" had worked long enough in his soul for him to experience it with understanding.

The appearance of the spiritual being in the blue starry mantle and the giving of the letter to him are both experienced by the traveler to the Chemical Wedding without his own soul's free decision having led him to them. Then, however, he proceeds to other experiences through free decision. He enters a state like sleep that brings dream experiences that have reality. This is possible because, after the experiences he has already had, he can, through sleep, enter into a relationship with the spiritual world different from the usual one. Our ordinary experience during sleep does not link our soul to the spiritual world by bonds that would be capable of giving us valid concepts of reality.

But the traveler's soul is transformed. It is so strengthened inwardly that in the dream experience it can perceive the aspects of the experience that are connected with the spiritual world in which it dwells. The soul first experiences its own newly won relationship through such a dream experience — namely, through "the imagination of the tower" in which the dreamer is enclosed and from which he wishes to be freed.[10]

The traveler's soul experiences consciously what is experienced unconsciously in ordinary existence when the soul passes from sense experience to suprasensory existence in sleep. The experiences of cramping and distress in the tower express the soul's inner sensory experiences within the sphere from which it is separating. The life forces that engender growth bind the soul to the body in such a way that the result is ordinary sense experience. Under these forces alone, consciousness could never arise. What is merely living remains unconscious.

The arising of consciousness, together with illusion, serves the forces that destroy life. If we did not bear in ourselves all that leads us to physical death, we could certainly live in a physical body, but we could not develop consciousness within it. The connection between the death forces and consciousness remains hidden for ordinary consciousness. As with the one who experiences the Chemical Wedding, this connection must appear before the "spiritual eye" of anyone who wishes to develop a consciousness for the spiritual world.

We must realize that bound up with our existence is the "hoary-headed Ancient Man" — the being that, according to its nature, bears within it the forces of old age. The only souls who can participate in a vision in the realm of spirit are those who, while in this domain, observe the force hidden in ordinary life behind the ageing process working upon it. This force has power to tear the soul away from the realm of sensory experience. The reality of the dream lies in that through it the traveler to the Chemical Wedding becomes conscious that henceforth he can encounter nature and the human world with a mood of soul enabling him to perceive in both what is hidden from ordinary consciousness. Thus, he is ready for the experiences of the next day.

The Second Day

The beginning of the description of the second day immediately indicates that nature appears to the traveler in a new way.[11] The traveler is meant not only to see what is behind nature; he is to gain a deeper insight into the motives of human will and action than is possible with ordinary consciousness. The writer of *The Chemical Wedding* implies that ordinary consciousness understands only the external aspects of will and of action. With this consciousness, people become aware only of the outer aspect of their will and action. The underlying, spiritual impulses that pour out of the spiritual world into this willing and acting — forming human social life — remain unknown to ordinary consciousness.

We can live in the belief that a specific motive leads a person to act, but this motive is only the conscious mask for something that remains unconscious. Insofar as human beings regulate their "social life" with ordinary consciousness, forces lay hold of this common life that do not belong to the true, healthy purposes of human evolution. Against these forces, other forces must be placed in opposition — forces derived from suprasensory consciousness. These suprasensory impulses must then be incorporated into the social activity. It is to the knowledge of such forces that the traveler to the Chemical Wedding has to be led.

The traveler is to look through human beings and penetrate to their inner being, for this inner being is something quite different from what we believe it is and does not, of course, have anything to do with our position in the social order determined by ordinary consciousness. The image of nature as it is revealed to ordinary consciousness is very different from the image of the human social order. But the suprasensory forces of nature that spiritual consciousness comes to know are related to the suprasensory forces that work in the human social order.

Therefore the alchemist strives for a way of knowing nature that will be the foundation of a true way of knowing humanity. The traveler to the Chemical Wedding seeks the path to such knowledge. Not just this path, however, but several are shown to him.[12]

The first path leads to a region where the intellectual ideas of ordinary consciousness, won through sense perception, influence the process of suprasensory experience. Through the resulting working together of both spheres of experience, insight into reality is killed.

The second path shows that the soul may lose patience when it has to wait a long time for spiritual revelations to allow what initially can be received only as incomprehensible revelation to ripen.

The third path demands people who, through their already attained, but still unconscious readiness, are allowed to see in a brief time what others have to attain only through long struggle.

The fourth brings a person to meet all the forces that, from the suprasensory world, becloud and alarm consciousness when it wishes to tear itself free from sensory experience.

Which path a soul takes depends upon the state it has attained through the experiences of ordinary consciousness before entering on the spiritual journey. It cannot "choose" in the ordinary sense, for the choice would come from physical consciousness, which is not adapted for making decisions about suprasensory things. The traveler to the Chemical Wedding recognizes the impossibility of such a choice. But he also knows that his soul has been sufficiently strengthened to conduct itself in a suprasensory world so as to be directed rightly when such direction comes from the spiritual world itself. The imagination of being set free "from the tower" gives him this knowledge.[13]

The imagination of the "black raven," which snatches the offered food from the "white dove," evokes in the soul of the traveler a certain feeling; and this feeling, produced out of suprasensory, imaginative perceptions, leads along the way that ordinary consciousness would not have been permitted to choose.[14]

On this path he comes to perceive human beings and human relationships in a light inaccessible to experience in a sense body. He passes through a portal into a dwelling where people behave in accordance with the suprasensory forces that pour into their souls. Through the experiences he has in this dwelling he will awaken to the new life he will have to lead when enough of his experience is grasped by suprasensory consciousness.[15]

Many of those who have pronounced judgment on *The Chemical Wedding of Christian Rosenkreutz* have expressed the opinion that it is nothing more than a satirical romance about the activity of a certain sect, or of wild alchemists, or something of the kind. Perhaps, however, a true insight into the experiences the author of this book assigns to the traveler "at the portal" shows that the satirical mood of later parts of the work is really to be traced to soul experiences of such seriousness that they assume a form of mere satire only to those who wish to remain in the sphere of the senses. It would be well to bear this in mind in the perusal of the further experiences of the traveler to the Chemical Wedding. The second day's labor brings to the soul experiences that decide whether the seeker of the spirit Johann Valentin Andreae is describing will attain the faculties for true spiritual perception or whether his soul will be surrounded by a world of spiritual error. For his capacity of perception these experiences are clothed in the imagination of "entering a castle" where the world of spiritual experience is administered.

Not only genuine but also false seekers of the spirit can have such imaginations. A soul may come to them when following certain trends of thought and feeling that allow it to imagine surroundings not derived from impressions of the senses. From the way Andreae describes the company of false seekers of the spirit within which the "Brother of the Red Rose Cross" finds himself on "the second day," we realize that the secret of the difference between the true and the untrue seeker is well known to him. Anyone in a position to estimate rightly such inner proof of the spiritual insight of the author of *The Chemical Wedding* can no longer be in doubt concerning the true character of this book nor the intentions of Andreae, its author.

The Chemical Wedding is obviously written to show serious seekers of the spirit the connection between the sense world and the spiritual world, and to explain to them the forces for social and moral life that can be awakened in the human soul through knowledge of the spiritual world. The unsentimental, humorously satirical mode of Andreae's presentation does not contradict but confirms the deep seriousness of his goal. Not only can we feel this seriousness in the apparently unimportant scenes, but we also realize that Andreae presents his pictures like one who does not wish to confuse his readers' minds with sentimentality about the mysteries of the spiritual world, but would rather create in his readers a soul-free, self-conscious, and reasonable attitude toward that world.

Although the control of thought and feeling can enable anyone to form imaginations of the spiritual world, this faculty by no means guarantees that these imaginations will bring one into a genuine relation to the spiritual world. In this field of imaginative experience the Rosicrucian brother finds himself surrounded by numerous souls who indeed live in imaginations of the spiritual world but who, through their inner condition, are not able to come into genuine contact with it. The possibility of such genuine contact depends upon how the seeker of the spirit relates his soul to the sense world before he approaches the threshold of the spiritual world. This relationship creates a mood of soul that is carried across the threshold and reveals itself in the spirit world by the acceptance or rejection of the seeker.

The right disposition of soul is attained only by the seeker's readiness to leave behind everything that conditioned his relation to the world of sensory reality — to lay it aside at the threshold. All impulses of heart and mind that through his outer position in life and destiny gave him the sense of the character and the worth — the weight — of his personality must cease to be active while he is in the spiritual world.

If the necessity to become again as a little child is felt to be difficult, it seems more repugnant still to ordinary feelings to suppress the kind of judgment by which one finds one's way in the sensory world. One must acquire insight into the fact that this latter kind of judgment applies and has value only in this world. It is within the spiritual world itself that we must be ready to learn how to judge in the spiritual world.

From the moment of his entrance into the castle, the Rosicrucian brother — the traveler — develops the mood of soul that springs from a feeling for these necessities. He does not allow himself to be led into a room where the others would spend the first night within the castle, but remains in the hall, which he has reached through all that is possible as a result of his participation in the events of the second day. Thus he guards himself from bringing his soul into a region of the spiritual world he is not yet able to connect himself with worthily in his innermost forces. This mood of soul, which prevents him from penetrating further into spiritual places than the experiences of the second day warrant, works in his soul throughout the night and equips him with a power of perception and will that he will need on the following day.

Those seekers of the spirit who accompanied him but do not have the faculty of this soul mood must be rejected by the spiritual world on the following day because they cannot develop the fruits of this mood. Without these fruits it is impossible for them through actual inner forces to unite the soul with that world by which it is, so to speak, only outwardly surrounded.

The events at the portals,[16] the encounter with the lion,[17] the reading of the inscriptions on the two pillars at the entrance, and various events of the second day are experienced by the Rosicrucian brother so that one sees that his soul lives in the mood I have just described. The traveler brother experiences things in such a way that everything related only to the ordinary intellect bound up with the sense world remains unknown to him, and he perceives only the part that appears to his deeper soul forces in a spiritually visible connection.

The encounter with "the terrible grim Lion" at the second portal forms part of the spiritual seeker's self-knowledge. The Rosicrucian brother experiences it so that it works as an imagination on his deeper soul forces, but he does not know what it signifies for his position in the spiritual world. This judgment, of which he is ignorant, is pronounced by the "Guardian"[18] who stands near the lion, which he calms, and who addresses these words to the traveler that are in accord with the contents of a letter that, again, are unknown to the traveler: "Now welcome in God's Name to the man whom I would have liked to see long ago."

The suprasensory picture of the "terrible lion" is the result of the Rosicrucian brother's state of soul. This condition of soul is reflected in the formative forces region of the spiritual world and produces the imagination of the lion. In this reflection a picture of the seer's own self is presented. In the sphere of spiritual reality he is a different being from what he is during his existence in the sense world. The active forces of the sense world mold him into a physical human image. However, in the domain of the spirit he is not yet "human," but is a being that can be imaginatively expressed by the animal form. All that displays itself within physical existence as instincts, emotions, impulses of feelings and will is held in fetters within this existence through the life of ideas and perception bound to the sensory body, itself the outcome of the sensory world.

If we desire to leave this sensory world we must become aware of all that, outside this world, is no longer attached to us through the gifts of the sense world, and we must be led into the right path through new gifts emanating from the world of spirit. We must behold ourselves as we were *before* becoming human in the sensory world.

This perception is given to the Rosicrucian brother through his meeting with the lion, which is the picture of his own being *before* becoming a human. To avoid misunderstanding, it may here be noted that the form in which we existed before becoming human, which our essential essence considers in a spiritual way, has nothing to do with the animal state that Darwinism considers to be connected with the descent of the human race. For the animal form that appears to spiritual vision is such as can, through its very nature, belong only to the world of formative forces. Within the sense world it can exist only as a subconscious part of human nature. The fact that one encounters this part of one's being, which is usually fettered to the sensory body, is expressed in the soul mood of the Rosicrucian brother as he enters the castle. He is nonjudgmental about what he is to experience, and does not allow the latter to be obscured by judgments originating from the intellect bound to the sense world.

Later, the traveler must observe this obscuring by judgments in those who have come without the right mood of soul. These also have seen and passed the "terrible Lion," for this depends only upon their having taken into their soul the appropriate thoughts and feelings. But in their case the effect of this spiritual vision was not strong enough to induce the laying aside of the faculty of judgment that belongs to the sense world. In the spiritual realm their way of judging appears to the spiritual eye of the Rosicrucian brother as vain boasting. They presume to see Plato's ideas, to count the atoms of Democritus, to pretend to see the invisible, whereas in truth they see nothing.

This shows that they cannot unite their inner soul forces with the world that now surrounds them. They lack consciousness of the real demands made by the spiritual world upon those who strive to see. The Rosicrucian brother — our traveler — is able to form the connection between his soul powers and the realm of the spirit during the following days because during the second day he admits to himself that he is unable to see and do the things the intruders claim to see and do. His feeling of helplessness later becomes the power to experience spiritually. He must allow himself to be fettered at the end of the second day because he is to feel the fetters of soul impotence in face of the spiritual world until this helplessness has been exposed long enough to the light of consciousness to be transmuted into power.

The Third Day

Andreae wants to show how the "Seven Liberal Arts" — into which people in the Middle Ages organized knowledge attainable in the sensory world — should function as a preparation for spiritual knowledge. These Seven Liberal Arts or seven branches of knowledge were Grammar, Rhetoric, Logic, Arithmetic, Geometry, Music, and Astronomy. From his description in *The Chemical Wedding* it is clear that Andreae considers that the Rosicrucian brother and his legitimate companions, as well as the intruders, are all equipped with the knowledge attainable through these "liberal arts" — though their possession of it differs.

The legitimate seekers of the spirit, and above all the Rosicrucian brother (our "traveler") whose experiences are being described, have made this knowledge their own. By possessing it, their souls have developed the power to receive from the spiritual world what was still unknown for the Seven Liberal Arts. These arts have prepared their souls so that not only do they know what is to be known by and through them, but this knowledge can give them the necessary weight for having experiences in the spiritual world. For intruders, however, the weight of these arts has not become weight of soul. Their souls have not acquired the true world content that these arts contain.

On the third day, the brother of the Rose Cross participates in "weighing the souls." This is described by an imagination of the scales upon which the souls are weighed to ascertain whether they have added to their own weight what corresponds to the seven other weights. These seven weights are imaginative representations of the "Seven Liberal Arts."[19]

The Rosicrucian brother carries in his own soul not only the content of the Seven Liberal Arts that has grown out of the seven weights but also a surplus. This benefits another person who is not considered sufficiently mature in himself. And this person is made safe from expulsion from the spiritual world by the true seeker of the spirit. In mentioning this episode, Andreae demonstrates how well acquainted he is with the secrets of the spiritual world.

For of all the soul forces already developed in the sense world, love is the only one that can remain unchanged by the passage of the soul into the spiritual world. In the sense world, we can help one who is weaker than we attain forces we ourselves possess. And the same can be accomplished through what is bestowed upon us in the realm of the spirit.

Andreae's description of the "illegitimate intruders' expulsion" from the spiritual world shows that by his writing he desires to make his contemporaries conscious of how far removed one can be from the spiritual world and therefore from true reality when, although familiar with various descriptions of the way to this world, one has remained a stranger to consciousness of real inner soul change. An unbiased reading of *The Chemical Wedding* shows that one of the author's aims is to reveal to his contemporaries how destructive for true human evolution are those who interfere with life through impulses that place themselves into illegitimate relationship to the spiritual world. Andreae envisions — for his own time — how right knowledge of the spiritual foundations of existence leads to right social, moral, and other communal human goals. Hence, in his description, he throws a clear light upon all that becomes injurious to human progress because its aims are derived from an unsound relationship with the spirit world.

On the third day, therefore, after having experienced the expulsion of the unlawful intruders, the brother of the Rose Cross feels the possibility arising of using his faculties of understanding in a way suited to the spiritual world. His possession of this capacity appears before his soul in the imagination of "the unicorn bowing before a lion."

Roaring, the lion calls a dove who brings him an olive branch, which he swallows.

Were we to consider this as a symbol rather than a real imagination, we might say that it pictures an event in the soul of the spiritual seeker through which he feels himself capable of thinking what is spiritual. But such an abstract idea would not express the full essence of the soul event that we are considering. For the event is experienced in such a manner that the sphere of personal sensory perception is extended beyond the boundary of the physical body. In the spirit realm the seer experiences beings and events external to his own essential being just as we experience processes going on within our own bodies during usual waking consciousness. When such extended consciousness arises, mere abstract conceptions cease, and the imagination appears as the necessary form of expression for what is experienced.

When we try to express these experiences in abstract ideas, as we must today for the wider communication of knowledge derived from the science of spirit, then these imaginations must be brought into the appropriate ideas. Andreae omits this in *The Chemical Wedding,* for he aims at describing, without alteration, the experiences of the spiritual seeker in the middle of the fifteenth century, when it was not customary to translate experienced imaginations into ideas and concepts.

When imaginative perception reaches the stage of maturity, as it does in the case of the Rosicrucian brother on the third day, the soul with its inner life is enabled to enter the realm of reality where imaginations originate. With the attainment of this faculty, a person can observe in a new way — from a viewpoint in the spiritual world — the beings and events of the sense world. One sees the extent to which these beings and events flow from their true suprasensory source. Andreae explains that the Rosicrucian brother succeeds in acquiring this power to a greater degree than his companions. He reaches the stage where he sees the "library of the castle" and the "burial of the kings" from a spiritual point of view.

This is possible because he can use his own will to a high degree in the imaginative world. His comrades can perceive only what comes to them from external powers, without such strong activity of their own will. The Rosicrucian brother learns more from "the burial of the kings" than is "found written in all books." The view of these burials is brought into direct connection with seeing the glorious "Phoenix." In the beholding of these, the secret of death and of birth is revealed.

These two threshold life events rule only in the sense world. In the spiritual world, birth and death do not correspond to a becoming and passing away, but represent a transmutation of one form of life into another. The nature of birth and death can be understood only when viewed from a standpoint removed from the sense world into a realm in which they themselves do not exist.

In recording how the Rosicrucian brother makes his way to the "burial of the kings" and sees the rise of a new kingly power out of the death of the old kings in the image of the phoenix, Andreae seeks to describe the particular path of a spiritual seeker in the middle of the fifteenth century, which was a turning point for human spiritual experience. The way of approaching the spiritual world that had been valid for many previous centuries changed then. In the outer life of human beings, this change arose through the growing mode of "modern thinking" in natural science and other transformations in the human life. This passing away of one particular tendency of the human soul and the beginning of another may be found in the spiritual realm where the scientist of the spirit searches for the secrets of existence. Despite all the other revolutionary events in the historical progress of humanity, the character of spiritual vision remained practically unchanged from Greco-Roman times until the fifteenth century. The spiritual, instinctive understanding rooted in the human heart and mind was still the essential characteristic of human soul powers, and this had to be transferred to the realms of spiritual reality and there transmuted into the power of spiritual perception. From the middle of the fifteenth century, in place of this soul power, an understanding arose that was liberated from the instinctive forces and worked in the light of full self-knowledge. To raise this understanding to the power of "perceptive" consciousness is the task of the spirit seeker.

In Christian Rosenkreutz, the leading brother of the Rose Cross, Andreae describes a person who has entered the spiritual world by a method that ended in the fifteenth century. The experiences of *The Chemical Wedding* present to the eye of his soul the end of one approach and the beginning of another. Consequently, he must understand certain secrets that the castle's rulers (who would rather continue to administer the spiritual life in the old ways) would willingly hide from him. Andreae wishes to portray to his contemporaries the foremost spiritual investigator of a declining era — one who perceives in the spiritual realm the death of that era and the birth of a new one. Andreae found that his contemporaries were still content with the traditions of the old era. They still preferred to open the way to the spiritual world using their traditional methods. But Andreae wanted to tell them, "Your path is useless; the greatest who has most recently followed it, has seen this. Realize what he has perceived and you will develop a sense for a new path."

Andreae wanted to set up Christian Rosenkreutz's spiritual path as the legacy of fifteenth-century spiritual investigation. He wanted to show that a new way of spiritual investigation had to begin. Contemporary spiritual scientists who understand the signs of the times find themselves continuing the efforts begun by Johann Valentin Andreae. They meet the strongest opposition from those spiritual seekers who still attempt to open the way into the suprasensory world through a renewal of old spiritual scientific traditions.

Andreae subtly and gently indicates what kind of knowing must emerge through perceptive human consciousness after the middle of the fifteenth century. Christian Rosenkreutz finds his way to a great globe, through which the dependence of earthly events on extra-earthly, cosmic impulses is presented to his soul. This indicates the first glimpse into a new "knowledge of the heavens," beginning with the Copernican view of the universe — which, however, Christian Rosenkreutz considers able to provide only what is meaningful for the physical world. To this day, modern natural science still investigates in terms of this Copernican beginning. In its worldview, modern science sees Earth surrounded by "heavenly events," which it tries to under-stand through intellect alone. It seeks within the earthly sphere itself the forces behind the essential processes of earthly events. When in-vestigating the conditions under which the seed of a new being arises within the maternal being, it notes only the forces that are related to the earthly ancestors in the stream of heredity. It is quite uncon-scious of the fact that during the forming of the seed "the earth's heavenly periphery" is working into the earthly happenings, and the maternal being is merely the place within which the extraterrestrial cosmos shapes the seed. This mode of thought seeks the causes of historical events exclusively in facts preceding these events in earthly life. It ignores the supra-earthly impulses that fertilize earthly facts so that events of a subsequent epoch may proceed from events of a preceding one. This way of thinking admits extra-earthly influence as working merely upon lifeless earthly processes.

The prospect of an organic, a spiritual "knowledge of the heavens" is revealed to Christian Rosenkreutz; but this can have nothing in common with the ways of ancient astrology. Rather, it rests upon the same foundations for the suprasensory as Copernicanism does for the sense world.

We may note how competently Andreae treats the imaginative life in *The Chemical Wedding.* All the wisdom that comes to Christian Rosenkreutz as revelation and without the exercise of his own will, Andreae shows as appearing through forces represented in *images of a feminine nature;* and where the personal will of the spiritual investigator makes its way is pictured through the male element by *images of boys leading the way.*

In the human being, whether physically man or woman, male and female hold sway as polar opposites. Andreae gives his characteriza-tions with this in view. What has to do with concepts and thoughts will be put in the correct relation to the nature of will when this rela-tion is represented in images reminding us of male and female in the world of the senses. Once more it should be noted, as a precaution against misunderstanding, that the imagination of male and female is not to be confused with the relation between man and woman in the sensory world — any more than the imagination of the animal form appearing to perceptive consciousness has to do with the animal nature related by current Darwinism to humankind. At present many people think that they can penetrate to hidden secrets of existence through the physiology of sex. Even a superficial knowledge of the real science of the spirit should convince them that such efforts, instead of leading toward the mysteries of existence, lead far away from them. In any case, it is nonsense to connect the teaching of such a personality as Andreae in any way with the physiology of sex.

Andreae points with great clarity to something important when he secretly includes in *The Chemical Wedding* a description of the "virgin" and brings this "virgin" into particularly close relationship with the seeker of the spirit. The "virgin" is the imaginative representation of suprasensory knowledge, which, instead of being gained on the physical plane like the "seven liberal arts," has to be drawn from the realm of the spirit. In a somewhat enigmatic way the virgin gives her name — it is *alchemy*. By this Andreae wishes to show that true alchemy is a different science from those evolved from ordinary consciousness. For Andreae, alchemists accomplish their work with perceptible substances and forces, not because they wish to investigate effects in the sensory world, but because they wish to allow what is suprasensory to manifest through the physical process. Alchemists seek to penetrate to suprasensory processes through physical processes. What alchemists do — their research — differs from the research of the ordinary scientist in how they look at the physical process.

The experiences of the "third day" include completely overcoming the belief that the kind of judgment we are used to in the sensory world can, without changing it, be a guide in the suprasensory world. Among the company in which Christian Rosenkreutz finds himself, questions are propounded, all leading to the end that decisive answers are withheld. Reality is richer than the faculty of judgment based upon the intellect nurtured by the sense world. After the description of these experiences Andreae also introduces a "Duchess." Thus, he brings Christian Rosenkreutz into relationship with the suprasensory kind of knowledge she characterizes: Theology. How this is to affect the human heart and soul is then pictured.

Of special significance is the fact that after all these experiences, the spiritual seeker is visited again on the following night by a *dream* in which he is shown a door he wishes to open but which offers him considerable and prolonged resistance. This image is produced in his soul by the idea that all his previous experiences should not be thought of as possessing any intrinsic value by their immediate content. Rather, his previous experiences are generators of a force that will have to be subject to still further effort.

The Fourth Day

The "fourth day" is decisive for the spiritual traveler insofar as his position in the suprasensory world is concerned. Once more he meets the lion. "The ancient inscription," brought to him by the lion, contains essentially the demand that he should approach the source from which inspirations flow from the spiritual world. The soul satisfied with mere imaginative experience could only allow itself to be addressed, as it were, from the spiritual world and to use the power of its own will to make these revelations comprehensible. If the full power of the I is to enter the suprasensory world, this I must carry its own consciousness into that world. The soul must rediscover the I and its sensory experiences in the spiritual world.

In a certain way the memory of the kind of experiences one has in the sensory world must emerge in the suprasensory world. Andreae makes this clear by introducing on the fourth day a "comedy," that is, a phantom image of events in the physical world. In beholding this phantom picture obtained in the suprasensory realm, the spirit seeker's I is strengthened so that he feels a firm connection between the aspect of his soul that experiences in the suprasensory world and the part that is active through the body in the world of the senses.

Andreae's effective method of description convinces us that he wants to address his contemporaries in a most serious manner about a path into the spiritual world appropriate to the epoch of human development in the sixteenth century — at the beginning of which the author of *The Chemical Wedding* feels himself placed. The fact that initially serious obstacles hindered a realization of the idealistic claims Andreae placed before his contemporaries was due to the devastating confusion of the Thirty Years' War and all that it brought into the more modern era.[20]

Progress in human evolution is possible, however, only when personalities of an attitude similar to that of Johann Valentin Andreae oppose the retarding forces of certain world currents with impulses of a truly constructive nature. We can determine whether Andreae succeeded in describing Christian Rosenkreutz as a spiritual seeker able to point effectively from his spiritual experiences of a past epoch to the new path appropriate for the new era only if we can show that the last "days" of *The Chemical Wedding* relate experiences that open a perspective into this period — in other words, if we can show that Christian Rosenkreutz is able to carry his I over into the new period.

The most significant experience for Christian Rosenkreutz on the fourth day is his introduction to the kings, and their subsequent beheading.

The author of *The Chemical Wedding* indicates the nature of this experience by "symbolic figures standing on a small altar." In these symbols the human soul can behold its relationship to the universe and its evolution. Spiritual investigators have always tried by such symbols to bring intimately before the soul how their own being lives within the cosmic being. The "book" points to human thinking, which, in conformity with the human organization, is an influx of objective cosmic-creative thought into the soul. The "little light" indicates that these world-creative thoughts are active as light ether in the universe; they become productive of knowledge and illumination in humankind. The role of Cupid, who blows on the light, refers to the spirit seeker's perception that light and love are the two forces that, as polar opposites, are etherically at the basis of all existence and becoming. We judge this perception correctly, however, only if we see in physical light and the love active on the physical plane the materially effective revelations of original spiritual forces. The creative thought element of the world lives freely in the primal spiritual force of light, and the creative will element lives in love.

Among the symbols is a "sphere" to indicate how human experience, in encountering cosmic life, becomes a member of that life. The "clock" indicates how the soul is interwoven with the progress of cosmic time, just as the sphere is interwoven with its spatial existence. The "little well," from which blood-red water flows, and "the skull and serpent" demonstrate the seer's vision of birth and death as based in the "cosmic-all." Such symbols are among the very oldest.

Valentin Andreae uses such symbolic figures in a similar way to that used in ancient meeting places that served societies admitting people for initiation into the mysteries of life. Because Andreae uses them in the same way, he shows that, in his opinion, such symbols are imaginations based on the evolution of the human soul and can stimulate it to perceive the mysteries of existence.

We must ask, What is the meaning of the "Hall of the Kings" into which Christian Rosenkreutz is led? And what was experienced in the presence of the "Kings who were beheaded"? The symbols show the answer. Spiritual seekers are meant to bear witness to how they are grounded in cosmic being with their own being. They should perceive in the world what is within them; what is within the world they should perceive in themselves. They can do this only when they see in things and events cosmic images of what works and weaves within them — when they no longer view inner experiences simply as ideas proceeding from their own souls, but perceive them as images representing the growth and becoming of the whole cosmos. The kings stand before Christian Rosenkreutz to say, as it were, "Thus your soul forces live within your own being."

The kings' experiences reflect events that must take place in the soul under certain conditions. Christian Rosenkreutz faces what happens in the "Hall of the Kings:" his whole soul sees itself in it. The beheading of the kings is an event in his own soul's evolution. He arrived in the "Hall of the Kings" with forces of cognition that are the same as they were before he gained entry to the spiritual world. By living into this world, however, those "forces of cognition" have experiences that are also related to the material world. Not only does the spiritual world light up when faced by the soul, but the material world also reveals itself before the soul — in forms that cannot be seen in their full meaning by those whose powers of observation remain in the material realm. The revelation of our divided human nature is a part of these experiences. The forces that are the basis of physical growth are shown to be also active in phenomena usually considered to be of a soul nature. The power of memory and the impulses for forming thoughts prove to be dependent upon the same kind of physical condition as growth. The forces of growth develop progressively in childhood and youth; after this they decrease, finally becoming the cause of death. Memory and the forces for forming ideas, on the other hand, can decline from an early period of life. While we are awake, these forces pass through the same process of decline that the whole organism experiences in the second half of life until death. Conversely, while we sleep this decline is compensated for, and memory and the forces of forming ideas undergo a resurrection. The soul organism is grafted — like a parasite — upon the whole human organism. The soul can supply the condition for memory and representations because in the course of a day the soul follows the same path to death that the whole organism traverses in the course of earthly life. Hence, for the spiritual investigator, the soul organism becomes a metamorphosis of the whole organism.

The soul organism thus appears as the part of the complete organism that develops more intensely the forces responsible for manifesting life between birth and death. These forces can therefore become the basis for the soul's conceptual life. Creative cosmic thought being flows into the daily decline of the forces of the soul organism and becomes human conceptual life.

It is essential for the spiritual seeker to perceive the material foundation of soul processes as transmuted outer, material processes of the whole organism. It is a paradoxical fact that one first sees the material conditions of the soul life when on the way to the spirit. The realization can mark the beginning of a temptation. One can remain at the point of discovery that soul events manifest themselves in their material form and, while seeking the spirit, can be driven into a materialistic world conception. If one really penetrates what is in question, however, the opposite takes place. One observes the creative spiritual powers that reveal themselves in the formation of substances in the material basis of soul life, and thereby becomes able to recognize spirit at the basis of the whole organism and its life course.

Christian Rosenkreutz is thus confronted with the important experience that reveals to him an alchemy accomplishing its work within the processes of nature. The material processes of the whole organism are transformed before his spiritual eye. They become something out of which the soul events flash forth like the light in the external process of combustion. But in so doing these soul events also reveal where they reach their limits. They correspond to the processes in the organism that lead to death. Christian Rosenkreutz is brought before the "kings" of his own soul being, before his powers of knowledge. They appear to him as a metamorphosis of the whole organism. But the forces of growth change into cognitional powers only by accepting death into themselves. For this reason they carry in them only the knowledge of what is dead. Death is included in all natural processes in such a way that the nonliving exists in everything. Our ordinary process of knowledge is directed upon what is nonliving. Because it itself is dead it grasps the inorganic; it understands the plant and all that is living only insofar as they are touched by the nonliving. Every plant contains inorganic processes, over and above what it is as a living entity. Ordinarily our forces of knowledge grasp these inorganic processes; but they do not grasp what is living. What is living becomes visible only insofar as it manifests itself in the nonliving. Christian Rosenkreutz witnesses the death of his "soul kings," his forces of knowledge, as these arise from the metamorphosis of the material forces of the whole organism without the human being passing over from the "alchemy of nature" to the "alchemy of art." This has to take place in such a way that, within one's soul, one gives the forces of knowledge a character they do not possess through their merely organic evolutionary processes. What is essential in the ascending powers of growth, where death has not yet encroached, has to be awakened in the forces of cognition. Natural alchemy must be carried further.

The Fifth Day

This further development of natural alchemy becomes the work during the "fifth day" of *The Chemical Wedding.* The spiritual seeker's vision must penetrate the processes that nature causes as she produces growing life. The seeker of the spirit must lead this creative activity of nature into the forces of knowledge — without allowing death to prevail in the transition from processes of growth to those of soul.

The seeker receives the forces of knowledge from nature as dead entities. Then he or she must animate these by restoring all that nature withheld from them when it brought about their alchemical transmutation into forces of cognition. As we move toward this goal, a temptation approaches us. We must descend into the region where through the force of love, nature charms life from what, of its own nature, strives toward death. Here the seeker is in danger of the vision being seized by those instincts that prevail in the lower regions of substances. One must learn to recognize how in matter, which bears the stamp of death, lives an element related to the love that underlies the renewal of life.

The soul's exposure to temptation is strikingly described by Andreae when he makes Christian Rosenkreutz appear before Venus while Cupid plays his role.[21] Here we are clearly shown how temptation does not stop the spiritual seeker from continuing on the path by his or her own soul forces alone, but also by the working of other powers.

If Christian Rosenkreutz had to tread only his own path of knowledge, the latter could have ended with the temptation. The fact that this is not the case indicates Andreae's intention. On his spiritual path Christian Rosenkreutz is meant to show the way from one epoch to the dawn of another. The active powers of the courses of time help him to permeate his I with the powers of knowledge suitable for the new period. Therefore he can proceed on his journey to the "tower" by participating in the alchemical process through which the dead powers of cognition experience their resurrection. Thereby he also possesses the power of listening to the "Siren's Song" of love without falling victim to its seductions.[22] The spiritual primeval force of love must work upon him, but he may not allow its manner of manifestation in the sense world to divert him from his way.

The permeation of the dead cognitional forces with those impulses that in the ordinary human organism hold sway only in the process of growth occurs in the "Tower of Olympus."[23] We are shown how Christian Rosenkreutz is allowed to take part in this event because his soul development is to proceed in accordance with the changing forces of the times. Instead of going to sleep he goes into the garden, looks up at the starry heavens and observes, "Because I thus have a good opportunity to ponder astronomy I discovered that, on this night, a conjunction of planets takes place such as is seldom seen."

The Sixth Day

Detailed descriptions are given in the experiences of the "sixth day" of the various imaginations that make it clear to Christian Rosenkreutz's soul how the dead forces of cognition evolved by the organism in the ordinary journey through life are transmuted into suprasensory powers of perception. Each of these imaginations corresponds to an experience of the soul in relation to its own powers when it realizes how what until now could be permeated only by death, becomes capable of knowingly allowing the living to stir within it.

Other spiritual seekers than Andreae would differently describe individual images. Yet it is not a question of the content of individual images, but of the transformation of our human soul forces through having before us in a succession of imaginations, pictures reflecting this transformation.

Christian Rosenkreutz is portrayed in *The Chemical Wedding* as the spirit seeker who feels the approach of that period when humanity will view natural phenomena differently than in the epoch that ended with the fifteenth century. In the following period, human beings will no longer be able to perceive the spiritual content of natural objects and events when they observe nature. This fact could lead to a denial of the spiritual world if one does not at the same time admit the existence of a path of knowledge that can penetrate the material basis of the soul life and receive the being of the spirit.

To be able to effect this, one must be able to shed spiritual light upon this material basis. One must be able to perceive how nature proceeds — as it shapes its active forces into a soul organism that reveals death — in order to be able to hear from the being of nature itself the mystery of how spirit can confront spirit when the creative activity of nature is guided to awaking the dead cognitive forces to a higher life. Thereby, a way of knowing may be developed that, as spiritual knowledge, finds its place within reality.

Knowledge of this kind is a further shoot on the living being of the world. This way of knowing continues the evolution of reality that has prevailed from the first primeval beginnings of existence up to human life.

Something is developed exclusively into higher forces of knowledge. As a seed it is conditioned by nature, but it is held back from the activity of nature itself at the point where, in the metamorphosis of existence, the cognition of what has died should be developed. Some would argue that such a continuation of natural activity beyond what it attains in the human organism leads beyond reality and into the unreal. Those who penetrate the evolution of nature will never make such an objection themselves. Evolution is always a progress of arresting the forces of growth at certain points to reveal the endless possibilities of new forms at certain stages of human existence. Thus the human organism itself is likewise an arresting of a possible form. Just as in the green leaf of the plant a possible form is arrested, and yet the formative forces of the plant's growth advance beyond this form, making the colored leaf of the blossom appear at a higher stage — so human beings too can progress from the formation of cognitive forces that are directed toward what is dead to a higher stage of these forces. We experience the character of reality in this progress by becoming aware that through it we receive into ourselves the soul organ for the understanding of spirit in its suprasensory revelation. Just so, the transformation of the green leaf into the colored flower organ of the plant prepares the capacity that expands itself into the formation of the fruit.

The Seventh Day

After the artistic alchemical process is completed, Christian Rosenkreutz is named *Knight of the Golden Stone*.[24] One would have to
enter deeply into a purely historical discussion to explain the name
"Golden Stone" from the literature and point out its meaning and
use.[25] To enter this literature — some trustworthy, but for the most
part fraudulent — is not however the purpose of this article. We may
nevertheless simply indicate some conclusions concerning the use of
this name derived from a reading of the literature. Those who have
used the name "The Golden Stone" — and are to be taken seriously —
wished to indicate by this designation that one can observe dead
"stone nature" in such a way as to grasp its relation to what is alive
and evolving. Serious alchemists believed they could produce "artificial" processes of nature in which what is dead and of a "stony"
character is used in such a way that, when rightly observed, something can be recognized of what goes on when nature herself weaves
what is dead into what is living and evolving.

Through the perception of quite distinct processes in what is dead,
serious alchemists would grasp traces of nature's creative activity and,
with it, the presence of the spirit ruling in the phenomena. The symbol
for what is "dead" but is recognized nevertheless as the revelation of
the spirit is *"The Golden Stone."*

Whoever examines a corpse in its essential, actual nature, recognizes how what is dead is gathered up into the general process of
nature. The form of the corpse, however, protests against this general nature-process. This form can only be the result of life permeated
by spirit. The universal natural processes must destroy what has been
formed by such "spirit-permeated life." Alchemists believe that what
ordinary human knowledge can grasp of the whole of nature is only
as much as may be identified of a human being from a corpse. Higher
knowledge should discover in a natural phenomenon what "spirit"
is related to it — in the sense that spirit-permeated life is related to
the corpse. This is the striving for "The Golden Stone."

Andreae speaks of this symbol in such a way that he clearly means
only those who have experienced what he describes as "the six days'
work" can understand what to do with "The Golden Stone." He
seeks to show that anyone who speaks of it without knowing the
nature of the transformation of the cognitive forces can have only
an illusion in mind. In the figure of Christian Rosenkreutz, Andreae
strives to describe a personality who can speak in an authoritative

way about something that is often spoken of without authority. He wishes to defend the truth against what is wrongly spoken about the search for the spiritual world.

Christian Rosenkreutz and his companions, after they have become actual workers on "The Golden Stone," receive a memento with the two sayings: "Art is the servant of nature," and "Nature is the daughter of time."[26] They are to work with these guiding principles out of their spiritual knowledge. The principles resume and exemplify their six days' experiences. Nature reveals its mysteries to those who can continue its creative work through their art. But one cannot succeed in this unless one has first listened to the meaning of nature's will in one's art, and unless one has recognized how nature's revelations arise through its infinite faculty of evolution, coming forth from the womb of time in finite forms of existence.

In his connection with the king on the seventh day, we are shown how Christian Rosenkreutz as a seeker of the spirit now stands in relation to his transformed faculties of knowledge. We are shown how, as "Father," Rosenkreutz himself gave birth to these faculties of knowledge.[27]

Christian Rosenkreutz's relationship to the "First Gatekeeper"[28] is really a relationship to a part of his own being — in other words, a relationship to that part of his being which as "Astrologer" searched for the laws determining human life but was unable (before the transformation of his cognitive powers) to face a temptation like the one at the beginning of the fifth day when Christian Rosenkreutz confronted Venus. Those who succumb to this temptation cannot gain entrance to the spiritual world. They know too much to be entirely shut away from it, but they cannot enter. They must stand guard before the door until another appears and falls victim to the same temptation.

Christian Rosenkreutz supposes himself to have succumbed and thus to have been condemned to take over "The Office of Watchman." But this watchman is part of himself, and because he can survey it with his other, transformed part, he is able to overcome it. He becomes the watchman of his own soul life. But this guardianship does not stop him from establishing free connection with the spiritual world.

Because of his seven days' experience Christian Rosenkreutz has become a knower of the spirit who, with the power conferred on him by his experience, can work in the world. What Christian Rosenkreutz and his associates accomplish in external life will flow from the spirit from which nature's own works flow. Through their work they will bring harmony into human life that will depict the harmony of nature that is capable of conquering disharmony. The presence of such people in the social order is a continuously effective impulse toward a healthy way of life.

When people ask what are the best laws for living together, for the social life of human beings on Earth, Andreae points to Christian Rosenkreutz and his companions. To the question of the best laws, he answers that the social order cannot be regulated by ideas expressed in thoughts about how this or that should be done, but by what those who strive to live in the spirit that manifests itself through existence may say.

What guides souls who, following Christian Rosenkreutz, wish to work in human life, is expressed in five sentences:

1. They should not think out of any spirit other than that which reveals itself in the creations of nature, and they should see human works as a continuation of nature's works.

2. They should not place their work in the service of human impulses, but make those impulses mediate the works of the spirit.

3. They should lovingly serve human beings, so that the creative spirit could reveal itself in the relationship of one human being to another.

4. They should not allow themselves to be led astray from the value that the spirit confers upon all human labor by any value that the world can give.

5. They should not, like bad alchemists — "puffers" — fall into the error of confusing what is physical with what is spiritual. (Bad alchemists believe that the physical prolongation of life and other similar objectives are the highest good. They forget that what is physical has value only when its existence properly manifests the spirit underlying it.)

At the end of the narrative of *The Chemical Wedding*, Andreae describes Christian Rosenkreutz's "homecoming." In all externals he is the same as he was before his experiences. His new condition of life is different from the old only in that henceforth he will carry his "higher human" within himself, as the ruler of his consciousness, and what he accomplishes will be what the "higher human" can effect through him. The transition from the last experiences of the seventh day to finding himself at home in his ordinary surroundings is not described. It says: "Here two or three pages are missing." One could imagine there might be people who would be especially curious about what these "missing pages" contain.

Only those who have themselves undergone an individual experience of the transformation of their soul nature can know what those pages contain. Such people know that everything leading to this experience has a universal human significance that is communicated as one communicates the experience of a journey. What an ordinary person experiences is, on the contrary, something quite personal; it is different for everyone and cannot be understood by another in the same way as by the one who has experienced it.

That Valentin Andreae did not describe the transition into the ordinary conditions of life can serve as further proof that *The Chemical Wedding* expresses true knowledge of what it describes.

The above exposition has attempted to describe what is expressed in *The Chemical Wedding* solely through a consideration of the content of this work as revealed to the author. It should confirm the judgment that in this writing published by Andreae, the direction is shown that must be followed when anything concerning the true character of higher knowledge is to be known. And this exposition seeks to make clear that in *The Chemical Wedding* we have a picture of the special kind of spiritual knowledge demanded since the fifteenth century.

For those who understand this document as does the author of this exposition, it is a historical account of a European spiritual stream going back to the fifteenth century, a stream seeking to acquire knowledge about the relationship of everything that lies behind the phenomena of the external world.

A fairly extensive literature exists concerning the work of Johann Valentin Andreae. Here there is much discussion as to whether his published writings can be regarded as actual proof of the existence of a spiritual stream of this nature. In these writings, this stream is said to be that of Rosicrucianism. Certain investigators consider the whole affair of Andreae and his Rosicrucian writings to be simply a literary joke intended to ridicule the sentimentality to be found wherever the mysteries of higher knowledge are discussed. From this point of view, this Rosicrucianism would be a fantasy picture created by Andreae for the express purpose of making fun of the wild talk of sentimentalists or of fraudulent mystics.

The author of this exposition, however, considers it unnecessary to trouble his readers with much of what is advanced in this way against the seriousness of Andreae's intentions. He is of the opinion that a correct study of what *The Chemical Wedding* contains affords sufficient basis for understanding what it means to convey. Evidence based on material other than these contents can have no effect upon this opinion. Anyone who recognizes the full weight of inner reasons will be convinced that outer documentary evidence should be valued according to inner reasons, and not that the inner should receive its value from the outer. Therefore if what is said here takes its position outside the purely historical literature concerning Rosicrucianism, no adverse criticism of historical research is intended. All that is meant here is that the point of view taken in this exposition makes a full discussion of Rosicrucian literature unnecessary.

Let me therefore add only a few remarks. It is a known fact that the manuscript of *The Chemical Wedding* was completed by 1603. It made its first public appearance in 1616 — after Andreae, in 1614, had published his other Rosicrucian document, the *Fama Fraternitatis R.C.* It was this publication above all that gave rise to the belief that Andreae spoke only in jest of the existence of a Rosicrucian Society. This belief was later supported by Andreae's own statement that Rosicrucianism was not a thing he would have cared to defend. There is much in his later writings and in his letters to support the interpretation that his sole purpose was to invent stories concerning this spiritual stream for the mystification of fanatics and the curious. As a rule. in making use of such evidence, no heed is paid to what misunderstandings works like those of Andreae are exposed. What he himself later said about this can be rightly estimated only when one realizes that he was obliged to speak in that manner after enemies had appeared who severely condemned this spiritual movement as heresy, and that adherents had come forward who were fanatical or were alchemical swindlers, distorting everything for which Rosicrucianism stood. But even if all this is taken into consideration and one is willing to accept the idea that Andreae, who later seems to be a pietistic writer, showed himself (soon after the publication of the Rosicrucian writings) to be averse to owning as his what was communicated in those writings, one does not reach any solid conclusion on the relation of this personality to Rosicrucianism. Indeed, even if one is willing to go so far as to deny Andreae the authorship of the *Fama* on historical grounds, one cannot deny him authorship of *The Chemical Wedding*.

There is another point of view from which this matter must be considered historically. The *Fama Fraternitatis* appeared in 1614. We may first of all leave undecided whether with this work Andreae wished to approach serious readers in order to tell them about the spiritual path known as Rosicrucianism. But two years after the appearance of the *Fama, The Chemical Wedding,* which had been completed thirteen years before, was published. In 1603 Andreae was still a very young man (seventeen years of age). Are we to suppose that he was sufficiently mature to have started a ghost among the sentimentalists of his day by presenting them with Rosicrucianism, an image of his power of fantasy, as a sop for their mockery? Besides, if in the *Fama,* which was already being read in manuscript in the Tyrol by 1610, Andreae wished to speak of Rosicrucianism in a serious way, how was it that as a quite young man he composed in *The Chemical Wedding* a document that he published as information concerning true Rosicrucianism two years after the *Fama?*

In fact, the questions about Andreae seem to become so entangled that this complicates any merely historical solution. We should not be able to protest against any merely historical investigator trying to make it credible that Andreae may have lighted upon the manuscripts — perhaps in possession of his family — of *The Chemical Wedding* and the *Fama,* that he published them for some reason in his youth, but later repudiated the spiritual bent expressed in them. Was this a fact, however, why did Andreae not simply announce that this was the case?

With the help of spiritual science, one can reach a totally different conclusion. There is no need to connect *The Chemical Wedding* with Andreae's age at the time he wrote it, nor with his powers of judgment. As far as the content is concerned, *The Chemical Wedding* shows that it was written through *intuition.* People can write down things of this kind with a certain aptitude for them, even if their own powers of judgment and experience in life take no part in what is written. Nevertheless, what is written down can convey full reality. On the basis of its content one is compelled to accept *The Chemical Wedding* as a communication about a spiritual current that actually exists. The assumption that Valentin Andreae wrote it out of *intuition* illuminates his later attitude toward Rosicrucianism. As a young man he had the capacity to give a picture of this spiritual current without calling upon his own means of knowledge. Andreae's own path of knowledge found its development later when he became the pietistic theologian, whereas his spiritual receptivity that could reflect *intuition* receded in his soul. Later he himself philosophized about what he had written in his youth. He did this as early as 1619 in his *Turris Babel* (Tower of Babel).

The connection between the later Andreae and the youthful Andreae who wrote from intuition was not clear to him. If we consider Andreae's attitude toward what *The Chemical Wedding* contains in this light, we are obliged to keep in mind only what the document contains — without relation to anything expressed by him at any time concerning his connections with Rosicrucianism. What it was possible to reveal about this spiritual stream in Andreae's day was presented by a person suited to do so. Whoever believes from the outset that it is impossible for the spiritual life as it takes effect in world phenomena to be revealed in such a way as this, will certainly be constrained to reject what is said here. There may be people, however, who, without superstitious prejudices, will quietly consider the "case of Andreae," and by it gain the conviction of the possibility of this kind of revelation.

Part 4

ROSICRUCIANISM AND MODERN INITIATION

— e l e v e n —

The Life of the Spirit in the Middle Ages

*With the next four lectures, which make up a cycle or course of lectures —
a continuous, coherent narrative — Steiner's language and the mode of presentation change. The lectures were the concluding act of his laying of the
Foundation Stone for the new, refounded Anthroposophical Society of which
he himself was the head (previously he had not been part of the society, but
had functioned solely as its "teacher.") All this happened during the period
extending through the Holy Nights (Christmas and New Year) 1923–24.
A year and a half later, Steiner was dead. The time remaining to him was
therefore critical. Whether because of this, or because of the changing nature
of the times and his relationship to anthroposophy, he began to speak much
more directly and straightforwardly, and in "ordinary language." These lectures, therefore, while being in a sense the most "anthroposophical" of the
lectures in this book, are at the same time among the most accessible for
those who are willing to enter into the spirit of Steiner's endeavor.*

*The first lecture begins with the Middle Ages: how advanced human
beings (philosophers, theologians, alchemists) in the period between the
ninth and the thirteenth centuries thought when they thought about and*

researched nature, humanity, and the cosmos. This was before what we know as historical Rosicrucianism arose, but for Steiner it marks an important moment in the new beginning of the spiritual-scientific movement whose twentieth-century continuer he saw himself to be. Therefore Steiner felt it was important that we know how to understand what they wrote. They were, after all, proto-Rosicrucians and proto-anthroposophists. It is upon their researches and deep consciousness that we must build.

Toward the end of this lecture, Rudolf Steiner comes to an important aspect of Rosicrucianism — the description of humanity as the "fourth hierarchy." No phrase better resumes the high responsibility this tradition places on us.

— ◆ —

Following up on what I brought before you in the lectures given at our Christmas Foundation Meeting, I would like to speak now of the movement leading us to research into the life of the spirit.

I refer to the movement spoken of under the name of Rosicrucianism (or some other esoteric designation). I should like to take this opportunity to give you a picture of its inner aspect and nature. For this, I must first of all, by way of introduction, say something about the whole way of forming ideas that had become customary around about the ninth, tenth, and eleventh centuries, and has since then only gradually disappeared. It could be found here and there among stragglers, as it were, even as late as the nineteenth century. I do not intend today to go into the whole history of the movement, but rather to present some views and ideas that you are to think of as experienced inwardly by certain people belonging to those earlier centuries. It is not generally realized that we merely need to go back a comparatively short time in history to find that the scholars of earlier times possessed a world of ideas altogether different from our own.

Today, we speak of chemical substances. We enumerate seventy or eighty distinct chemical elements, but we have no idea how very little we are saying when we name one substance oxygen, another nitrogen, and so on. Oxygen, for instance, is something that is present only under certain definite conditions — conditions of warmth, for example — and no reasonable person can unite a view of reality with something that, when the temperature is raised by so and so many degrees, is no longer present in the same measure or manner as it is under the conditions that obtain for human physical life on Earth.

The realization of facts like this underlay research during the earlier centuries of the Middle Ages. The research of those times set out to get beyond what has only relative existence to arrive at real existence.

I have frequently spoken of a transition between the ninth and tenth centuries. Up to that time human perceptions were still altogether spiritual. It would never have occurred to a philosopher of the ninth century, for example, to imagine Angels, Archangels, or Seraphim as having less reality — that is, pure reality — than those physical human beings seen with physical eyes. You will find that before the tenth century, scholars always spoke of the spiritual beings, the "cosmic intelligences," as one speaks of beings one actually meets in life. The people of that time were of course well aware that the day was long past when the "beholding" of spiritual beings was a common human experience, but they knew that in certain circumstances some apprehension of their presence could still be had. One must not, for instance, overlook the fact that on into the ninth and tenth centuries countless priests of the Catholic Church were quite conscious of how, in the course of their celebration of the Mass, it would happen that in this or that act of the ritual they encountered spiritual beings, intelligences of the cosmos.

With the coming of the tenth century, however, all such direct and immediate contact with the cosmic intelligences began to disappear from human consciousness. In its place consciousness of the elements of the cosmos arose — the earthy element; the fluid, or watery, element; the airy element; and the warm, or fiery, element. Just as previously people had spoken of cosmic intelligences ruling the movements of the planets, leading the planets across the constellations of the fixed stars, and so forth, now they began to speak rather of the immediate environment of the earth. They spoke of the elements of earth, water, air, fire. Of chemical substances in the modern sense of the word, they had as yet no knowledge; that came much later.

Indeed, it would be a great mistake to imagine that philosophers of the fourteenth century, even in some sense those of the eighteenth century, had ideas concerning the elements — warmth, air, water, earth — that resembled ideas we have today. Today, we speak of warmth merely as a condition in which bodies exist. No one speaks any more of an actual "warmth ether." Air and water have likewise become completely abstract for people today. It is time we studied the ideas of these earlier centuries and learned to enter into a true understanding of them. Today, therefore, I should like to give you a picture, showing you how a philosopher of those times would speak to his pupils.

When I wrote my *Outline of Esoteric Science,* I had to make the account of Earth's evolution fit just a little with the prevailing ideas of the present day. In the thirteenth century one would have been able to give the account quite differently. The following might then have been found, for example, in a certain chapter of *An Outline of Esoteric Science.*

An idea would have been called up, to begin with, of the beings who may be designated as the beings of the first hierarchy: Seraphim, Cherubim, Thrones. The Seraphim would have been characterized as beings with whom there is no subject and object, with whom subject and object are one and the same; they would not say, "Around me are various objects," but, "The world is, and I am the world, and the world is I." Such beings know only of themselves, and this knowledge of themselves is for them an inner experience of which human beings have a weak reflection when they are filled, let us say, with burning enthusiasm. It is often quite difficult to make people today understand what is meant by "burning enthusiasm." In the beginning of the nineteenth century people still knew better what it is than they do today. In those days it could still happen that when some poem or other was read aloud people were filled with enthusiasm — forgive me, but it was so. People today would say they had all gone out of their minds — they were so moved, so warmed! Nowadays people freeze up just when you expect them to be "enthused." Now, by lifting this experience of "enthusiasm" into consciousness — by letting it completely fill consciousness — people could form an idea of the inner life of the Seraphim. The idea of the Cherubim, on the other hand, people then experienced as a bright, clear element in consciousness — as an experience full of light, one in which thought turns at once into light, illuminating everything. The element of consciousness of the Thrones, for its part, was conceived of as "sustaining" — "bearing" — the worlds in grace.

There you have one sketch that could have been drawn for that earlier consciousness. I could go on speaking about it for a long time. For the moment, I simply wanted to tell you how in those days one would first of all have tried to describe the Seraphim, Cherubim, and Thrones in the true qualities of their being.

One would then have gone on to say that the choirs of Seraphim, Cherubim, and Thrones work together, in such a way that the Thrones found and establish a kind of seed or kernel; the Cherubim let their own light-filled being stream forth from this center; and the Seraphim wrap the whole in a mantle of warmth and enthusiasm that radiate deep into cosmic space. [Here Rudolf Steiner draws on the blackboard.]

All that I have drawn is beings: in the middle, the Thrones; around them, the Cherubim; and on the periphery, the Seraphim. All is essential being — beings who move and weave one into another, who act, think, will, feel in one another. It is all being. And now, if some other being having the right sensitiveness were to take its path through the space where the Thrones have in this manner established a kernel, where the Cherubim have made a kind of circling around it, and where the Seraphim have, as it were, enveloped the whole — if a being with the required sensitiveness were to come into this realm of activity of the first hierarchy, it would feel warmth in varying differentiations: here greater warmth, there less. Everything would be a soul experience, and yet at the same time a sensory experience; that is to say, when the being felt warm in soul, the feeling would be the feeling you have when you are in a well-warmed room.

Such a united building-up by beings of the first hierarchy did actually once take place in the universe; it formed what we call "Saturn" existence. The warmth is merely the expression of the fact that these beings are there; it is nothing more than the expression of the fact that the beings are there.

Let me try to make clearer to you what I mean. Suppose you have an affection for a certain person. His presence gives you warmth. But now someone comes along who is frightfully abstract and says, "The person himself does not interest me; I will think him away. I am interested in the warmth he gives off around him." Or suppose he or she doesn't even say, "The warmth this person sheds around him is all that interests me," and instead says, "The warmth as such is all that interests me." This is nonsense, of course, and you see that at once, for if the person who sheds the warmth is not there, then the warmth is not there. The warmth is only there when the person is there. In itself the warmth is nothing. The person must be there, if the warmth is to be there. Even so must Seraphim, Cherubim, and Thrones be there; if the beings are not there, neither is the warmth. The warmth is merely the revelation of Seraphim, Cherubim, and Thrones. Now in the time we are speaking of, everything was just as I have described it, even to the picture that I have drawn on the blackboard. People spoke of elements. By the element of warmth they understood Cherubim, Seraphim, Thrones, and that is the Saturn existence; that is Saturn.

And then the description would have gone further. It would have been said that the Seraphim, Cherubim, and Thrones alone have the power to produce something of the nature of Saturn. None but the highest hierarchy is capable of placing such an existence into the cosmos. But once this highest hierarchy had placed it there to start a new world creation, then evolution could go further. This "Sun" of Seraphim, Cherubim, and Thrones could carry evolution further. This happened as follows.

Beings of the second hierarchy — Kyriotetes, Dynamis, Exusiai — beings generated by the Seraphim, Cherubim, and Thrones, pressed into the space that had been "formed" through the working of Seraphim, Cherubim, and Thrones, formed and fashioned to Saturn warmth. Then younger, cosmically younger, beings entered. And how do these cosmically younger beings work? Whereas Cherubim, Seraphim, and Thrones revealed themselves in the element of warmth, the beings of the second hierarchy take form in the element of light. You have Saturn; it is dark, it gives warmth. And now within the dark world of Saturn something new begins to arise through the working of the sons of the first hierarchy, through the Exusiai, Dynamis, and Kyriotetes. What is it that is now able to arise within the Saturn warmth? The penetration of the second hierarchy signifies an inner illumination. Saturn warmth is inwardly shone through with light. (At the same time it also becomes denser; instead of the warmth element alone, there is now also air.) Thus we have the entry of the second hierarchy, coming to revelation in light.

You must clearly understand that it is in very deed and truth beings who press their way into the Saturn existence. One who has the requisite power of perception sees the event as a penetration of light; the light reveals the path of the beings. And where light enters, there we find, too, under certain conditions, shadow, darkness, dark shadow. Through the penetration by the second hierarchy in the form of light, shadow also comes about.

What was this shadow? It was air. Right on into the fifteenth and sixteenth centuries people knew for a fact what air is. Today we know only that air consists of oxygen, nitrogen, and so forth, which is much the same as saying that a watch consists of glass and silver. That really tells me nothing at all about the watch as watch. And nothing at all is told about air as a cosmic phenomenon when it is said to consist of oxygen and nitrogen. We tell very much, on the other hand, if we know that air comes forth from the cosmos as the shadow of light. In actual fact, with the entry of the second hierarchy into the Saturn warmth, we have the entry of light and of the shadow of light, air.

And therewith we have "Sun." Such is the way one would have had to speak in the thirteenth century.

And what follows after this? The further evolution comes about through the working of the sons of the second hierarchy: the Archai, Archangels, and Angels. The second hierarchy accomplished the entry of the element of light. This light has drawn after it its shadow, the darkness of air, which is not the indifferent, neutral darkness that belongs to Saturn — the darkness that is simply absence of light — but the darkness that is the antithesis of light. And now to this element of light the third hierarchy — Archai, Archangels, Angels — add by virtue of their nature and being a new element, an element that is like our human desire, like our impulse to strive after something, to long for something.

Thereby the following comes to pass.

Imagine that some Archai (or Archangel) enters, and encounters an element of light, encounters, as it were, a place of light. In this place of light, the being (the Archai or Archangel) will then receive, through its very receptivity for the light, the urge, the desire for darkness. The Angels carry light into darkness, or they may carry darkness into light. These beings thus become mediators, messengers between light and darkness. As a result, what previously has shone only in light and drawn after it its shadow, the darkness of air, now begins to shine in color, to glow in a play of color. Light begins to appear in darkness, darkness in light. The third hierarchy create color; from light and darkness they conjure color.

Here we may turn to something historical, to something that is documented. In the time of Aristotle people still knew, when they gave themselves up to contemplation in the Mysteries, whence colors come; they knew that it is the beings of the third hierarchy who have to do with color. Aristotle himself, in his color harmony, declares that color signifies a working together of light and darkness. But this spiritual element in human thought, whereby Aristotle knew that behind warmth were beings of the first hierarchy, behind light and its shadow darkness, beings of the second hierarchy, and behind the iridescent play of color shimmering in a great cosmic harmony, beings of the third hierarchy — this spiritual element in human thought has been lost. And nothing is left today but the unhappy Newtonian theory of color. Initiates continued to smile at Newton's theory until the eighteenth century; then it became an article of faith for professional physicists.

A person must really have lost all knowledge of the spiritual world to speak of Newton's color theory. People who are still inwardly stimulated by the spiritual world, as was the case with Goethe, will resist it. They will try to place the truth of the matter before public opinion, as Goethe did, and attack Newton's theory with all their might. Goethe never censured so severely as he censured Newton; he went for him and his theory hammer and tongs. Such a thing is incomprehensible nowadays, for the simple reason that in our time anyone who does not recognize the Newtonian theory of color is a fool in the eyes of the physicists. But things were different in Goethe's time. He did not stand alone. True, he stood alone as one who spoke openly on the matter, but there were others who knew, even as late as the end of the eighteenth century, whence color comes, who knew with absolute certainty how color wells up from within the spiritual.

Let us follow evolution further. We have seen that air is the shadow of light. And when light arises, under certain conditions we find the dark shadow. Similarly, when color is present and works as a reality — which it can do when it penetrates and flames up into the air element, when in a word it *is* something, is a reality flashing and sparkling in the element of air — when this is so, then, under certain conditions we get pressure, counter-pressure, and out of the quite real color the fluid element of water comes into being. As, for cosmic thinking, the shadow of light is air, so is water the reflection, the creation of color in the cosmos.

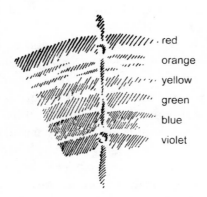

red
orange
yellow
green
blue
violet

You will say, No, I cannot understand that. But try just once to comprehend color in its truest meaning. Red — you certainly do not think that red, in its essence, is the neutral surface it is generally thought to be. Red is something that "attacks" you. I have often spoken of this. You want to run away from red; it thrusts you back. Blue-violet, on the other hand, you want to run after. It runs away from you all the time; it grows deeper and deeper. In the colors everything is alive. The colors are a world in themselves, and the soul element in the world of color simply cannot exist without movement; we ourselves, if we follow the colors with soul experience, must follow with movement.

People gaze wide-eyed at a rainbow. But if you look at a rainbow with a little imagination, you may be able to see elemental beings. They are full of activity and demonstrate that activity in a most remarkable way.

Here (at yellow) you see some of them flowing from the rainbow, continually coming out of it. They move across, and the moment they reach the lower end of the green they feel drawn to it. You see them disappear at this point (green). On the other side they come out again. To one who views it with imagination, a whole rainbow reveals the spirit — flowing out and disappearing again within. It is in fact like a spiritual cylinder, wonderful to behold. And you may observe too how these spiritual beings come forth from the rainbow with extreme fear, and then how they go in with an absolutely invincible courage. When you look at the red-yellow, you see fear streaming out, and when you look at the blue-violet you have the feeling that there all is courage and bravery of heart.

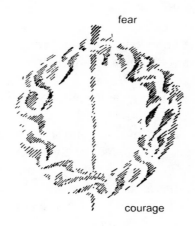

fear

courage

Picture it to yourself: What I see before me is not just a rainbow. Here beings are coming out of it; there beings are disappearing into it. Here is anxiety and fear; there is courage. And now the courage disappears again. That is the way to look at the rainbow. But now, imagine it is there before you in all its colors — red, yellow, and so on; and it receives a certain density. You can easily imagine how this will give rise to the element of water. And in this watery element spiritual beings live, beings that are actually a kind of copy of the beings of the third hierarchy.

There is no doubt about it: if we want to approach those who were possessed of real knowledge in the eleventh, twelfth, and thirteenth centuries, we must be ready to understand such things. As a matter of fact, without this we cannot approach even the philosophers of still later times. We cannot understand Albertus Magnus, if we read him with the knowledge we have today. We must read him with a kind of knowledge that takes account of the fact that spiritual things such as we have been considering were still a reality for him: only then will we understand how he uses his words.

Thus we have air and water, coming into existence as a reflection of the hierarchies, first air and then water. The hierarchies themselves dive in, as it were. The first hierarchy pour in their very selves as warmth, the second enter in the form of light, and the third hierarchy as color. And therewith we have reached our Earth's Moon stage.

We come then to the "fourth" hierarchy. I am telling you this, remember, as it was thought of in the twelfth to thirteenth centuries. Today, we do not speak of the fourth hierarchy, but people still did so then. What is this fourth hierarchy? It is we. We — human beings — are the fourth hierarchy. But the fourth hierarchy did not mean the two-legged beings who go about the world today, ageing year by year. To one who had true knowledge, human beings as we know them on Earth today would have seemed strange beings indeed. No, in those times they spoke of original Humanity, of Humanity before the Fall, which still bore a form that gave it power over the earth, even as the Angels and Archangels and Archai had power over our Earth's Moon stage, the second hierarchy over the Sun stage, and the first hierarchy over the Saturn stage. They spoke of the Human Being in original existence as Earth Human, and then they were right to speak of Earth Human as the fourth hierarchy. And with this fourth hierarchy came *life* — as a gift, it is true, of the higher hierarchies, but they had been holding it only as a possession they did not themselves use but guarded and protected. Into the world of color, into the iridescent world of changing color, of which I have been able to give you only the merest hints and suggestions, came life.

You will say, Was then nothing alive before this time? My dear friends, you can understand how it was by looking at the human being. Your I and astral body do not have life, yet they have being, they are. What is of the soul and spirit does not need life. Life begins with your etheric body. And the etheric body is external, it is of the nature of a sheath. Thus it is only after the Moon stage, only with the present Earth stage of existence that life enters the evolution to which our Earth belongs. The world of moving, glancing color is quickened to life. And now, not only do Angels, Archangels, and Archai experience a longing desire to carry darkness into light, and light into darkness, thereby calling forth the play of color in the planet — now a desire becomes manifest to experience this play of color as something inward, to feel it all inwardly: when darkness dominates light, to feel weakness, lassitude; when light dominates darkness, to feel activity. For what is really happening when you run? When you run, light is predominating in you over darkness; when you sit and are lazy and indolent, then darkness is predominating over light. It is all a play of color, an iridescent play of color, not physical, but of the soul. Color permeated with life, in its iridescence penetrated with life — this is what appeared with the coming of the fourth hierarchy, humankind. And in this moment of cosmic becoming, the forces that had been active in the play of color began to build contours, began to fashion forms. Life, as it rounded off and molded the colors, called into being the hard, firm form of the crystal. And thus we come to the Earth stage of existence.

The kinds of things I have been describing to you were once fundamental truths to medieval alchemists, esotericists, Rosicrucians, and others who flourished (though history tells us little of them) from the ninth century to about the fifteenth century. And, as I say, some stragglers may be found as late as the eighteenth and even at the beginning of the nineteenth century. In later times, however, they were always considered strange and eccentric. Only then, let us say with the turn of the nineteenth century, did the knowledge become entirely hidden. Only then did people begin to acquire a view of the world that led them to a point of view that I would like to indicate in the following way.

Imagine, my dear friends, that here we have a human being. Suppose I cease to have any interest in this person, but I take his clothes and hang them on a coat hanger that has a knob here above. From now on I take no further interest in the person and I tell myself: There is the person — I have no concern with what can be put into these clothes. That, the coat hanger with the clothes on it, is the person. This is what really happened with the elements. It did not interest people any longer that behind warmth, or fire, is the first hierarchy;

behind light and air, the second hierarchy; behind what we call chemical (or color) ether and water the third hierarchy; and behind the life element and earth the fourth hierarchy, humankind. The peg, with the hanger, and on it the clothes — that is all that counts.

There you have the first act of the drama. The second act begins with Kant. There is the hanger, and the clothes hanging on it; and clever people begin to philosophize in true Kantian fashion as to what the "thing-in-itself" of these clothes may be. And they come to the conclusion that the "thing-in-itself" of the clothes cannot be known. Very clever, very clever indeed. Do away with the human being and have only the coat hanger with the clothes, and you can of course proceed to philosophize over the clothes, you can make most beautiful speculations. You can either philosophize in the way Kant did, and say, "The 'thing-in-itself' cannot be known," or in the fashion of Helmholtz and think to yourself, "But these clothes, they cannot of themselves have forms; there is nothing really there but tiny, whirling specks of dust, tiny atoms, which hit and strike each other, and behold, the clothes are held in their form."

Yes, my friends, that is the way thought has developed in recent times. It is all abstract, shadowy. And this is the kind of thinking we live in today, this speculative way of thinking; it gives the stamp to our whole natural-scientific outlook. And when we do not admit that we think in this atomistic way, then we do it most of all. For we are far from being ready to admit that it is quite unnecessary to dream in this way of a whirling dance of atoms, and that what we have rather to do is to put the being back into the clothes. This is however the very thing the renewal of spiritual science must now set out to do.

I wanted to indicate to you today, in a series of pictures, how people thought in earlier centuries and to help you see what is really contained in the older writings, although it has been obscured. The obscurity has led to incidents that are not without interest. A Swedish scientist of today has reprinted a passage from the writings of Basil Valentine and interpreted it in terms of modern chemistry.[1] He could not possibly come to any other conclusion than that it is nonsense, for that is what it appears to be if, in the modern sense, one thinks of a chemist standing in a laboratory, making experiments with retorts and other up-to-date apparatus. What Basil Valentine gives in this passage is a fragment of embryology, expressed in pictures. Yes, that is what he gives — a fragment of embryology. If you approach it from the modern standpoint, it looks like a laboratory experiment, which then proves to be nonsense. You cannot possibly expect to reproduce the real processes of embryology in a retort, unless you are like the Wagner of Goethe's *Faust*, who is still inclined to see things more from the perspective of earlier centuries.

It is time these things were understood. And in connection with the great truths of which I was able to speak during the Christmas Foundation Meeting, I shall have something still further to say concerning the history and destiny of the spiritual life of humankind during the last few centuries.

— twelve —

Hidden Centers of the Mysteries
in the Middle Ages

Steiner now moves to the immediate precursors of historical Rosicrucianism. As befits his new, direct style, the presentation is clear and unambiguous. We learn of the thirteenth and fourteenth century backgrounds. Reading what he has to say of the beginning of this period, we might think well of Brunetto Latini and Dante Alighieri. Then, speaking of Ramon Lull, he is more explicit. The message is clear. As Steiner says, "it is to such efforts to find knowledge that we must trace the rise of Rosicrucianism."

Yesterday I began to speak to you of the search for knowledge of the spiritual during the tenth century or so after Christ. We learned how such efforts were still seriously undertaken as late as the end of the eighteenth and beginning of the nineteenth century and I tried to tell you something of their results. Today I should like to touch particularly on their historical aspect.

We have to remember that the Mysteries of ancient times were of such a nature and character that in the Mystery centers an actual meeting with the gods could take place. In the lectures recently given at the Christmas Foundation Meeting, I described how the human being who was an initiate or was about to receive initiation did truly meet with the gods. And it was actually possible in those times to discover places that by their very locality were expressly fitted to induce such meeting with the gods.[1]

The founding impulses for all the more ancient civilizations arose from such centers. Gradually, however, they disappeared, and from the fourth century onward were no longer to be found in their original form. Here and there we may come upon survivals, but the knowledge is no longer so exact or reliable. Not that initiation ever ceased;

it was the form in which the candidates found their way that changed. I have already indicated how things were in the Middle Ages. I have told you how here and there were individuals, living simple, humble, unpretentious lives, who did not gather around them a circle of official students in one particular place, but whose students were scattered in various directions in accordance with karma — with the karma, that is, of humankind or with the karma of some people or nation. I have described one such instance in what I said about Johannes Tauler in my book *Mystics after Modernism*.

There is no need for me to speak about that here. I should like however to tell you of another typical example, one that had very great influence, lasting from the twelfth and thirteenth on into the fifteenth centuries. The spiritual streams that were working during these centuries are in large measure to be traced to the events I would like to speak of now. Let me give you first a sketch, as it were, of the situation.

The time when these events took place is around A.D. 1200. There were at that time a great number of people, especially younger people, who felt within them the urge for higher knowledge, for a union with the spiritual world — one may indeed truthfully say, for a meeting with the gods. And the whole situation and condition of the times was such that very often it looked as though a person who was searching and striving in this way found his or her teacher almost by chance. (In those days one could not find one's teacher through books; it could come about only in an entirely personal way.) But although it might look from without like a chance happening, in reality deep connections of destiny were at work in the event. And it was so in the case of the student of whom I want now to tell you.

This student found a teacher in a place in Middle Europe through such an apparently chance event. He met with an older man of whom he at once had the feeling: He will be able to lead me farther in that search that is the deepest impulse of my soul. And now let me give you the gist of a conversation between them. I do not of course mean that only one such conversation took place; I am compressing several into one.

The student speaks to the teacher and tells him of his earnest desire to be able to see into the spiritual world; but it seems to him as though the nature of the human being as it is in that time — somewhere about the twelfth or thirteenth century — does not allow him to penetrate to the spiritual worlds. "Nevertheless," he says, "I cannot but feel that in nature one has something that is the work, the creation, of divine-spiritual beings. When one looks at what the objects of nature are in their deeper meaning, when one observes how the processes of nature take their course, one is bound to recognize that behind these creations stands the working of divine-spiritual beings. One cannot however get through to them."

The student, who was a young man somewhere between twenty-five and twenty-eight, felt strongly and definitely that the human being of his time, because of the particular kind of connection that the physical body has with the soul, could not reach the divine-spiritual beings because of internal obstacles.

The teacher began by putting him to the test. He said to him, "You have your eyes, you have your ears. Look with your eyes on the things of nature, hear with your ears what goes on in nature; the spiritual reveals itself through color and through tone, and as you look and listen, surely you cannot but feel how it reveals itself in these."

The student replied, "Yes, but when I use my eyes, when I look out into the world, with all its color, it is as though my eye stops the color, as though the color suddenly turns numb and cold when it reaches the eye. When I listen with my ear to tones, it is as though the sounds turn to stone in my ear; and these frozen colors and dead, hard sounds will not let the spirit of nature through."

"But," said the teacher, "is there not also revelation — the revelation of the religious life? In religion you are taught how gods made and fashioned the world, and how the Christ entered the evolution of time and became human. What nature cannot give you, does not revelation give?"

And the student said, "Revelation does indeed speak powerfully to my heart, but I cannot comprehend it; I cannot connect what is out there in nature with what revelation says to me. It is impossible to bring the two into relation with one another. Just as I do not comprehend nature, just as nature reveals nothing to me, so neither do I comprehend the revelation of religion."

And the teacher answered, "I understand you well. If you must speak thus, if it is with your heart and soul as you say, then you cannot, as you stand in the world today, comprehend either nature or revelation: For you live in a body that has undergone the Fall [such was the manner of speaking in those days], and the 'fallen' body is not in accord with the earthly environment in which you are living. This environment does not afford the conditions for using your senses, your feeling, and your understanding in such a way that you may behold in nature and also in revelation a light, an enlightenment that comes from the gods. If you are willing, I will lead you out of the nature of your earthly environment, which is simply unsuited to your being; I will lead you away from it and give you the opportunity of coming to a better understanding both of revelation and of nature." And the teacher and student discussed when this should take place.

Then, one day, the teacher led the student up a very high mountain, whence the surface of the earth with its trees and flowers could no longer be seen at all. As the student stood there with his teacher, all he could see below him was a kind of sea of cloud, which completely covered the earth he was familiar with. You know how this often is so on high mountains. Up there, the student was far removed from the affairs of Earth — at all events, the situation suggested this. He looked out into space above, and saw great billowing clouds, and below him, too, could see only a surging sea, as it were, composed entirely of cloud. Morning mist, and the breath of morning in the air! Then the teacher began to speak to the student. He spoke of the wide spaces of the worlds, of the cosmic distances, and of how, when one gazes out into these far spaces in the nighttime, one sees the stars shining forth from afar. And as he continued telling him many things, gradually the heart of the student was removed far away from the earth, and wholly given up to nature, to nature in the essential features of her existence.

The preparation continued until the student came into a mood of soul that may be indicated by the following comparison. It was as though — and not just for a moment, but for quite a long time — all that he had ever experienced during his life on Earth in this incarnation was something he had dreamed. The scene that lay spread out before him, the surging waves of cloud, the wide sea of cloud with here and there a drift rising up to nearer view like the crest of a wave, the far spaces of the universe, broken here and there by rising shapes of cloud, and scarcely even that, for there was no more than a glimpse now and then of cloud forms in the far distances — this whole scene, showing so little variation, having so little content in comparison with the manifold variety of his experiences down below on the surface of the earth, was nevertheless for the student now the content of his waking consciousness. Everything he had ever experienced on Earth was no more than the memory of a dream he had dreamed. Now, now, so it seemed to him, he had woken up. And as he grew gradually more and more awake, behold, from a cleft in a rock that he had hitherto not noticed, a boy came forth — a boy ten or eleven years old. The boy made a strange impression upon him, for he at once recognized in him his own self in his tenth or eleventh year. What stood before him was indeed the spirit of his youth.

... The student thus stood before the spirit of his boyhood, his very self. He, with his twenty-five or twenty-eight years, stood face to face with the spirit of his youth. And a conversation took place, guided by the teacher, but nevertheless actually taking place between the student and his own younger self. Such a conversation has a unique character.... For when people are face to face with the spirit of their own youth — and such a thing is always possible — then they give something of riper understanding to the childlike ideas of the spirit of their youth, and at the same time the spirit of their youth gives something of its freshness, its childlikeness, to what the older person possesses; and through the fact of this mutual interchange, the meeting becomes peculiarly fruitful. This conversation had the result that the student came to understand revelation — the revelation that is given in religion.

The conversation turned especially on Genesis, the beginning of the Old Testament, and on the Christ becoming Human. Under the guidance of the teacher and because of the special kind of fruitfulness that the conversation possessed, it ended with the student saying these words: "Now I understand what spirit works in revelation. Only when one is transplanted, as it were, far away from the earthly into the heights of the ether, there to comprehend the etheric heights with the help of the power of childhood — this power being projected into the later years of life — only then does one understand revelation correctly. And now I understand why it is that the gods have given us revelation — for human beings are unable, in their earthly state, to see through the works of nature and discover the working of the gods behind them. Therefore the gods gave them revelation, which is incomprehensible to mature reflection, but can be understood when childhood comes to life again in the years of maturity. Thus to understand revelation is really something abnormal."

All this made a powerful impression on the student. And the impression remained; he could not forget it. The spirit of his youth vanished. The first phase of the instruction was over. A second had now to come. And the second took its course in the following way.

Once more the teacher led the student forth, but this time on a different path. He did not now lead him up to a mountaintop, but took him to a mountain where he knew there was a cave through which they could pass to deep inner clefts, going down as far as the strata of the mines. Thus the student was now with the teacher, not in the etheric heights high above the earth, but in the depths, far below the surface of the earth.

Once again it was for the consciousness of the student as if all he had ever experienced on Earth went past him like a dream. For he was living down there in an environment in which his consciousness was particularly awakened to perceive how he himself was related to the depths of the earth. What took place for him was really none other than what lies behind legends like those told, for example, of the Emperor Barbarossa and his life in Kyffhäuser, or of Charlemagne and his life beneath a mountain near Salzburg. It was something of this nature that actually happened for the student, although of course only for a short time: he experienced a life in the depths of the earth, far removed from human life on the earth's surface.

The teacher was able this time, by speaking with the student in a special way, to bring to his consciousness the fact of his union with the very depths of the earth. There came forth from a wall an old man, who was less easily recognizable to the student than the spirit of his youth had been. Nevertheless he had the feeling that after many years he would himself become that old man. He felt, in fact, that there before him stood his own self in future old age. Then followed a similar conversation, this time between the student and himself as an old man — once again a conversation under the guidance of the teacher.

What resulted from the second conversation was altogether different from what followed from the first; for now a consciousness began to arise within the student of his own physical organization. He began to follow the circulation of the blood in his body, moving with it as it coursed through all the individual veins. He began to follow also in the same way the nerve fibers. He could moreover feel all the different organs of his organism and the meaning and significance of each for the whole. And he could feel too how what is related to the human being in the cosmos works into the human being. He felt the inward activity of the plant world, in its blossoming, in its rooting; he felt also how the earth's mineral element is at work in the human organism. Down there in the depths, he could feel how the forces of the earth, when brought into the human organism, circulate within the human being, how they create within us, undergoing change themselves, now destroying, now building up substances. He felt how the earth creates and weaves and has being — in us, in human beings. And the result of this conversation was that when the old man, who was himself, had disappeared, the student could say: "Now the earth, in which

I have been incarnated, has at last really spoken to me through her very being; a moment has come in my life when I have seen through the things and processes of nature, seen through them to the work of the gods that is behind the things and processes of nature."

The teacher then led the student out again onto the earth, and as he took leave of him, said, "Look now! Today, people and the earth are so poorly suited to each other that you have had to receive the 'revelation of religion' from the spirit of your own youth, receiving it on the mountain high above the earth. And you have had to receive the 'revelation of nature' deep within the earth, in clefts far below its surface. If you can now succeed in illuminating what your soul has felt in the hollow clefts of the earth with the light it has brought from the mountain, then you will attain wisdom."

Such was the path by which a deepening of the soul was brought about in those times — it was about A.D. 1200; this was how the soul became filled with wisdom. The student of whom I have been telling you was thereby brought to initiation. Now he knew what power he must put forth in his soul to rouse to activity the light of the heights and the feeling of the depths. Further instruction was then given by the teacher, showing him how self-knowledge really always consists in this: one perceives on the one hand what is high above earthly humankind, and on the other hand what is deep below it; and these two have to meet in humankind's inner being. Then human beings will be able to find within their own being the power of God the Creator.

The initiation I have described is a characteristic example of the initiations that led afterward to what we may designate as "medieval mysticism." It was a mysticism that sought self-knowledge, but always with the idea of finding in the self the way to the Divine. Later, this mysticism tended to become abstract, and the concrete union with the external world that was given to these students who were carried up into the etheric heights and down into the earth's depths, was no longer sought. Consequently we do not find in it the same deep stirring of the soul, nor did the whole experience attain such a degree of intensity. But there was still the search, there was still the impulse to seek within for God — God the Creator. Fundamentally speaking, all the seeking and striving of Meister Eckhart, of Johannes Tauler, and of the later mystics I have described in my book *Mystics after Modernism* owed its impulse to these earlier medieval initiates.

Those who worked faithfully in the sense of such medieval forms of initiation were however very much misunderstood, and it is by no

means easy for us to find out in our day what the students of the
medieval initiates were really like. It is, as you know, possible to go a
considerable distance along the path into the spiritual world. Those
who follow actively and resolutely what is given in my book *How
to Know Higher Worlds* do find the way into the spiritual worlds.
And everything that has been physically real in the past is of course
to be found now only in the spiritual world. Therefore such scenes
as I have been describing are also now only to be found there, for
there are no material documents that record them. There are however egions of the spiritual world that are hard to access, even for
a very advanced stage of spiritual power. In order to research into
these regions, we must have reached the point of actually communi-
cating with the beings of the spiritual world, in a quite simple, natural
way, as we communicate with people on Earth. Only when we have
attained so far shall we come to perceive and understand the connection between the initiates I have told you of and their students —
such a student, for example, as Ramon Lull, who lived from 1235 to
1315 and who, in what history can tell of him, seems to leave us full
of doubts and questions.

What you can learn of Ramon Lull by studying historical documents is indeed very scanty. But if you are able to enter into a personal
relationship with Ramon Lull — if you will allow me to use the expression; perhaps in the light of all I have been telling you lately, it
will not now sound paradoxical — if you are able to do this, then
Ramon Lull shows himself to you as someone quite different from
what the historical documents make him out to be. For he shows
himself to be preeminently a personality who, under the influence
and inspiration of the very initiate of whom I have spoken to you as
the "student," resolved to use all his power to bring about a renewal
in his own time of the way that the mysteries of the Word, or Logos,
lived among humankind in ages past. He determined to do this by
means of that self-knowledge for which, as I have been telling you,
so powerful an impulse was working in the twelfth and thirteenth
centuries. It is in the light of this resolve that we should read his so-
called *Ars Magna*. Ramon Lull said to himself: "When a human being
speaks, then what we have in speech is really a microcosm. What a
human being utters in speech is truly the whole being concentrated
in the organs of speech; the secret and mystery of each single word is
to be sought in the whole human being — and therefore in the great
world, in the cosmos."

And so Ramon Lull came to see that one must look for the secret of

Ramon Lull
Ars Magna

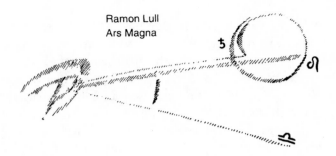

speech first in ourselves — by diving down, as it were, from the speech organs into the whole organism of the human being — and then in the cosmos; for the whole human organism can be explained and understood only through the cosmos. Let us suppose, for example, that we want to understand the true significance of the sound A (as in "father"). The point is that the sound A, which comes about through the forming and shaping of the outgoing breath, depends on a certain posture or gesture of the etheric body, which you can easily learn today. Eurythmy will show it to you, for this attitude of the etheric body is carried over in eurythmy to the physical body and becomes the eurythmic movement for the sound "ah."[2]

This was by no means fully clear to Ramon Lull; with him it was all more of an intuitive "divining." He did however come so far as to follow the inner attitude or gesture of the human being out into the cosmos, and then say, for example: If you look in the direction of the constellation of the Lion (Leo), and then in the direction of the Balance (Libra), the connection between the two lines of vision will give you A. Or again, say you turn your eye in the direction of Saturn. Saturn stops your line of vision, gets in the way. And if Saturn stands in front, for example, of the Ram (Aries), you have, as it were, to go around the Ram with Saturn. Then you receive from the cosmos the feeling of "oh."

Intuitive perceptions of this nature led Ramon Lull to find certain geometrical figures, whose points and sides he named with the letters of the alphabet. And he was quite sure that when one experiences an impulse to draw lines in the figures — diagonals, for instance, across a pentagon, uniting the five points in different ways — then one has to see in these lines different combinations of sounds; and these combinations of sounds express certain secrets of the World-All, the cosmos. Thus did Ramon Lull look for a kind of renaissance of the secrets of the Logos, as they were known and spoken of in the ancient Mysteries.

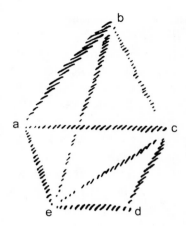

You will find all of this quite misrepresented in the historical documents. But when one enters little by little, as it were, into a personal relationship with Ramon Lull, then one comes to see how in all these efforts he was trying to find again the solution of the riddle of the Cosmic Word. And it is a fact that the students of the medieval initiates continued for several centuries to spend their lives in endeavors of this kind. It was an earnest and intensive striving, first to immerse oneself in the human being, and then to go forth from the human being and rise up into the secrets of the cosmos.

Thus did these sages — for we may truly call them such — seek to unite revelation with nature. They believed — and much of their belief was well founded — that in this way they could go behind both the revelation of religion and the revelation of nature. For it was quite clear to them that human beings, as they are now living on Earth, were destined and intended to become the fourth hierarchy, and that they had "fallen" from their true and proper nature and become more deeply involved in physical existence than they should be — and on this account lack the power to develop soul and spirit.

We must trace the rise of the Rosicrucians to such efforts to find knowledge.

At a place of instruction of the Rosicrucians, of the first, original Rosicrucians, the scene I have depicted to you today — the scene between the teacher and the student, at first upon a high mountain and then down in a deep cleft of the earth — reemerged like a kind of fata morgana, came again, as it were, like a ghost. We find the scene reflected there as knowledge. It taught the Rosicrucian students in that school to recognize how we must attain two things by inner effort and striving — two things, that is, if we wish to come to true self-knowledge and to recover our rightful place on Earth and be able at last to become in actual reality a member of the fourth hierarchy. For within the Rosicrucian school the possibility was given to recognize what students experienced when they saw before them in bodily form the spirit of their youth — namely, they recognized that the astral body, which was stronger at that moment than it otherwise ever is in life, had been loosened and that it was in this loosening of the astral body that one came to know the meaning and significance of revelation. And again, what had been experienced in the depths of the earth — that also was made clear to students in the Rosicrucian School. This time the astral body was seen to have been indrawn, so that it was deep within, and this enabled one to apprehend the certainty of one's own inner being.

Exercises also were found within Rosicrucianism, comparatively simple exercises. Symbolic figures were put before the students, to which they had to surrender in devotion and meditation. The force and power that possessed the soul through practicing devotion to these figures enabled students on the one hand to loosen the astral body and become like the student in the etheric heights on the mountaintop, and on the other hand, through compression, contraction of the astral body, to become like the student in the clefts of the earth. And it was then possible without the help, as before, of the external environment, simply through performing a powerful inner exercise, to enter one's inner being.

I have given you here a picture of something I have alluded to slightly in the preface to the new edition of my book *Mystics after Modernism*. I said there that what we find in Meister Eckhart, in Johannes Tauler, in Nicolas Cusa, in Valentine Wiegel, and the rest is a late product of a magnificent striving of humankind that preceded them. And this earlier striving in the spirit, this search for self-knowledge, in connection on the one hand with revelation and on the other hand with the illumination of nature, I wanted to bring before you today as one of the currents that run their course in the so-called Dark Ages — "so-called," because people have conjured darkness into the Middle Ages out of their own imagination. In reality there were in those times many enlightened persons; but those who today consider themselves the most highly enlightened are incapable of understanding the "light" of these medieval searchers after truth, and consequently remain themselves in the dark.

It is indeed quite characteristic of modern times that people take light for darkness and darkness for light. If, however, we are able to look into what lies behind the literature of those earlier times and see something of what the literature only reflects, then we may receive a powerful and lasting impression....

— thirteen —

The Time of Transition

Steiner now moves to reconsider the immediate context of the arising of the Fraternitas — the Brotherhood of the Rose Cross.

I spoke to you yesterday of the special form in which the results of research in the realm of spiritual knowledge were communicated in the Middle Ages. This form was, so to speak, the last experience vouchsafed to human beings before a door was shut for the evolution of the human spirit, a door that had been open for many centuries and had given entrance by way of natural gift and faculty into the spiritual world. The door was shut when the time came for human beings, so far as their instinctive faculties were concerned, to be placed outside the kingdom of the divine-spiritual will that had been controlling them. From that time forward they had to find in their own inmost being, in their own will, the possibility to evolve conscious freedom in the soul.

But, as you know, all such momentous movements of evolution take place slowly, step by step. And we can trace how the experience that the pupil had attained when led by the teacher up into the etheric heights and down into the deep clefts of the earth — an experience that was for the pupil directly connected with Nature (though not with Nature on the earth's surface) and that even in those times was no longer possible in the form it had taken in the ancient Mysteries — began now to come to human beings in a different, in a more unconscious, way.

Think for a moment how it was with those who were searching for knowledge about the year 1200 and through the following century. They would hear tell of how, only a short time before, a pupil had still been able to find a teacher like the one we were speaking of yesterday; they themselves however were now being directed to thought —

to human thinking — as the means of attaining knowledge. And in the succeeding years of the Middle Ages we can see this thinking developing and spreading, asserting itself in an impressive manner. It sets out on new paths with zeal, with sincere and wholehearted devotion, and the paths are followed by large circles of knowledge seekers.

At the same time what may truly be called spiritual science, knowledge of the spirit, continued, and after a few centuries we come to the time that saw the rise of Rosicrucianism. That event is connected with a change that took place in the whole spiritual world with respect to human beings. I can best describe the change by giving you once again a picture.

Mysteries in the old sense of the word were no longer possible in this time. There were, however, people who yearned for knowledge in the sense of the ancient Mysteries, and such people experienced severe conflicts of soul when they heard how in the past pupils had been led up to mountaintops and down into deep clefts of the earth; and they made great efforts, exerting themselves inwardly in all sorts of ways, hoping thereby to rouse the soul within them, that it might yet find the way. And one who is able to see such things can find in those times, as we have said, not places of the Mysteries, but gatherings of knowledge seekers who met together in an atmosphere warmed through and through with the glow of genuine piety. What appears later as Rosicrucianism — sound and genuine Rosicrucianism, as well as the degenerate and charlatan varieties — is to be traced back to people who came together in this simple way and sought so to temper their souls that it might be possible again for genuine spiritual knowledge to be found on Earth. In such a gathering, one that took place in quite unpretentious surroundings, just the simple living room of a kind of manor house, a few persons once met who, through certain exercises done in common by them all — exercises half thoughtful and meditative in character, half of the nature of prayer — had developed a mystical mood in which all shared. It was the same mystical mood of soul that was cultivated in later times by the so-called Brothers of the Common Life, and later still by the followers of Comenius and by many other Brotherhoods; and in the small circle I am telling of, it showed itself with a peculiar intensity. While these few people were gathered together in this intense mystical atmosphere of soul, making devotion, so to say, of their ordinary consciousness, of their whole intellect, it happened that a being came to them, not a being of flesh and blood like the teacher who led the earlier pupil up the mountain and down into the clefts of the earth, but a being who was able to appear in this little company only in an etheric body. However, he revealed himself as the very being who had guided that pupil about the year 1200. He was now in the after-death state, and descended to these people from the spiritual world; they had drawn him from beyond through the mood of soul that prevailed in them, one that was mystical, meditative, and pious.

My dear friends, so that no misunderstanding may arise, let me expressly emphasize that here there is no question of any sort of mediumistic power. The little company who were gathered there would have looked upon any use or any sanctioning of mediumistic powers as deeply sinful; they would have been led to do so by certain widely accepted ideas belonging to old and honored tradition. Particularly in those very communities of which I am telling you, to be a medium with all that went with it was considered to be not merely harmful, but sinful. This is because those people knew that being a medium accompanies a peculiar constitution of the physical body; they knew it is the physical body that gives the medium powers, spiritual powers. But they looked upon the physical body as "fallen," and could not but regard information that came by the help of mediumistic talents, under any circumstances, as acquired by the help of ahrimanic or luciferic powers.

In the times we are speaking of, all this was still clearly and exactly known. We should not, therefore, think of anything mediumistic in this connection. Everything was in the mood of mysticism and meditation, and in that alone. And it was the enhancing and strengthening of this mood through fellowship of soul that, so to speak, enchanted into the circle — but of his own free will — that disembodied human being, who was purely spiritual, and yet at the same time human. And now the being spoke to them, in a deeply solemn manner. "You are not quite prepared for my appearance. I am among you discarnate, without physical body, inasmuch as a time has come when for a short period of Earth existence the initiates of olden times are unable to appear in a physical body. The time will come when they can again do so — when the Michael period begins. I am come to reveal to you that the inner being of humankind remains unchanged, that the inner being of humankind, if it bears itself aright, can yet find the way to divine-spiritual existence. For a certain period of time, however, the human intellect and understanding will be so constituted that they will have to be suppressed in order for what is of the spirit to be able to speak to the human soul. Therefore remain in your mystic and pious mood. You have now received from me, all of you together, the picture, the imagination. What I have been able to give you is no more than an indication of what will come to fulfillment within you; you will go on further and find a continuation of what you have here experienced."

And now, from the number gathered there together three were chosen to establish a special union with the spiritual world, once more not at all through any kind of mediumistic powers but through a further development of the mystic, meditative, pious mood of soul. These three, who were particularly guarded and protected by the rest of the circle, really closely and intimately cared for by them, experienced from time to time a kind of "absence of mind." They were at such times, in their external bodily nature, wonderfully lovely and beautiful; their countenances shone like the Sun. And they wrote down, in symbols, revelations they received from the spiritual world. These symbolic revelations were the first pictures that revealed to the Rosicrucians what it behooved them to know of the spiritual world. The pictures contained a kind of philosophy, a kind of theology, and also a kind of medicine.

And the remarkable thing was that the others (it seems to me as though the others were four in number, so that the whole was a company of seven), after the experience they had had with their brothers — beholding how their eyes shone like the Sun and how their countenances were bright and radiant — these other four were able to give again in ordinary language what was in the symbols. The brothers whose destiny it was to bring the symbols from the spiritual world could only transcribe them and say, when they returned again into their ordinary consciousness, "We have been among the stars and among the spirits of the stars, and have found the old teachers of the esoteric knowledge." They could not themselves turn the symbolic pictures they drew into ordinary human speech. The others could, and did. And this is really the source of a great deal of the knowledge that passed over into the literature of theology that was philosophical in character (the theology not of the Church but rather of the laity) and into the literature of medicine.

And what had been thus received from the spiritual world in symbols was afterward communicated to small groups organized by the first Rosicrucians.

Again and again, in the time from the thirteenth to the fifteenth centuries, the possibility arose in certain very small groups for experiences of this nature. Revelations from the spiritual world came frequently to people in this or some similar way. Those who had to translate what was revealed in pictures were not always capable of rendering it quite faithfully; hence the want of clarity in much that has come down to us of the philosophy of this period. One has to discover for oneself what it really means, by seeking it again in the world of the spirit. However, those familiar with this kind of revelation that can be received from the spiritual world have always had the possibility of connecting with such revelations.

But picture to yourselves, my dear friends, what strange feelings must gradually have come over the people who had to receive the very highest knowledge (for what was given them was recognized as such) from a direction that was growing more and more foreign to them, indeed almost uncanny — for they could no longer see into the world from which the secrets came; ordinary consciousness could not reach so far.

It will readily be understood that such things could all too easily lead to charlatanism and even to fraud. Indeed at no time in human evolution have charlatanism and the highest and purest revelation stood so close to one another as in this period. It is difficult to distinguish the true from the false — and this is what has led many to regard the whole of Rosicrucianism as charlatanism. One can understand it, for the true Rosicrucians are extraordinarily hard to find among the charlatans, and the matter is all the more difficult and problematic because one has continually to bear in mind that the spiritual revelation comes from sources whose real quality and nature were in those days quite hidden.

The small circles gathered by the first Rosicrucians grew to a larger brotherhood, who went about unrecognized, appearing here and there in the world, generally with the calling of a physician, healing the sick and at the same time spreading knowledge as they went. And it was true that the spreading of very much of this knowledge was not without a certain embarrassment, inasmuch as those who carried it were not able to say anything at all about their connection to the spiritual world.

But in this pursuit of spiritual research we can detect the development of something of very great beauty. There are, as we said, the three brethren and the four. The three are able to attain their goal only when the four work with them; the two groups are absolutely interdependent. The three receive the revelations from the spiritual world; the four are able to translate the revelations into ordinary human language. What the three give would be nothing but utterly unintelligible pictures, were the four not able to translate them. And again, the four would have nothing to translate if the three did not receive their revelations, in picture form, from the spiritual world. This interdependence gave rise to the development within such communities of an inner brotherhood of soul, a brotherhood in knowledge and in spiritual life, which in those days was held in some circles to be among the very highest of human achievements. Such small groups of people did indeed learn to know the true worth of brotherhood. And gradually they came more and more to feel how in the evolution of humanity toward freedom the bond between human beings and gods would be completely severed were it not kept whole by this kind of brotherhood, where the one looks to the other, where the one is in very truth dependent on the other.

We have before us here a quality of soul that is wonderfully beautiful. And much that was written in those days possesses a charm that we understand only when we recognize how this atmosphere of brotherhood, which permeated the spiritual life of many circles in Europe in those times, has shed its radiant light into the writings.

We have however also to see how a mood that made people anxious began gradually to pervade this whole striving for knowledge. If one was unable oneself to approach the sources of spiritual revelation, it was in the last resort impossible to know whether these revelations were good or evil; and so, along with the recognition of what was good in them, anxiety began to be felt in regard to some of the influences. This anxiety then spread over large circles of people, who came in time to have fear, intense fear, of all knowledge.

The gradual development of the mood I speak of may be particularly well studied in two men. One is Raimund of Sabunda, who lived in the fifteenth century (he was born about 1430). Raimund of Sabunda is a remarkable man. If you study carefully what remains to us of his thought, you will have the feeling that this is surely almost the very same revelation that was communicated in full consciousness about the year 1200 by the teacher who took his pupil to the mountaintops and to the deep clefts of the earth! In Raimund of Sabunda, however, who belongs, as we saw, to the fifteenth century, it is all given in a more vague, impersonal style, philosophical in character, theological too, and medical. This is due to the fact that Raimund of Sabunda received his revelations by way of the genuine Rosicrucians, that is to say, by the path that had been opened by the great initiate of the twelfth century, whose work and influence I described to you yesterday and who continued to inspire people from the spiritual world in all that I have been relating to you today. For the revelation that came through Rosicrucianism is to be traced originally to this great initiate and those who were with him in the spiritual world; he set the mood and feeling of the whole teaching. By now, as I said, a certain anxiety regarding the teaching was beginning to take hold of people. Raimund of Sabunda, however, was a bold, brave spirit, one of those who are able to value ideas, who understand how to live in ideas. And so, although we notice in him a certain vagueness due to the fact that the revelations have their source, after all, in the spiritual world, in him we find as yet no trace of anxiety or fear in regard to knowledge.

All the more striking therefore is another — and very character- istic — example of that spiritual stream: Pico della Mirandola, who also belongs to the fifteenth century.

The short-lived Pico della Mirandola is a remarkable figure. If you make an intensive study of the fruits of his thought and con- templation, you see how the same initiative I have just described is everywhere active in them, a continuation of the wisdom of that old initiate by way of the Rosicrucian stream. But in Pico della Miran- dola you will observe a kind of shrinking back before the knowledge. Let me give you an instance. He makes, for example, the following declaration: Everything that happens on Earth — stones and rocks coming into being, plants living and growing and bearing fruit, ani- mals living out their lives — all this cannot be attributed to the forces of Earth. If anyone were to think: There is Earth, and it is the forces of Earth that produce what is on Earth, then he would have quite a wrong notion of the matter. The true view, according to Pico della Mirandola, is that up there are the stars and what happens on Earth is dependent on the stars. One must look up to the heavens if one wants to understand what happens on Earth. Speaking in the sense of Pico della Mirandola, we would have to say: You give me your hand, friend, but it is not just your feeling alone that is the cause of your giving me your hand; it is the star standing over you that gives you the impulse to hold out your hand. Ultimately everything that comes about has its source in the heavens, in the cosmos; what happens on Earth is but its reflection.

Pico della Mirandola expresses this as his firm conviction, and yet at the same time he says: But it is not for human beings to look up to these causes in the stars; human beings have to account only for the immediate cause on Earth.

From this point of view, Pico della Mirandola combats the astrology that he finds prevalent — and that is a most significant fact! He knows well that the old and genuine astrology expresses itself in the destinies of human beings. He knows that: it is for him a truth. And yet he says that one should not pursue astrology, that one should look only for the immediate causes, for the causes nearest at hand.

Note well what we have before us here. For the first time we are confronted with the idea of *boundaries* to knowledge. The idea shows itself however in a singular manner; it is still, let me say, quite human in character. Later, in Kant, in Du Bois-Reymond, you will be expressly told, "Human beings cannot cross the boundaries of knowledge." For them that is a fact, resting on an inner necessity. Not so with Pico della Mirandola, in the fifteenth century! He says, "What is on Earth has undoubtedly come about through cosmic causes. But human beings are called upon to forgo the attainment of a knowledge of these cosmic causes; they have to limit themselves to Earth." Thus we have in the fifteenth century, in such a markedly characteristic person as Pico della Mirandola, voluntary renunciation of the highest knowledge.

My dear friends, we have here reached an event in human history that is of the greatest imaginable importance. Human beings are making the resolve: We will renounce knowledge! And it is actually so that what comes to pass externally in such a person as Pico della Mirandola has also its counterpart in the spiritual.

It was again in one of those simple gatherings of Rosicrucians that, on the occasion of a ritual arranged for the purpose — it was during the latter half of the fifteenth century — people's knowledge of the stars was, in deeply solemn manner, offered up. What took place in that ritual, a ritual enacted with all the reverence proper to such a solemn occasion, may be expressed as follows. People stood before a kind of altar and said: "We resolve to feel ourselves at this moment responsible not for ourselves alone, nor for our community or our nation alone, nor even for the people of our time alone; we resolve to feel ourselves responsible for all people who have ever lived on Earth, we resolve to feel ourselves belonging to the whole of humankind. And we feel that what has really happened with human beings is that they have deserted the rank of the fourth hierarchy and have descended too deeply into matter [for the "Fall" was understood in this sense]. And so that humanity may be able to return to the rank of the fourth hierarchy, may be able to find for itself of its own free will what in earlier times gods have tried to find for it and with it, let now the higher knowledge be offered up for a season."

And certain beings of the spiritual world, who are not of humankind, who do not come to Earth in human incarnation, accepted the sacrifice in order to fulfill therewith certain purposes in the spiritual world. It would take us too far to speak of these here; we will do so another time. But thereby was the impulse for freedom made possible for human beings. This possibility was granted them by the spiritual world.

I tell you of this ritual to show you how everything that takes place in the external life of the physical senses has its spiritual counterpart; we merely have to look for it in the right place. For it can happen that such a ritual, enacted — I will not say, in this instance, with full knowledge, but enacted by persons who stand in connection with the spiritual world, can have very deep meaning; from it can radiate impulses for a whole culture, for a whole stream of civilization. For it is a fact that if we want to come to a clear knowledge of the fundamental coloring and tone of a particular epoch of history, we must look for the source in the spiritual; the spiritual spring whose forces stream through that epoch of time. Whatever, in the years that followed, showed itself to be of a truly spiritual nature was a kind of echo sounding on of this creative working out of unknown spiritual worlds. Side by side with the external materialism that developed in the succeeding centuries, we can always find here and there individuals who are living under the influence of that renunciation of higher knowledge.

I should like to give you a brief description of a type of person who might be met from the fifteenth century onward, right through the sixteenth, seventeenth, and eighteenth centuries. You might find such a person in some village, gathering herbs for an apothecary, or engaged in some other simple calling. If you are one who takes an interest in special forms and manifestations of the being of humankind as they show themselves in this or that individuality, then you may meet such persons. At first you will find them very reserved; they will speak but little, perhaps they will even turn your attention away from what you are trying to find in them by talking in a trivial way on purpose, to make you think it is not worthwhile to converse with them. If, however, you know better than to look merely at the content of what people say, if you know how to listen to the sound of the words, if you can hearken to the way the words come out, then you will go on listening, despite all discouragement. And if then out of some karmic connection such people receive the impression that they really should talk to you, they will begin to do so, carefully and guardedly — and you will discover that they have a kind of wisdom. But what they are telling is not earthly wisdom. Neither does it contain much of what we now call spiritual science. It is warm words of the heart that they speak, far-reaching ethical teachings. Not that there is anything sentimental about their way of uttering them; they express themselves rather in proverbs, in short, pithy sayings.

They might say something like this. "Let us go over to yonder fir tree. My soul can creep into the needles and cones, for my soul is everywhere. And when my soul creeps into the cones and needles of the fir tree, it sees through them; my soul looks out through them into the deep distances of worlds beyond; and then I become one with the whole world. That is the true piety, to become one with the whole world. Where is God? God is in every fir cone. And if we do not recognize God in every fir cone, if we look for God somewhere else than in every fir cone, then we do not know the true God."

I want to give you only a kind of picture of how these people spoke — people you might meet in the way I have described. And then they might go on to say more: "Yes, and when one creeps into the cones and needles of the fir tree, one finds how God rejoices over the human beings in the world. And when one descends deep into one's own heart, into the abysses of the innermost of human nature, there too one finds God; but then one learns to know how God is made sad through the sinfulness of human beings."

In such wise did these simple sages speak. A great number of them possessed what might be described in modern language as "new editions" of the geometrical figures of the old Rosicrucians. These they would show to persons who approached them in the right way. However, when they spoke about these figures — which might be quite unpretentious, even badly drawn — then the conversation would unfold in a strange manner. There were in those days many who felt interested in the unpretentious wise person before them, but were at the same time overcome with curiosity about what these strange Rosicrucian pictures really meant, and would ask questions about them. But they received from these wise persons, who were as a rule regarded as rather strange and eccentric, no clear or exact answer. They would receive only the advice that if one studied these figures with the right deepening of soul, then one could see through them, as through a window, into the spiritual world. These sages might give as it were a description of what they themselves had been able to feel from contemplating the figures, but they were not ready to offer any explanation or interpretation of them. And it was often the case that when one had heard these expressions of feeling in connection with the figures, one could not put them into thought at all — for it was not thoughts that these simple sages gave. What they gave had, however, an after-working that was of immense significance. One would come away, not only with warmth in one's soul, but also with the feeling: I have received a knowledge that lives in me — a knowledge I cannot possibly bring into intellectual concepts.

This, then, was one of the ways — I have also described others to you — in which, during the period from the fourteenth and fifteenth centuries right down to the eighteenth, the knowledge of the nature of the human being and of the nature of the Divine was communicated to wide circles of people through the medium, as it were, of feeling. We cannot quite say without words, but without ideas, although not on that account without content.

In this period it was actually so that much intercourse went on among people by means of a silencing of thought. No one can truly imagine the character of this period who does not know how much was brought to pass in those days through this silencing of thought, when people interchanged not mere words but their very souls.

I have given you, my dear friends, a picture of one of the features of that time of transition when freedom was first beginning to flourish among human beings. I shall have more to say on this from many aspects....

— f o u r t e e n —

The Relationship between Humankind and the Sun

To end this cycle of lectures, Steiner brings the story into the present. From some points of view, this is the most important task: to make Rosicrucianism contemporary. We must become twenty-first century students of Christian Rosenkreutz. Steiner is very clear, however, that this is not an easy task. Yet cosmic evolution requires that we acquire spiritual knowledge once more. It is demanded of us that we continue the human spiritual path of knowledge and love. And the time is right for it!

What I have been telling you in recent lectures needs to be carried a little further. I have tried to give you a picture of how spiritual knowledge took its course through the centuries, and of the form it has assumed in recent times. I have shown you how from the fifteenth century until the end of the eighteenth and even on into the beginning of the nineteenth, the spiritual knowledge that previously had been present in human beings as clear and concrete (though instinctive) knowledge, now manifested more in a devotion of heart and soul to the spiritual in the world.

We have seen how a direct knowledge of nature, and of how the spiritual world works in nature, is still unmistakably present in the eleventh, twelfth, and thirteenth centuries. In Agrippa of Nettesheim, for example, whom I have described in my book *Mystics after Modernism*, we have a personality who still knew quite well that in the several planets of our system are spiritual beings of specific character and kind.

In his writings, Agrippa of Nettesheim assigns to each single planet what he calls the Intelligence of the planet. This points to traditions that were extant from ancient times and were even in his day still something more than traditions. To look up to a planet in the way that became customary in the later astronomy and is still customary today would have been quite impossible to a man like Agrippa of Nettesheim. For him, the external planet, even every single star, was no more than a sign, an announcement, so to say, of the presence of spiritual beings, whom human beings could look up to with the eye of the soul when they turned their gaze in the direction of the star. And Agrippa of Nettesheim knew that the beings who are united with the single stars rule the inner existence of that star or planet, rule also its movements in the universe, hold sway indeed over its whole activity. And he called such beings the Intelligence of the star.

And Agrippa knew how, at the same time, hindering beings are at work there, beings who undermine the good deeds of the star, working both from the star and also into it. These beings he called the Demon of the star. And together with this knowledge went an understanding that Earth too was a heavenly body having its Intelligence and its Demon. This understanding of star Intelligence and star Demonology, with all its implications, has been completely lost. Let us look for a moment at what it implied.

Earth was looked upon as ruled in her inner activity, in her movement in the cosmos, by a group of Intelligences that could be grouped under the name of the Intelligence of the Earth star. But what, for the people of Agrippa's time, was the Intelligence of the Earth star? It is exceedingly difficult today even to speak of these things, because people's ideas have traveled so very far away from what was accepted as a matter of course in those times by persons of insight and understanding. The Intelligence of the Earth star was humanity itself. The people of those times saw human beings as beings who had received a task, a mission, from the spirituality of the worlds, which was not merely, as people today believe, to walk about on Earth, to travel over it by train, to buy and sell, to write books, and so on. No, they saw human beings as beings to whom the world spirit had given the task to rule and regulate Earth, to bring, as it were, law and order into all that has to do with the place of Earth in the cosmos. Their view of humankind was expressed by saying: Through what they are, through the forces and powers they bear within their being, human beings give to Earth the impulse for her movement around the Sun, for her movement altogether in cosmic space.

There was in those days still a feeling for this. It was known that such a task had once been allotted to humankind. The world spirituality had really made humankind the lord of Earth, but in course of evolution it had not been equal to the task and had fallen from its previous high estate. When people speak of knowledge today, it is seldom indeed that one can catch even a last echo of this view. What we find in religious belief concerning the Fall goes back ultimately to this view, for there the point is that originally humanity had quite another status on Earth and in the universe, that it has in fact fallen from its high estate. But apart from this religious view, wherever people think they have attained knowledge by correct methods of thought, it is only here and there that we may still find today an echo of the ancient knowledge that once proceeded from instinctive clairvoyance, and that was well aware of humanity's true calling and of its Fall into its present narrow limitations.

It may happen, for example, that one is having a conversation with a person (I am relating fact) who has thought very deeply and who has also acquired a deep knowledge of spiritual matters. The conversation turns to whether human beings, as they exist on Earth today, are really self-contained creatures who bear their whole being within themselves. And such a person will say to you that this cannot be. Humankind must in reality be a far more comprehensive being — otherwise we could not have the striving we have now, we could not develop the great idealism of which we can see such fine and exalted examples; in its true nature humankind must be a great and comprehensive being that has somehow or other committed a cosmic sin, as a consequence of which it has been banished within the limits of this present earthly existence, so that today it is really imprisoned as it were in a cage. You may still meet here and there a stray survival, as it were, of this view. But, speaking generally, where shall we find one considered to be a qualified scientist giving serious attention to these great and far-reaching questions? And yet it is only by facing such questions that humanity can ever find its way to an existence worthy of calling itself human.

It was, then, really so: humanity was regarded as the bearer of the Intelligence of the Earth. But now, such a person as Agrippa of Nettesheim ascribed to Earth also a Demon. When we go back to the twelfth or thirteenth century, we find that this Demon of the Earth could become what it did become on Earth only because it found in humanity a ready tool for its activity.

In order to understand this, we must acquaint ourselves with the way people thought in those days about the relationship of Earth to the Sun, or rather of Earth Human to the Sun. And if I am now to describe to you how they understood this relationship, then I must again speak in imaginations: for these things will not suffer themselves to be confined in abstract concepts. Abstract concepts came later, and they are very far from being able to span the truth; we must therefore begin here to speak in pictures, in imaginations.

I have described in my *Outline of Esoteric Science* how the Sun separated itself from Earth, or one may say, separated Earth from itself. For the Sun, you must remember, is the original abode of humanity; ever since the Saturn time humanity has been united with the whole planetary system including the Sun. Humankind is not at home on Earth, but has on Earth only a temporary resting place. It is in reality, according to the view that prevailed in those ancient times, a Sun being. In its whole nature and existence it is united with the Sun. And it ought, as human being, as a Sun being, to have an altogether different relation to Earth than it has. What should happen is that Earth, first of all, should obey her impulse — to bring forth out of the mineral and plant kingdoms the seed of the human being in etheric form, and the Sun should then fructify the seed. Thence should arise the etheric human form that, by establishing its own relationship to the physical substances of Earth, should then take on Earth substantiality. The contemporaries of Agrippa of Nettesheim — Agrippa's own knowledge was, unfortunately, somewhat clouded, but better contemporaries of his did really hold the view — held that human beings ought not to be born in the earthly way they are now, but ought to come to being in etheric bodies through the interaction of Sun and Earth, and then, going about on Earth as etheric beings, give themselves earthly form. The seeds of humankind should grow up out of the earth with the purity of plant life, appearing here and there as ethereal fruits of the earth, darkly gleaming. These should then in a certain season of the year be illuminated by the light of the Sun, and thereby assume human form, but etheric still. Then human beings should draw to themselves physical substance — not from the body of the mother, but from the earth and all that is thereon, incorporating physical substance into themselves from the kingdoms of the earth. That, in the view of Agrippa's contemporaries, should have been the manner of human appearance on Earth, in accordance with the purposes of the cosmic spirituality.

The development that came later was attributed to the fact that human beings had allowed to awaken within themselves too deep an urge, too intense a desire for the earthly and material. Thereby they forfeited their connection with the Sun and the cosmos, and could find their existence on Earth only in the form of the stream of inheritance.

And that gave the opportunity for the Demon of the Earth to begin its work. The Demon of the Earth would not have been able to do anything with human beings who were Sun-born. Sun-born human beings on Earth would have been in very truth the fourth hierarchy. If one wanted to place humankind, one would have had to say: first hierarchy: Seraphim, Cherubim, Thrones; second hierarchy: Exusiai, Dynamis, Kyriotetes; third hierarchy: Angels, Archangels, Archai; fourth hierarchy: humankind (three different stages or gradations of the human, forming together the fourth hierarchy).

But because human beings gave rein to their strong impulses in the direction of the physical, they became, not the being on the lowest branch, as it were, of the hierarchies, but instead the being at the summit — on the topmost branch — of the kingdoms of Earth. Mineral kingdom, plant kingdom, animal kingdom, human kingdom — this became the picture of how humankind stood in the world.

Moreover, because humankind has not found its proper task on Earth, Earth herself does not have her rightful and worthy position in the cosmos. For since humankind has fallen, the true lord of Earth is not there. What has happened? The true lord of Earth is lacking, and it has become necessary for Earth's place and course in the cosmos, not being regulated from Earth herself, to be regulated from the Sun. The tasks that should really be carried out on Earth have fallen to the Sun. The human being of medieval times looked up to the Sun and said: In the Sun are certain Intelligences. They determine the movement of Earth in the cosmos; they govern what happens on Earth. Humankind ought, in reality, to do this; the Sun forces ought to work on Earth through human beings. Hence that significant medieval view that was expressed in the words: The Sun, the unlawful prince of this world.

And now reflect, my dear friends, how infinitely such views deepened the feeling of medieval people for the Christ impulse. The Christ became for them the spirit who no longer wanted his task to be on the Sun and was unwilling to remain among those who directed Earth in an unlawful way from without. He wanted to make his way from the Sun to Earth, to enter into the destiny of humanity and into the destiny of Earth, to experience Earth events, to follow the path of Earth evolution, sharing the lot of human beings and of Earth.

Thus, for medieval people, Christ was the being — the only being — who saved humanity's task on Earth for the cosmos. There you have the connection. And now you can see why, in Rosicrucian times, again and again it was impressed upon the pupil: "Listen, you are not what you are; the Christ had to come to take up your task so that he could perform it in your place."

A great deal in Goethe's *Faust* has come over from medieval views, although Goethe himself did not understand this. Recall, my dear friends, how Faust conjures up the Earth Spirit. With these medieval views in mind, we can enter with feeling and understanding into the way this Earth Spirit speaks.

> In the tides of Life, in Action's storm,
> fluctuant wave,
> shuttle free, Birth and the Grave,
> An eternal sea,
> A weaving, flowing life, all glowing,
> Thus at Time's humming loom 'tis my hand prepares
> The garment of Life that the Deity wears.[1]

Who is it really that Faust is invoking? Goethe himself, when he was writing *Faust,* most assuredly did not fully comprehend. But if we go back from Goethe to the medieval Faust, in whom Rosicrucian wisdom was living, we find that he too wanted to conjure up a spirit. And who was it he wanted to conjure up? He never spoke of the Earth Spirit — he spoke of humankind. The longing and striving of medieval people was: to be a human being. For they felt in the depths of their soul that the earth human is not truly the human being. How can true humanity be found again? The way Faust is rebuffed, is pushed aside by the Earth Spirit, is a picture of how humankind in its earthly form is repelled by its own being. And this is why many accounts of "conversion" to Christianity in the Middle Ages show such extraordinary depth of feeling. They are filled with the sense that people have striven to attain the true humanity that has been lost, and have had to give up in despair, have rightly despaired of being able to find in themselves, within earthly physical life, the true and genuine human being; and so they have come to the point where they have to say: Humankind's striving for true humanity must be abandoned; earthly humankind must leave it to the Christ to fulfill the task of the earth.

This was a time in human history when the human relationship to true humanity as well as to the Christ was still understood in a way that may be called both personal and suprapersonal; it was a time when spirit knowledge, or spirit vision, was still real and still a matter of experience. This ended in the fifteenth century, and then came that amazing change that no one has fully understood. However, those with knowledge of such things are aware of how, during the fifteenth to sixteenth centuries and even later, there was a Rosicrucian school, isolated and scarcely known to the world, where again and again a few pupils were educated and where, above all, care was taken that a certain holy tradition should be preserved and not forgotten. I will give this to you as a narrative.

Let us say, a new pupil arrived one day at some such lonely spot to receive preparation. The first thing to be set before him was the so-called Ptolemaic system in its true form, as it had been handed down from an older era — not in the trivial way it is explained nowadays as something that has long ago been supplanted, but in an altogether different way. The pupil was shown how Earth really and truly bears within herself the forces needed to determine her path through the universe. So to have a correct picture of the world, it has to be drawn in the old Ptolemaic sense: Earth in the center of the universe, and the other stars controlled and directed in their corresponding revolutions by the earth. And the pupil was told: If one really studies to find what are the best forces in the earth, then one can arrive at no other view of the world than this. Actually, however, it is not so. It is not so on account of human sin. Through human sin, Earth has gone over, in an unauthorized, unjustifiable manner, into the kingdom of the Sun; the Sun has become the regent and ruler of earthly activities. And so, over against a world system given by the gods with Earth in the center, another world system has now been set that has the Sun in the center and Earth revolving around the Sun — the system, that is, of Copernicus. And then the pupil was taught that here a mistake, a cosmic mistake, had been brought about by human sin. This was the knowledge entrusted to the pupil, who had to engrave it deeply in heart and soul. Humans have overthrown the old world system, the teacher would say, and set another in its place; and they do not know that this other is the outcome of their own guilt, is really nothing else than the expression — the revelation — of human guilt, while all the time they are imagining it to be the right and correct view of the cosmos. And the teacher would go on to say: What has happened in recent times? Science has suffered a downfall through human guilt. Science has become a science of the Demonic.

About the end of the eighteenth century such communications became impossible, but until that time there were always at least a few pupils here and there who received in some lonely Rosicrucian school their spiritual nourishment — receiving it with "feeling," receiving it as a knowledge of the heart.

Even such a person, for example, as the great philosopher Leibniz was led by his own thought and deliberation to try to find somewhere a place of learning where one could arrive at a correct view of the relationship between the Copernican and Ptolemaic systems. He was not able to discover any such place.

Things like this need to be known if one is to understand aright, in all its shades of meaning, the great change that has come about in the last centuries in the way humankind looks on itself and on the universe. And with this weakening of humankind's living connection with itself, with this estrangement of human beings from themselves, came afterward the tendency to cling to the external intellect, which today rules all. Think for a moment about this external intellect — is it truly human experience? Not by any means. Were it human experience, it could not live so externally in humankind as it does. The intellect has really no sort of connection with what is individual and personal, with the single individual person; we could almost call it a convention. It does not spring from inner human experience; it approaches humans as something external to them.

You can sense how external the intellect has become by comparing the way Aristotle taught logic to his pupils with the way it was taught much later — say in the seventeenth century. In the time of Aristotle, logic was still thoroughly human. Those who were taught to think logically felt (if I may be allowed to express myself again in imaginative terms) as though their heads were dipped in cold water, thus becoming estranged from themselves momentarily. Or they had a feeling like the one Alexander expressed when Aristotle wanted to teach logic to him — as though Aristotle were compressing his skull. Logic was experienced as external. By the seventeenth century, this external quality was a matter of course. People learned that from the major and minor premises, the consequent must be deduced. They learned what we find treated so ironically in Goethe's *Faust:* "The first was so, the second so, therefore the third and fourth are so. Were not the first and second, then the third and fourth had never been.... There will your mind be drilled and braced, as if in Spanish boots it were laced."[2]

Whether, like Alexander, one feels the bones of one's head pressed together, or whether with all this first, second, third, fourth, one feels laced up in Spanish boots — we have each time a picture of the same experience. But this externality of abstract thought was no longer experienced in the time when logic began to be taught in the schools. Today, of course, this has for the most part ceased; logic is no longer a subject in the curriculum. It is rather as if there had once been a time when hundreds of people had been ordered to put on the same uniform and had done it with enthusiasm, and then later on came a time when they went on doing it of their own accord, without giving it a thought.

But, now, during all the time when the logic of the abstract was gaining the upper hand, the old spiritual knowledge could not flourish. Even spiritual knowledge becomes external, assuming a form exemplified in the writings of Eliphas Levi or in the publications of Saint-Martin. Such writings are the last offshoots of the old spirit knowledge and spirit vision.

What do we find in a book like Eliphas Levi's *The Dogma and Ritual of High Magic?* In the first place there are all manner of signs — triangles, pentagrams, and so forth. Then there are words from languages that were in use in bygone ages, especially from the Hebrew. And what in earlier times was life as well as knowledge and could pass over into human deeds and into human ideas we find has on the one hand become bereft of ideas and on the other hand degenerated into external magic. There is speculation about the symbolic meaning of this or that sign, concerning all of which modern people, if they are honest, are obliged to confess that they can see nothing in it. Allusion is made to horrible practices connected with all manner of rites, while those who spoke of these rites and frequently practiced them were far from having any notion at all of their spiritual connection. Such books are invariably pointers to what was once understood in earlier times, was once an inward knowledge-experience, but, at the time when Eliphas Levi, for example, was writing his books, was no longer understood. As for Saint-Martin, you can read what I have written about him in the *Goetheanum Weekly.*

Thus we see how what had once been interwoven into the soul and spirit of human life could not be held there but fell victim to complete want of understanding.

Sincere and genuine was the common impulse and striving for the Divine that showed itself in people's feeling life from the fifteenth to the eighteenth and nineteenth centuries. Beautiful things and sublime are to be found in it. Much that has come down from those times and that is far too little noticed today has about it quite a magic breath of the spiritual. Side by side with it, however, a seed is sprouting, a hard seed, tending to ossify — the seed of inability to understand the old spiritual truths. At the same time it becomes also more and more impossible to approach the spiritual in a way that is in right accord with the age. We come across people of the eighteenth century who speak of a destruction of all that is human, and of the rise of a terrible materialism. Often it seems as though what these people of the eighteenth century say could just as well be applied to our own time. And yet it is not so; what they say does not apply to the last two-thirds of the nineteenth century. For in the nineteenth century a further stage has been reached. What was still regarded in the eighteenth with a certain abhorrence because of its demonic character, has come to be taken quite as a matter of course. People of the nineteenth century no longer had the power to say that the Copernican system is fine, but is a view of the universe that could arise only because human beings did not become what they should have become on Earth; they were no longer revolted by such a view.

We are deeply moved by what happened — that Earth was left without a ruler, that the function passed to the illegitimate lords of the world (this expression occurs again and again in medieval writing), and that Christ then left the Sun and united with the destiny of Earth. Only now, at the end of the nineteenth century, has it again become possible to look into these things with clear vision, with such clear vision as human beings possessed originally — only now in the Michael Age! We have spoken repeatedly of the dawn of the Michael Age, and of its character. But there are tasks that belong to this Michael Age, and it is possible now to point to these tasks, after all that we have been considering in the Christmas Meeting and since about the evolution of spirit vision as it has taken its course through the centuries.

Part 5

ROSICRUCIAN MEDITATION

— fifteen —

Meditating the Rose Cross

Rosicrucianism is, above all, a path of practice. Throughout his life Rudolf Steiner gave many indications and meditation practices to his students that were explicitly Rosicrucian in nature. Some of these follow.

We begin with the description of how to meditate the Rose Cross from Steiner's major cosmological (hermetic and alchemical) work, An Outline of Esoteric Science.

We can rise to a state of suprasensible consciousness only from ordinary waking consciousness, the state the soul lives in prior to its ascent. Training provides the soul with methods that will lead it out of the ordinary waking state. Among the first methods provided by the training discussed here are some that can still be described as functions of ordinary waking consciousness.

The most important of these methods consists of silent activities of the soul, in which the soul devotes itself to certain specific mental images that have the intrinsic power to awaken certain hidden faculties in it. Such mental images are different from those of our daily waking life, whose purpose is to depict outer things — the more truly they do this, the "truer" such images themselves are, and it is part of their essential nature to be "true" in this sense — but this is not the purpose of the mental images the soul concentrates on when its goal is spiritual training. Images intended for spiritual training are not structured so as to reproduce anything external, but to have an awakening effect on the soul.

The best mental or thought pictures for this purpose are symbolic ones, but others can also be used. The content of these mental images is not essential; the point is that the soul devotes all its energies to having nothing in its consciousness other than the mental image in question.

In our everyday soul life, the soul's energies are divided among many different things and our mental images shift rapidly. In spiritual training, the point is to concentrate the soul's entire activity on a single mental image that is freely chosen as a focus for consciousness. For this reason, symbolic images are better than ones that represent outer objects or processes and have a point of contact with the outer world, since these do not force the soul to rely on itself to the same extent as it does with symbols that it creates out of its own energy. What is imagined is not important. What is important is that the process of visualizing the image frees the soul from dependence on anything physical.

By recalling what happens in memory, we can begin to grasp what it means to immerse ourselves in a visualized image.

For example, if we look at a tree and then turn away from it so that we can no longer see it, we can reawaken the mental image of the tree out of our memory. The mental image we have of a tree when it is not actually present before our eyes is the memory of the tree.

Let us imagine that we retain this memory in our soul. We allow the soul to rest on this memory image and attempt to exclude all other images until the soul is immersed in the memory image of the tree. But in this case although the soul is immersed in a mental image, the image is a copy of something perceived by our senses. However, if we now attempt the same thing with an image that we insert into our consciousness through an act of free will, we will gradually be able to achieve the necessary effect.

I will illustrate this with a single example of contemplating or meditating on a symbolic mental image. First, this mental image must be built up in the soul. I can do this as follows: I imagine a plant taking root in the ground, sprouting one leaf after another, and continuing to develop up to the point of flowering. Then I imagine a human being alongside this plant. In my soul, I bring to life the thought that this human being has qualities and abilities that can be called more perfect than those of the plant. I think about how human beings are able to move around in response to their feelings and intentions, while plants are attached to the ground. But then I also notice that although human beings are certainly more perfect than plants, they also have characteristics that we cannot perceive in plants, characteristics whose absence can actually make plants seem more perfect than humans. Human beings are filled with desires and passions, which their actions obey, and certain errors result from these drives and passions. In contrast, I see how plants obey the pure laws of growth as they develop one leaf after another and open their flowers without passion to the Sun's chaste rays. I can say that human beings have an advantage over plants with regard to a certain type of perfection, but that the price they have paid for this perfection is to allow urges, desires, and passions to enter their nature alongside the forces of the plants that seem so pure to me.

Next, I visualize the green sap flowing through the plant. I imagine this as an expression of the pure, passionless laws of growth. Then I visualize the red blood flowing through human arteries and imagine it as an expression of urges, desires, and passions. I allow all this to arise in my soul as a vivid thought.

Then I think about how human beings are capable of development, how they can use the higher soul faculties to cleanse and purify their urges and passions. I think about how this destroys a baser element in these urges and passions, which are then reborn on a higher level. The blood may then be imagined as the expression of these cleansed and purified urges and passions.

For example, in the spirit I see a rose and say: In the red sap of the rose blossom I see the color of the plant's green sap transformed into red, and the red rose, like the green leaf, obeys the pure, passionless laws of growth. Let the red of the rose symbolize the blood that is an expression of purified urges and passions. They have been stripped of their baser element and are now similar in purity to the forces that are active in the red rose.

At this point, I try not only to assimilate these thoughts with my intellect, but also to bring them to life in my feeling. I can have a blissful sensation when I imagine the growing plant's purity and absence of passion; I can generate a feeling in myself for the price human beings must pay for greater perfection by acquiring urges and desires. This can transform my earlier bliss into a serious feeling. Next, a feeling of liberating happiness can stir in me as I devote myself to the thought of the red blood that can become the vehicle of inwardly pure experiences, just like the red sap of the rose blossom. It is important not to think the thoughts that serve to build up a symbolic mental image unaccompanied by feeling.

After living in these thoughts and feelings for a while, we can transform them into a symbolic image as follows. We imagine a black cross. Let this be the symbol of the baser element that has been eliminated from our urges and passions. We imagine seven radiant red roses arranged in a circle where the two beams of the cross intersect. Let these be the symbol of the blood that is an expression of cleansed, purified passions and urges.[1] This symbolic image must now be called up before our mind's eye in the way described earlier with regard to a memory image. A symbolic mental image such as this has the power to awaken our souls when we inwardly immerse ourselves in it and devote ourselves to it. We must try to exclude all other mental images while we are immersed in this one. We must allow only this symbol to linger before our mind's eye in the spirit, and it must be as vivid as possible.

It is important that this symbol was not immediately proffered as a soul-awakening image but was first built up by specific ideas about plants and human beings, because the effectiveness of a symbol like this depends on its being put together in this way before it is used for meditation. If we imagine it without first having gone through this buildup in our own souls, the symbol remains cold and is much less effective than if it has received its soul-illuminating power through this preparation. During meditation, however, we should not summon up all of these preparatory thoughts. We should allow only the image to linger vividly before us in the spirit while permitting the feeling we had as a result of these preparatory thoughts to resonate. In this way, the symbol becomes a token of this experience of feeling, and its effectiveness is due to the fact that the soul dwells on this experience. The longer we can dwell on it without a different and disruptive image intervening, the more effective the whole process will be. However, it is a good idea to frequently repeat the process of building up the image — outside the time we actually set aside for the meditation — through thoughts and feelings of the type described above, so that the feeling doesn't fade away. The more patience we have in renewing it, the more significant the image becomes for our souls. . . .

This symbol of the Rose Cross was intended to illustrate the process of effective meditation. In spiritual training, any number of images of this sort could be used, and they could be built up in many different ways. Certain sentences, phrases, or single words may also be assigned as subjects for meditation. The goal of all of these methods of meditation, however, is to tear the soul away from sensory perception and to rouse it to activity in which physical sense impressions are meaningless and the development of dormant inner soul faculties becomes the essential thing.

— sixteen —

Meditation with the Rose Cross

In the following short section, a few of the meditations that Steiner gave have been gathered together.

1.

Imagine the Cross, as if arising out of burning wood. Then, on the Cross, the seven reddish roses, separating from it, gradually becoming illuminated.

> First Rose, lighting up:
> the left half of the head:
> May your warmth warm through me.
>
> Second Rose, lighting up:
> the right half of the head:
> May your light shine through me.
>
> Third Rose, lighting up:
> left hand:
> May your awakeness stream through me.
>
> Fourth Rose, lighting up:
> right hand:
> May your peace pour through me.
>
> Fifth Rose, lighting up:
> left foot:
> May your ray move powerfully through me.

Sixth Rose, lighting up:
right foot:
May your raising up penetrate me.

Seventh Rose, lighting up:
above:
I am in your sphere.

2.

Pour through me full of power,
flow wakefully streaming,
streaming from below upward,
strengthening above in the spirit,
strengthening through the source of life,
the source of life, that descends,
descends from the being of the Sun
through me.

> For Suse Karstsens,
> undateable (GA 266)

3.

I see seven Rose Stars gleaming
On the black wood of the Cross —
May they make me full of power
So that I may experience and sense
Seven World Powers within me
That work within my human being.

> 1915 or later (GA 267)

4.

Bright Rose Stars
On the black wooden Cross
May they be an image for me
Of my soul's divine spiritual powers
Streaming in the dark soul's ground
In me.

> c. 1913 (GA 267)

5.

On the black Cross
Bright Rose Stars
Image
In my soul's depths
Of strong shining spiritual powers
Active
In me.

                    November 9, 1913 (GA 267)

6.

Seven bright Rose Stars
On a black wooden Cross
Seven powerful soul forces
In the welter of life:
strength, peace, striving for wisdom,
the power of love, detachment, attention, trust/confidence.
With these signs I inscribe my soul.

                              June 1913 (GA 267)

7.

1. (evenings)
The image of a bright space, which becomes ever darker; a
    white Cross with seven green Roses.
In this sign I behold
The Revelation of the all-encompassing Spirit
A part of which is my own being —
Awake o holy longing
In my soul's deepest depths
To sense, to feel, to know
My own spirit in cosmic spirit.

2. (mornings)
Image of a dark space, which becomes ever brighter; a black
    Cross with red Roses:
I strive to enter

My soul's depths
So that out of the darkness
The light of the spirit might arise
And awaken in me
The spirit of this sign
To which I surrender myself.

May 1912 (GA 267)

8.

I raise my eyes
To the black wooden Cross
And surrender myself with my soul
Into the power of the World Spirit;
As the black cross gives itself
Wholly to the light.
I in me.

9. *Signature of the Rose Cross School*

Ex Deo nascimur
In Christo morimur
Per Spiritum Sanctum reviviscimus.

Munich, May 1907

From God, I am born
In Christ, I die
Through the Holy Spirit, I resurrect.

Malsch, April 1909

From God's being, the human soul arises
Dying, the soul can dip down into the essential ground
One day, it will unite death to the spirit.

Munich, August 1911

From the divine, the human being IS
In Christ, life becomes death
In the cosmic spirit thought, the soul awakens.

Dornach, January 1924

— afterword —

Rudolf Steiner and Rosicrucianism

Anyone threading their way through this volume alert to the subtext and its implications will have realized that, implicit in these lectures and writings, is the affirmation of the primacy of Rosicrucianism both for Rudolf Steiner personally and for anthroposophy, the spiritual science that he initiated. Rosicrucianism, in fact, is the golden, unifying thread that runs through Steiner's life and work. This Rosicrucianism is not, of course, identical either with that of the seventeenth century or with the hypothetical variant emerging in the ninth and tenth centuries, and even less with the originary Atlantean "Rosicrucianism" of the Tao. But it is related to these — as ancestors and generations are related, bearing the same seed and adapting it to the time.

In this sense, Rosicrucianism is a lineage. The lineage holders at any given moment mold the teaching and the practice to the evolutionary and historical circumstances of their time. Like any lineage, therefore, Rosicrucianism can also occur through transmission "outside the scriptures," outside the physical stream of incarnated beings, mind to mind, spirit being to spirit being. This is the kind of transmission that the Buddha exemplified in his "Flower Sermon." Without speaking, he held up a lotus flower before his disciples and suddenly one disciple, Mahakashyapa, entered Buddha-mind and understood.

Rudolf Steiner himself speaks of two initiatory encounters that in the light of this collection take on special meaning. The first is with the herb gatherer Felix Koguzki and the other with the Master "M.," traditionally taken to be Christian Rosenkreutz. For instance, in the so-called "Document of Barr," the autobiographical account penned for the French author and spiritual writer, Édouard Schuré, Steiner states (he is writing of his young adulthood):

> During that period [when, besides his official studies, he is intensively reading German idealist philosophy] I gained *a complete*

understanding of the concept of time. This knowledge was in no way connected with my studies and was grounded in the spiritual life. I understood that there is a backwards evolution, the occult-astral, which interferes with the forward one. This knowledge is the precondition for spiritual clairvoyance.

Then came the acquaintance with the agent of the M. . . .

I did not meet the M. immediately, but first an emissary who was completely initiated into the secrets of the plants and their effects and with their connection with the cosmos and human nature. . . .

Two things may be noted here, besides the mind-to-mind, being-to-being contact with Christian Rosenkreutz himself.

First, in relation to the "understanding of the concept of time," we may recall that in lecture eight, after speaking of what the Rosicrucian alchemists called "growth and decay," Steiner adds, almost enigmatically: "by observing nature, medieval theosophists learned the law of 'upward and downward evolution.' " Such a dual evolution clearly implies a two-way flow of time, progressing and regressing. This allows us to surmise a connection with Steiner's own breakthrough in understanding time, as described in the Barr document. At the same time, it also allows us to connect what he modestly calls his "spiritual life" with Rosicrucianism in general and the study of alchemical texts in particular. The second thing we might note in this regard is the strong association between Felix Koguzki and the plant world. This is important because in Steiner's exposition of Rosicrucian spiritual practice in the lectures in the first section of this book, the plant-nature of human blood becomes very clear. Thus, in lecture three, he says: "The human being is an inverted plant, while the animal is a semi-inverted plant. That is why the Rosicrucians told their students to look at the plant, with its root in the ground and its organs of reproduction stretched chastely toward the Sun. . . . "

The Rosicrucian directive, however, guides Steiner not only esoterically but also through modern science and philosophy and determines the form and content of the work that he does in these fields.

Note how in the first lectures he repeatedly proposes his own earliest epistemological works — *Truth and Knowledge* and *Intuitive Thinking as a Spiritual Path* — as paradigmatic of Rosicrucian study, thereby affirming the famous epistemology itself to be Rosicrucian.

It is Rosicrucianism, too, that requires of Steiner that he link himself to those other streams and channels of spiritual grace (Theosophy, Freemasonry, and Ritual Magic, for instance) that transmitted some aspect, however distant, of the historical reality of Christian Rosenkreutz.

The connection with Goethe, so important for Steiner, is also of course Rosicrucian. From this point of view, the Master of Weimar *is* in fact a Rosicrucian pure and simple. We see this not only in his poem "The Mysteries," his *Tale of the Green Snake and the Beautiful Lily* — explicitly Rosicrucian productions — and in his *Faust* and his great novels *Elective Affinities* and *Wilhelm Meister* (masterpieces permeated with secret teachings of the highest order), but also and above all in the hermetic, alchemical science of his nature studies and his color theory, for which, after all, Goethe thought he would be remembered long after his poems were forgotten.

All of this is to say that anthroposophy, as Steiner conceived it, marks the "return" of Rosicrucianism as he understood it. Around 1650, in the aftermath of the Thirty Years' War, the "true" Rosicrucian Brotherhood supposedly left Europe for the East, some say for the Baltic states, some for the Caucasus and beyond, some further east still. Remnants of teaching were transmitted by Masonry and other, less well-known, better hidden esoteric orders. During this time Christian Rosenkreutz himself — in the body, as well as out of it — continued to be active. But the earthly reality of the *Fraternitas* was no more. It was to bringing this reality once more into the earthly sphere of cosmic and human evolution that Rudolf Steiner dedicated his life.

Notes

Introduction

1. See the essay in the volume on the *Chemical Wedding*. More generally, a good case could be made that *An Outline of Esoteric Science* and indeed Steiner's whole cosmological and spiritual scientific worldview is alchemical. Goethe, too, after all, so important to Steiner, was deeply influenced by alchemy and hermetism.

2. See Maurice Aniane, "Notes on Alchemy, the Cosmological 'Yoga' of Medieval Christianity," *Material for Thought* (San Francisco, 1976). On alchemy generally, see Titus Burckhardt, *Alchemy: Science of the Cosmos, Science of the Soul* (London: Stuart & Watkins, 1967); Julius Evola, *The Hermetic Tradition* (Rochester, Vt.: Inner Traditions, 1996). Also a very rich resource: Adam McLean's Alchemy Website, http://www.levity.com/alchemy.

3. "Musical Theory and Ancient Cosmology," *World and I*, February 1994.

4. See *Homage to Pythagoras* (Hudson, N.Y.: Lindisfarne Books, 1994).

5. "Science and the Church: A Plea for Dialogue," an essay written for Science Secretariat Day at the Pax Romana Conference at St. Albans, England, September 24, 1998.

6. See Barbara Obrist, *Constantine of Pisa: The Book of the Secrets of Alchemy*, introduction, critical edition, translation, and commentary (Leiden and New York: E. J. Brill, 1990).

7. See the important early eighteenth-century Rosicrucian work by the Huguenot Douzetemps: *The Mysteries of the Cross*.

8. Paracelsus, quoted by Carlos Gilly, "Theophrastia Sancta: Paracelsianism as a Religion in Conflict with the Established Churches." J. R. Ritman Library: Bibliotheca Philosophica Hermetica. On the web at http://www.Ritmanlibrary. An enlarged, German-language version appears in *Analecta Paracelsiana* (Stuttgart: Steiner Verlag).

9. The primary documents may conveniently be found in Paul M. Allen, ed., *A Christian Rosenkreutz Anthology* (Blauvelt, N.Y.: Rudolf Steiner Publications, 1968); also Vaughan Waldenses et al., *A Rosicrucian Primer: Ancient Landmarks of the Rose Cross* (Edmonds, Wash.: Holmes Publishing Group, 1994); the *Fama* and the *Confessio* only may be found in the appendix to Frances Yates, *The Rosicrucian Enlightenment* (London and Boston: Routledge and Kegan Paul, 1972); there is a good translation of *The Chemical Wedding* by Joscelyn Godwin (Grand Rapids, Mich.: Phanes Press, 1991).

10. On Sendivogius, see Zbigniew Szydlo, *Water Which Does Not Wet Hands: The Alchemy of Michael Sendivogius* (Warsaw: Polish Academy of Sciences, 1994); also Rafal Prinke's masterly essay on Sendivogius in *The Rosicrucian Enlightenment Revisited*, ed. Ralph White (Hudson, N.Y.: Lindisfarne Books, 1999).

11. See Maurice Magre, *The Return of the Magi* (London: Philip Allen, 1931); also idem, *Magicians, Seers, and Mystics,* trans. Reginald Merton (New York: E. P. Dutton, 1932).

12. On Andreae, see John Warwick Montgomery, *Cross and Crucible, Johann Valentin Andreae (1586–1654), Phoenix of the Theologians* (The Hague: Martinus Nijhoff, 1973).

13. *On Mystical Theology; On the Divine Names; On the Celestial Hierarchy; On the Ecclesiastic Hierarchy;* and *Letters.*

14. For Rudolf Steiner, Hiram Abiff (builder of Solomon's Temple), Lazarus (St. John the Evangelist), and Christian Rosenkreutz represent the same entelechy.

15. For this and many other details of occult history, see the introduction to *The Transcendental Universe* (Hudson, N.Y.: Lindisfarne Books, 1993) by C. G. Harrison, who also claimed to be a "Rosicrucian."

16. See William R. Newman, *Gehennical Fire: The Lives of George Starkey, an American Alchemist in the Scientific Revolution* (Cambridge, Mass.: Harvard University Press, 1994).

17. See Christopher McIntosh, *The Rose Cross and the Age of Reason* (Leiden and New York: E. J. Brill, 1992).

18. For Boehme and the Behmenist tradition, see Arthur Versluis, *Wisdom's Children* (Albany: State University of New York Press, 1999).

19. See the lecture of September 27, 1911: "In 1785 all the esoteric ideas of the Rosicrucians were expressed in the work *Die Geheimen Figuren der Rosenkreutzer* by Hinricus Madathanus Theosophus. In a certain limited way this publication contains indications of everything that had been at work in the previous century, and which then was expressed only in certain works compiled and collected by Hinricus Madathanus. One hundred years later, we see again the effects of the Rosicrucian stream expressed in the work of H. P. Blavatsky, especially in the book *Isis Unveiled....* " Here another interesting fact may be noted. Steiner often said how, at the end of every century (or at least during its last third) a major Rosicrucian work would appear and inseminate the coming century. *Secret Symbols* was that work for the eighteenth century; and *Isis Unveiled,* according to Steiner, was that work for the nineteenth century. But what of the twentieth century? It is a pity this book did not appear eighteen months earlier — or perhaps the timing is not so precise.

20. See Ronald D. Gray, *Goethe the Alchemist* (Cambridge: Cambridge University Press, 1952).

21. See Rudolf Steiner, *The Archangel Michael: His Mission and Ours* (Hudson, N.Y.: Anthroposophic Press, 1994).

22. See Adam McClean "Bacstrom's Rosicrucian Society," *Hermetic Journal* 6 (1979). This article is also available on McLean's Alchemy Website (http://www. levity.com/alchemy), which also contains a transcription of *Rosicrucian Aphorisms and Process* attributable to Bacstrom and appended to the Tilloch document in the Ferguson Collection. See also A. E. Waite, *The Real History of the Rosicrucians* (first edition 1887; reprinted Blauvelt, N.Y.: Steinerbooks, 1977), and *The Brotherhood of the Rosy Cross* (first edition 1924; reprinted New Hyde Park, N.Y.: University Books, 1961); Joscelyn Godwin, *The Theosophical Enlightenment* (Albany: State University of New York Press, 1994).

23. Joscelyn Godwin's *The Theosophical Enlightenment* is an excellent historical guide to the period. See also A. E. Waite, *The Brotherhood of the Rosy Cross* and *The Real History of the Rosicrucians.* Also Christopher McIntosh, *Eliphas Levi*

and the French Occult Revival (London: Rider, 1972); R. Swinburne Clymer, *The Book of Rosicruciae: A Condensed History of the Fraternitas Rosae Crucae*, 3 vols. (Quakertown, Pa.: Philosophical Publishing Company 1946–1949).

24. See Ellic Howe, *The Magicians of the Golden Dawn: A Documentary History of a Magical Order 1887–1923* (London: Routledge and Kegan Paul, 1972).

25. George Adams, *The Mysteries of the Rose Cross* (London: Temple Lodge, 1989).

26. See his *Totality and Infinity* and *Otherwise Than Being.*

1. Tao and Rose Cross

1. This is also evidently the *Tao* of ancient China.

2. Not unrelatedly, dew plays a key role in alchemy. See, for instance, the images of the alchemist collecting dew in the *Mutus Liber.*

3. See Wilhelm Rath, *The Friend of God from the High Land: His Life according to the Records of the St. John's Hospice, the "Green Island," in Strasbourg*, trans. Roland Everett (Stroud, U.K.: Hawthorn Press, 1991).

4. See the account given by Rudolf Steiner in *The Occult Movement in the Nineteenth Century.* See also, C. G. Harrison, *The Transcendental Universe*, and Joscelyn Godwin, *The Theosophical Enlightenment.*

2. Who Are the Rosicrucians?

1. The actual documentation of this figure — Christian Rosenkreutz (or Rose Cross) — is limited to the three primary documents of Rosicrucianism: the *Fama*, the *Confessio*, and *The Chemical Wedding of Christian Rosenkreutz* (see introduction).

2. *Faust*, part 1.

3. "Spiritual science" is the designation Rudolf Steiner used to describe his method of initiation.

4. The "rules," as given in the *Fama*, run as follows:

1. No one should take upon himself any other profession than the healing of the sick, and this to no profit.

2. No one should be obliged to wear any distinctive dress on account of the brotherhood, but should adapt himself to the customs of the country.

3. Every year on the day C.[Christmas], they should meet together at the house Sancti Spiritus, or send reason for their absence.

4. Every brother should look for a worthy person who, after his death, might succeed him.

5. The word C.R. should be their seal, mark, and character.

6. The Fraternity should remain secret for one hundred years.

5. For this and other texts mentioned, see the bibliography at the end of this book.

6. Rudolf Steiner speaks here of certain aspects of theosophy and other manifestations of the "theosophical enlightenment," as well as his own "spiritual science," as Rosicrucianism for our time.

7. Rudolf Steiner uses the terms *Imagination, Inspiration,* and *Intuition* in an extraordinary sense. When we say "imagination," for example, we usually mean

"mental picturing" or "fantasy." These terms here represent stages of spiritually developed capacities. Steiner discusses these terms in greater detail in *The Stages of Higher Knowledge* and in lecture 3 of "Pneumatosophy" in *A Psychology of Body, Soul, and Spirit.* The term *imaginal* was introduced by the French scholar of Iranian theosophy Henry Corbin and fits Steiner's usage perfectly.

8. *Faust,* part 2, the last line.

9. See Plato's *Timaeus.*

10. Compare Rumi.

11. Amfortas is the wounded Fisher King of Grail legend.

12. See *An Outline of Esoteric Science* (p. 247ff).

13. Cf. Mary Settegast, *Plato Prehistorian* (Hudson, N.Y.: Lindisfarne Books, 1992).

14. See Rudolf Steiner, *Genesis.*

15. *Akashic record* (or chronicle) is the spiritual record of events read by those with clairvoyant sight. *Akasha* is the primordial substance of space, which contains the primordial substance of "memory," or time; see Steiner's *Cosmic Memory.*

16. *Tat vam asi,* as the Sanskrit of the Upanishads has it.

3. Rosicrucian Practice

1. Jacob Boehme (1575–1624). One of the greatest Christian gnostics and "alchemical philosophers" and closely linked to the Rosicrucian stream.

2. Dionysius the Areopagite, known as the Pseudo-Dionysius. Texts by this author (*Mystical Theology; The Divine Names; The Celestial Hierarchy; The Ecclesiastical Hierarchy;* and some letters), who claimed to be the pupil of St. Paul and the friend of St. John the Evangelist, first appeared in the fifth/sixth century. Scholars now assume the author to have been a contemporary Neoplatonist, perhaps Damascius, but Rudolf Steiner and the esoteric tradition take Dionysius's claim to have witnessed the darkening of the sky at the crucifixion and to have been converted and become a coworker with St. Paul at face value.

3. See bibliography.

4. See lecture 2.

5. Niflheim, Niflheimr. The northern world of the ice and unbearable cold, home of the Frost-Giants. One of the nine worlds of Norse mythology.

6. The German word for calyx also means "chalice."

5. Goethe's Rosicrucian Poem "The Mysteries"

1. Goethe, *Faust.*

6. Rosicrucian Symbols

1. See chapter 16, "Meditating the Rose Cross."

7. Who Was Christian Rosenkreutz?

1. Rudolf Steiner is here talking of what he calls elsewhere "spiritual economy." See the collection of lectures under that title.

2. This refers to the legendary statement by Christian Rosenkreutz: "I shall disappear from Europe toward the end of the century and proceed to regions of the Himalayas. I shall rest; I must rest. In eighty-five years, I shall be seen daily" (quoted by Isabel Cooper-Oakley in *Gnosis,* December 15, 1903).

3. Volume 1 of the three-volume work *The Secret Symbols of the Rosicrucians* contains the essay *"Aureum seculum redivivum"* by Hinricus Madathanus Theosophus (1590–1638). This name is an anagram of the Hadrianus a Munsicht ("Mynsicht" also being an anagram of the surname Symnicht, originally Seumenicht), a Paracelsian alchemist.

4. The current stage of Earth's evolution contains seven "cultural epochs," of which ours is the fifth. Steiner describes the stages of cosmic evolution and Earth's cultural epochs in *An Outline of Esoteric Science,* chapter 4.

5. For the "twelve tendencies of thought," see *Human and Cosmic Thought.*

6. See Isabel Cooper-Oakley, *The Comte de Saint Germain, the Secret of Kings* (Milan: G. Sulli-Rao, 1912; London: Theosophical Publishing House, 1927; reprinted since then); Jean Overton Fuller, *The Comte de Saint-Germain, Last Scion of the House of Rakoczy* (London: East-West Publications, 1988); also Rudolf Steiner, *The Temple Legend.*

7. Gotthold Ephraim Lessing (1729–1781) discusses reincarnation in his book.

8. In 1849, Maximilian Drossbach (1810–1884) wrote an article called "Reincarnation: Answering the Question of Immortality by Empirical Methods According to Natural Laws." Without revealing his identity, he offered 40 ducats of gold for the best explanation of the idea expressed in his article. Gustav Widenmann (1812–1876) was prompted to write "Ideas on Immortality as the Repetition of Life on Earth" (Vienna, 1851), which won the prize.

9. Theosophy refers to the current cycle of humanity's evolution as *Kalı Yuga* (period of darkness); here, "little" Kalı Yuga refers to the rise of materialism, particularly the advent of modern natural science at the beginning of the fifteenth century and ending around 1900. According to the Mahabharata, the Hindu term refers to one of the four ages in a world cycle: *Krita, Tretaa, Dvaapara,* and *Kali.* Each succeeding period declines in moral excellence, and in the Kali Yuga people forget their spiritual aim in life while captivated by the glitter of material things. Lifespans shorten, as does the duration of the Kali Yuga, which began in 3102 B.C. (with the death of Krishna) and will last 432,000 years (in contrast to 864,000 years for the previous period). The entire cycle of 4,320,000 years is called the *Mahaa Yuga,* the "Great Yuga."

8. The Teaching of Christian Rosenkreutz

1. Heinrich Khunrath (1560–1605).

2. Steiner discusses the antimony processes in terms of alchemical medicine in *Introducing Anthroposophical Medicine* and *The Healing Process.*

9. Christian Rosenkreutz and Gautama Buddha

1. *De revolutionibus orbium coelestium libre VI* (Nürnberg, 1543).

2. See Rudolf Steiner, *The East in the Light of the West,* chapter 9.

3. See Steiner's lecture course, *The Gospel of St. Luke.*

4. See Rudolf Steiner, *The Spiritual Foundation of Morality.*

5. See chapter 3 of *Theosophy,* "The Three Worlds," in which Steiner describes the "region of burning desire," or *kamaloka.* See also his lectures on the period between death and a new birth in *At Home in the Universe: Exploring Our Suprasensory Nature.*

6. For insights into Rudolf Steiner's involvement with the Theosophical Society,

see *From the History and Contents of the First Section of the Esoteric School 1904–1914* (Hudson, N.Y.: Anthroposophic Press, 1998).

7. Rudolf Steiner gave approximately forty lectures on the Gospels between November 1907 and September 1912; see bibliography, p. 263 below.

8. Buddha's first sermon after his enlightenment was on the "four noble truths" and the "eightfold path" — that is, on the causes of life's suffering and its alleviation.

10. *On* The Chemical Wedding of Christian Rosenkreutz

1. Bernus's main work on alchemy is *Alchymie und Heilkunst*, Verlag am Goetheanum, 1994. A French translation exists; no English translation has yet been made.

2. *The Chemical Wedding* is arranged in seven days — seven chapters.

3. He had said his prayers, conversed with his Creator, and was about to prepare in his heart, together with his "dear Paschal Lamb, a small, unleavened, undefiled cake."

4. "All on a sudden arises so horrible a tempest...."

5. Someone touches him on the back, and continues to tug on his coat.

6. Turning, he sees "a fair and glorious lady, whose garments were sky-color, and curiously (like heaven) bespangled with golden stars and in her right hand she bare a trumpet...."

7. The description of the lady continues: "... In her left hand she held a great bundle of letters of all languages, which she (as I afterward understood) was to carry into all countries... as soon as I turned about, she turned her letters over and over, and at length drew out a small one, which with great reverence she laid down upon the table, and without giving one word departed from me...." Then, the traveler, having fallen on his knees in prayer, "went to the letter, which was now so heavy as had it been mere gold it could hardly have been so weighty." The letter was sealed with a seal, upon which was a curious Cross with this inscription, IN HOC SIGNO VINCES (IN THIS SIGN YOU WILL CONQUER).

8.
> "*This day, this day, this, this*
> *The Royal Wedding is.*
> *Art thou thereto by Birth inclin'd,*
> *And unto joy of God design'd,*
> *Then may'st thou to the Mountain trend,*
> *Whereon three stately* Temples *stand,*
> *And there see all from end to end.*
> *Keep watch and ward,*
> *Thy self regard;*
> *Unless with diligence thou bathe,*
> *The Wedding can't thee harmless save:*
> *He'll damage have that here delays;*
> *Let him beware, too light that weights.*

Underneath stood *Sponsus and Sponsa* [Bride and Groom]."

9. The sign is the "Hieroglyphic Monad" of John Dee.

10. After pondering the invitation to the wedding, the traveler falls asleep, or almost — "For I was yet scarce fallen asleep, when methought, I, together with a numberless multitude of men lay fettered with great chains in a dark dungeon, wherein without the least glimpse of light, we swarmed like bees one over another,

and this rendered each others affliction more grievous. But although neither I nor any of the rest could see one jot; yet I continually heard one heaving himself above the other, when his chains or fetters were become ever so lighter, though none of us had much reason to shove up the other, since we were all captive wretches.... "

11. "I was hardly out of my cell into a forest, when methought that the whole heaven and all the elements had already trimmed themselves against this Wedding. For even the birds in my opinion chanted more pleasantly than before, and the young fawns skipped so merrily, that they rejoiced my old heart, and moved me to sing.... "

12. The traveler finds a tablet upon which is written: "... the Bridegroom offers you a choice between four ways, all of which, if you do not collapse on the path, can bring you to his royal court. The first is short but dangerous, and one which will lead you into rocky places, through which it will be hardly possible to pass. The second is longer and takes you roundabout; it is plain and easy if, by the help of the magnet, you turn neither to the left nor to the right. The third is that truly Royal road, which through various pleasures and pageants of our King affords you a happy journey. But so far this latter has hardly been granted to one in a thousand. By the fourth, no man will reach the place, because it is a consuming path, possible only for incorruptible bodies.... "

13. Faced with the "choice" of paths the traveler is distressed — all the ways seem dangerous or impossible — and yet, though "weighted down by my own unworthiness,...the dream still comforted me, that I was delivered out of the tower.... "

14. "...whereupon I was so variously perplexed, that for very great weariness, hunger and thirst seized me, whereupon I presently drew out my bread, cut a slice of it, which a snow white *dove* of whom I was not aware, sitting upon the tree, espyed and therewith...came down...to whom I willingly imparted my food, which she received....But as soon as her enemy, a most black *raven* perceived it, he straight darted himself down upon the dove.... "

15. After following the dove and the raven, the traveler spies in the distance "a stately portal." Providence leads him to it, "an exceeding Royal beautiful Portal, whereon were carved a multitude of most noble figures and devices, everyone of which had its own signification.... " The traveler stepped through the portal and was immediately welcomed and asked for "his letter of invitation" which, luckily, he had with him! Then he was greeted as "brother" and he himself now identified himself as "a brother of the Red-Rosy Cross.... "

16. Having passed through the first gate and been received, the traveler brother is asked for his bottle of water and in return is given a golden token and a sealed letter for the second porter. Thus he comes to the second gate, also adorned with images.

17. Under the second gate "lay a terrible grim Lion chain'd."

18. The second porter.

19. "...the Scales which were entirely of gold were hung up in the midst of the hall. There was also a little table covered with red velvet, and seven weights placed thereon.... " Then the Virgin began to speak:

> Who into a Painter's room does go
> And nothing does of painting know,
> Yet does in prating therof, pride it;
> Shall be of all the world derided.
> Who into the Artists' order goes,

And thereunto was never chose;
Yet with pretence of skill does pride it;
Shall be of all the world derided.
Who at a Wedding does appear
And yet was ne'er intended there;
Yet does in coming highly pride it;
Shall be of all the world derided.
Who now into this Scale ascends,
The weights not proving his fast
Friends,
And that it bounces so does ride it;
Shall be of all the world derided.

20. See, especially, Frances Yates, *The Rosicrucian Enlightenment* (London: Routledge and Kegan Paul, 1972). Also C. V. Wedgwood, *The Thirty Years' War* (New Haven: Yale University Press, 1939).

21. Rosenkreutz descends to the tomb of Venus. First, there comes the announcement, "Here Venus lies buried, the beautiful woman who has robbed so many noble men of fortune, honor, blessing, and well-being. . . . " Rosenkreutz descends into the tomb. There he beholds the lady Venus, stark naked, lying in such magnificence that he is paralyzed — impossible to say whether dead or alive. Behind the bed is written: "When the fruit of my tree fully melts, I will awaken and become the mother of a king." Then Cupid enters, angry that his mother has been thus discovered. Playfully, he "pricks" Rosenkreutz on the hand and warns the others to look out — Rosenkreutz will soon be growing old!

22.
There's nothing better here below,
Than beauteous, noble Love;
Whereby we like to God do grow,
And none to grief do move.
Wherefore let's chant it to the King,
That all the sea thereof may ring.
We question; Answer you.
What was it that at first us made?
'Twas love . . . etc.

23. " . . . The Virgin, having placed herself upon the middlemost stone, made a short oration, That we should be constant to our engagement, and not repine at the pains we were hereafter to undergo, but be helpful in restoring the present buried royal persons to life again, and therefore without delay to rise up with her to make a journey to the Tower of Olympus, to fetch from thence medicines useful and necessary for this purpose. . . . "

24. "After eight of clock I awaked, and quickly made myself ready, being desirous to return again to the Tower. . . . At last we all met again in the nethermost Vault, and habits entirely yellow were given to us, together with our golden Fleeces. At the same time the Virgin declared to us that we were Knights of the GOLDEN STONE, of which we were before ignorant. . . . "

25. See Antoine Faivre, *The Golden Fleece and Alchemy* (Albany: State University of New York Press, 1993).

26. "After we had now thus made ourselves ready, and taken our breakfast, the old man presented each of us with a medal of gold; on the one side stood these

words, AR. NAT. MI. On the other these, TEM. NA. F." *Ars naturae ministra,* "Art is the Priestess of Nature." *Temporis natura filia,* "Nature is the Daughter of Time."

27. After receiving the mementos or medals, they set sail; and sailed until they met the King and Queen; then after much din and joy they made land again. "We were all one after the other distributed amongst the Lords. But our old Lord, and I most unworthy, were to ride even with the King, each of us bearing a snow white Ensign, with a Red Cross: I indeed was made use of because of my age, for we both had long grey beards and hair. I had besides fastened my token around my hat, of which the young King soon took notice, and demanded if I were he, who could at the gate redeem these tokens. I answered in a most humble manner, Yea. But he laughed on me, saying, *There henceforth needed no ceremony; I was HIS Father....* "

28. "Herewith we came to the first gate where the Porter with the blue clothes waited.... I demanded of the King, what the condition of this Porter was? who friendly answered me, That he was a very famous and rare Astrologer, and always in high regard with the Lord, his Father. But having on a time committed a fault against Venus, and beheld her in her bed of rest, this punishment was therefore imposed upon him, that he should so long wait at the first gate, till someone should release him from thence. I replied, May he then be released? Yes, said the King, if any one can be found that has as highly transgressed as himself, he must stand in his stead, and the other shall be free.... "

11. The Life of the Spirit in the Middle Ages

1. Theodor Svedberg, author of a book published in German as *Die Materie* (1914).

12. Hidden Centers of the Mysteries in the Middle Ages

1. See Rudolf Steiner, *Mystery Knowledge and Mystery Centers;* also *The Christmas Conference.*

2. Readers unfamiliar with the movements in eurythmy for the sounds of speech are recommended to turn to the first three chapters of the book *Eurythmy as Visible Speech* by Rudolf Steiner.

14. The Relationship between Humankind and the Sun

1. *Faust,* part 1, act 1, scene 1. Bayard Taylor, trans.
2. *Faust,* part 1, act 1, scene 4.

16. Meditating with the Rose Cross

1. The point here is not the extent to which any particular natural-scientific view can or cannot find these thoughts justifiable. The point is to develop thoughts about plants and human beings that can be acquired by means of simple, direct observation without any theory whatsoever. These thoughts do have a value alongside other, more theoretical ideas (which are no less valuable in other respects) about things in the outer world. In this case, the purpose of these thoughts is not to present facts in a scientific way, but to build up a symbol that proves effective on a soul level, regardless of whatever objections may occur to one or the other individual as it is being built up. — R. Steiner.

Additional Sources

page 60: "Rosicrucian Practice" is from *Menschheitsentwickelung und Christus-Erkenntnis*, GA 100, translated by Catherine E. Creeger.

page 80: "Stages of Rosicrucian Initiation" is from *Natur- und Geistwesen, ihr Wirken in unserer sichtbaren Welt*, GA 98, translated by Catherine E. Creeger.

page 94: "Goethe's Rosicrucian Poem 'The Mysteries'" is from *Philosophie und Anthroposophie*, GA 35, translated by Catherine E. Creeger.

page 155: "On *The Chemical Wedding of Christian Rosenkreutz*," translated by Carlo Pietzner (revised), is in *A Christian Rosenkreutz Anthology*, compiled and edited by Paul M. Allen, published by Garber Communications, POB 799, Great Barrington, MA 01230.

page 193: "The Life of the Spirit in the Middle Ages" is lecture 1 in *Rosicrucianism and Modern Initiation*, translated by Mary Adams (revised), published by Rudolf Steiner Press, London.

page 206: "Hidden Centers of the Mysteries in the Middle Ages" is lecture 2 (revised translation) in *Rosicrucianism and Modern Initiation*.

page 218: "The Time of Transition" is lecture 3 (revised translation) in *Rosicrucianism and Modern Initiation*.

page 229: "The Relationship between Humankind and the Sun" is lecture 4 (revised translation) in *Rosicrucianism and Modern Initiation*.

page 244: "Meditation with the Rose Cross" is a selection from *Aus den Inhalten der esoterischen Stunden*, GA 266 and *Seelenübungen mit Wort- und Sinnbild-Meditationen*, GA 267, translated by Christopher Bamford.

Bibliography

Rosicrucianism (non-Steiner)

Allen, Paul M. *A Christian Rosenkreutz Anthology.* Blauvelt, N.Y.: Rudolf Steiner Publications, 1968.

Aniane, Maurice. "Notes on Alchemy, the Cosmological Yoga of Medieval Christianity." In *Material for Thought.* San Francisco, 1976.

Arnold, Paul. *Histoire des Rose-Croix et les Origines de la Franc-Maçonnnerie.* Paris: Mercure de France, 1955.

Bennell, Margaret, and Isabel Wyatt. *An Introductory Commentary on the Chemical Wedding of Christian Rosenkreutz.* Hawkwood College, 1965.

Burckhart, Titus. *Alchemy.* Louisville: Fons Vitae, 1997.

Case, Paul Foster. *The True and Invisible Rosicrucian Order.* York Beach, Me.: Samuel Weiser, 1989.

Clymer, R. Swinburne. *The Book of Rosicruciae.* Quakertown, Pa.: The Philosophical Publishing Company, 1949.

Cooper-Oakley, Isabel. *The Comte of Saint Germain, the Secret of Kings.* Milan: G. Sulli-Rao, 1912; London: Theosophical Publishing House, 1927.

Debus, Allen G. *Man and Nature in the Renaissance.* Cambridge: Cambridge University Press, 1978.

Edighoffer, Roland. *Rose Croix et societé ideal selon Johan Valentin Andreae.* Paris: Arma Artis, 1982, 1987.

Evola, Julius. *The Hermetic Tradition.* Rochester, Vt.: Inner Traditions, 1996.

Faivre, Antoine. *Access to Western Esotericism.* Albany: State University of New York Press, 1994.

Frick, Karl R. H. *Die Erleuchteten: Gnostischtheosophische und alchemistisch-rosenkreuzerische Geheimgesellschaften bis zum Ende des 18. Jahrhunderts.* Graz: Akademische Druck- und Verlaganstalt, 1973.

———. *Licht und Finsternis: Gnostisch-theosophische und freimaurerisch-okkulte Geheimgesellschaften bis an die Wende zum 20. Jahrhundert.* 2 vols. Graz: Akademische Druck- und Verlaganstalt, 1975, 1978.

Fuller, Jean Overton. *The Comte of Saint Germain: Last Scion of the House of Rákóczy.* London: East-West Publications, 1988.

Gilly, Carlos. "Theophrastia Sancta: Paracelsianism as a Religion in Conflict with the Established Churches." J. R. Ritman Library, Bibliotheca Philosophica Hermetica. On the web at http://www.Ritmanlibrary.

Godwin, Joscelyn, trans. *The Chemical Wedding of Christian Rosenkreutz.* Grand Rapids, Mich.: Phanes Press, 1991.

———. *The Theosophical Enlightenment.* Albany: State University of New York Press, 1994.

Gray, Ronald. *Goethe the Alchemist*. Cambridge: Cambridge University Press, 1952.

Hall, Manley Palmer. *Codex Rosae Crucis*. Los Angeles: Philosophical Research Society, 1971.

———. *The Secret Teachings of All Ages: An Encyclopedic Outline of Masonic, Hermetic, Qabalistic and Rosicrucian Symbolical Philosophy*. Los Angeles: Philosophical Research Society n.d.

Harrison, C. G. *The Transcendental Universe: Six Lectures on Occult Science, Theosophy, and the Catholic Faith*. Hudson, N.Y.: Lindisfarne Books, 1993.

Hirst, Désirée. *Hidden Riches: Traditional Symbolism from the Renaissance to Blake*. London: Eyre and Spottiswood, 1964.

Howe, Ellic. *The Magicians of the Golden Dawn: A Documentary History of a Magical Order 1887–1923*. London: Routledge and Kegan Paul, 1972.

Jennings, Hargrave. *The Rosicrucians, Their Rites and Mysteries*. London: Chatto and Windus, 1879.

Lapoukhin, I. P. *Characteristics of the Interior Church*. London: Watkins, 1909.

Lytton, E. Bulwer. *Zanoni*. Blauvelt, N.Y.: Garber Publications, 1997.

Magre, Maurice. *The Return of the Magi*. London: Philip Allen, 1931.

Merton, Reginald. *Magicians, Seers, and Mystics*. New York: E. P. Dutton, 1932.

McIntosh, Christopher. *The Rosy Cross Unveiled*. Wellingborough, Northampton: Aquarian Press, 1980.

———. *The Rose Cross and the Age of Reason: Eighteenth-Century Rosicrucianism in Central Europe and Its Relationship to the Enlightenment*. Leiden and New York: E. J. Brill, 1992.

McClean, Adam. See the "Alchemy Website" http://www.levity.com/alchemy.

Montgomery, J. W. *Cross and Crucible: J. V. Andreae (1586–1654)*. The Hague: Martinus Nijhoff, 1973.

Newman, William. *Gehennical Fire: The Lives of George Starkey, an American Alchemist in the Scientific Revolution*. Cambridge: Harvard University Press, 1994.

Obrist, Barbara. *Constantine of Pisa: The Book of the Secrets of Alchemy*. Leiden: E. J. Brill, 1990.

Pagel, Walter. *Paracelsus: An Introduction to Philosophical Medicine in the Era of the Renaissance*. Basel and New York: S. Karger, 1958.

———. *Joan Baptista Van Helmont, Reformer of Science and Medicine*. Cambridge: Cambridge University Press, 1982.

Peukert, Will-Erich. *Das Rosenkreuz*. Berlin: Erich Schmidt Verlag, 1973.

Ritman, J. R. "The Key to Hermetic Philosophy." *Hermetic Journal* 35 (1987).

Schuchard, Marsha Keith. "Freemasonry, Secret Societies, and the Continuity of the Occult Tradition in English Literature." Ph.D Dissertation, University of Texas, Austin, 1975.

Szydlo, Zbigniew. *Water Which Does Not Wet Hands: The Alchemy of Michael Sendivogius*. Warsaw: Polish Academy of Sciences, 1994.

Waite, A. E. *The Brotherhood of the Rosy Cross*. London: Rider, 1924.

———. *The Real History of the Rosicrucians*. Blauvelt, N.Y.: Steinerbooks, 1977.

Waldenses, Vaughan, et al. *A Rosicrucian Primer*. Edmonds, Wash.: Holmes Publishing, 1994.

White, Ralph, ed. *The Rosicrucian Enlightenment Revisited*. Hudson, N.Y.: Lindisfarne Books, 1999.

Yates, Frances. *The Rosicrucian Enlightenment*. London: Routledge and Kegan Paul, 1972.

————. *Giordano Bruno and the Hermetic Tradition.* London: Routledge and Kegan Paul, 1964.

————. *The Occult Philosophy in the Elizabethan Age.* London: Routledge and Kegan Paul, 1979.

Steiner Bibliography

The Archangel Michael: His Mission and Ours. Hudson, N.Y.: Anthroposophic Press, 1994.

At Home in the Universe: Exploring Our Suprasensory Nature. Hudson, N.Y.: Anthroposophic Press, 2000.

Background to the Gospel of St. Mark. London: Rudolf Steiner Press, 1968.

Between Death and Rebirth. London: Rudolf Steiner Press, 1975.

Building Stones for an Understanding of the Mystery of Golgotha. London: Rudolf Steiner Press, 1972.

The Christian Mystery. Hudson, N.Y.: Anthroposophic Press, 1998.

Christian Rosenkreutz. London: Rudolf Steiner Press, 1950.

The Christmas Conference for the Foundation of the General Anthroposophical Society 1923/1924. Hudson, N.Y.: Anthroposophic Press, 1990.

Correspondence and Documents 1901–1925. London: Rudolf Steiner Press, and New York: Anthroposophic Press, 1988.

Cosmic and Human Metamorphoses. Blauvelt N.Y.: Garber Communications, 1985.

Cosmic Memory. Englewood, N.J.: Rudolf Steiner Publications, 1959.

Earthly and Cosmic Man. London: Rudolf Steiner Publishing Co., 1948.

The East in the Light of the West. (with *The Children of Lucifer,* by Édouard Schuré). Blauvelt, N.Y.: Garber Communications, 1986.

Esoteric Christianity and the Mission of Christian Rosenkreutz. London: Rudolf Steiner Press, 1984.

Eurythmy as Visible Speech. London: Anthroposophical Publishing Co., 1956.

From Buddha to Christ. Hudson, N.Y.: Anthroposophic Press, and London: Rudolf Steiner Press, 1987.

From the History and Contents of the First Section of the Esoteric School 1904–1914: Letters, Documents, and Lectures. Hudson, N.Y.: Anthroposophic Press, 1998.

From Jesus to Christ. London: Rudolf Steiner Press, 1973.

Genesis: Secrets of the Bible Story of Creation. London: Anthroposophical Publishing Co., 1959.

The Gospel of St. John. Spring Valley, N.Y.: Anthroposophic Press, 1973.

The Gospel of St. Luke. London: Rudolf Steiner Press, and Hudson, N.Y.: Anthroposophic Press, 1988.

The Gospel of St. Matthew. London: Rudolf Steiner Publishing Co., 1946.

Guidance in Esoteric Training. London: Rudolf Steiner Press, 1994.

How to Know Higher Worlds: A Modern Path of Initiation. Hudson, N.Y.: Anthroposophic Press, 1994.

Human and Cosmic Thought. London: Rudolf Steiner Press, n.d.

Introducing Anthroposophical Medicine. Hudson, N.Y.: Anthroposophic Press, 1999.

Intuitive Thinking as a Spiritual Path: A Philosophy of Freedom. Hudson, N.Y.: Anthroposophic Press, 1995.

The Karma of Materialism. Spring Valley, N.Y.: Anthroposophic Press, and London: Rudolf Steiner Press, 1985.

Macrocosm and Microcosm. London: Rudolf Steiner Press, 1968.

Metamorphoses of the Soul: Paths of Experience. Vol. 2. London: Rudolf Steiner Press, 1983.

The Michael Mystery. Spring Valley, N.Y.: St. George Publications, 1984.

The Mission of Christian Rosenkreutz. London: R. Steiner Publishing Co., 1950.

Mystery Knowledge and Mystery Centers. London: Rudolf Steiner Press, 1973.

Mystics after Modernism: Discovering the Seeds of a New Science in the Renaissance. Hudson, N.Y.: Anthroposophic Press, 2000.

The Occult Movement in the Nineteenth Century. London: Rudolf Steiner Press, 1973.

An Outline of Esoteric Science. Hudson, N.Y.: Anthroposophic Press, 1997.

A Psychology of Body, Soul, and Spirit. Hudson, N.Y.: Anthroposophic Press, 1999.

Rosicrucian Esotericism. Spring Valley, N.Y.: Anthroposophic Press, 1978.

Rosicrucianism and Modern Initiation: Mystery Centres of the Middle Ages. London: Rudolf Steiner Press, 1982.

The Spiritual Foundation of Morality: Francis of Assisi and the Christ Impulse. Hudson, N.Y.: Anthroposophic Press, 1995.

The Stages of Higher Knowledge. New York: Anthroposophic Press, 1967.

Supersensible Knowledge. Hudson, N.Y.: Anthroposophic Press, 1987.

The Temple Legend. London: Rudolf Steiner Press, 1985.

Theosophy: An Introduction to the Spiritual Processes in Human Life and in the Cosmos. Hudson, N.Y.: Anthroposophic Press, 1994.

Theosophy of the Rosicrucian. London: Rudolf Steiner Press, 1981.

Truth and Knowledge: Introduction to "Philosophy of Spiritual Activity." Blauvelt, N.Y.: Steinerbooks, 1981.

During the last two decades of the nineteenth century, the Austrian-born Rudolf Steiner (1861–1925) became a respected and well-published scientific, literary, and philosophical scholar, particularly known for his work on Goethe's scientific writings. After the turn of the century he began to develop his earlier philosophical principles into an approach to methodical research of psychological and spiritual phenomena.

His multifaceted genius has led to innovative and holistic approaches in medicine, philosophy, religion, education (Waldorf schools), special education, economics, science, agriculture (Biodynamic method), architecture, drama, the new arts of speech and eurythmy, and other fields of activity. In 1924 he founded the General Anthroposophical Society, which today has branches throughout the world.

Printed in the United States
124272LV00003B/95/A

9 780880 104753